Country Music Annual 2002

Edited by
Charles K. Wolfe
and James E. Akenson

The University Press of Kentucky

Publication of this volume was made possible in part
by a grant from the National Endowment for the Humanities.

Copyright © 2002 by The University Press of Kentucky

Scholarly publisher for the Commonwealth,
serving Bellarmine University, Berea College, Centre
College of Kentucky, Eastern Kentucky University,
The Filson Historical Society, Georgetown College,
Kentucky Historical Society, Kentucky State University,
Morehead State University, Murray State University,
Northern Kentucky University, Transylvania University,
University of Kentucky, University of Louisville,
and Western Kentucky University.
All rights reserved.

Editorial and Sales Offices: The University Press of Kentucky
663 South Limestone Street, Lexington, Kentucky 40508-4008

06   05   04   03   02   5   4   3   2   1

ISBN 0-8131-0991-4 (pbk: alk. paper)

This book is printed on acid-free recycled paper meeting
the requirements of the American National Standard
for Permanence of Paper for Printed Library Materials.

Manufactured in the United States of America

Contents

Introduction	1
Conway Twitty: The Man and His Image **Jimmie N. Rogers**	3
The Bill Monroe Biography: Journalism Assisting Scholarship **Richard D. Smith**	15
"Man of Constant Sorrow": Antecedents and Tradition **John Garst**	26
The Selling Sound of Country Music: Class, Culture, and Early Radio Marketing Strategy of the Country Music Association **Diane Pecknold**	54
Tex Morton and His Influence on Country Music in Australia During the 1930s and 1940s **Andrew Smith**	82

Country Music Publishing Catalog Acquisition   104
   John Gonas, David Herrera, James I. Elliott, and Greg Faulk

Postcards and the Promotion of Early Country Music Artists   117
   Danny W. Allen

The Drive-by Truckers and the Redneck Underground: A Subcultural Analysis   130
   S. Renee Dechert and George H. Lewis

WPAQ Radio: The Voice of the Blue Ridge Mountains   151
   David B. Pruett

Politics and Country Music, 1963–1974   161
   Don Cusic

Honky-Tonk Angels and Rockabilly Queens: Oklahoma Divas in American Country Music   186
   George Carney

The Bristol Syndrome: Field Recordings of Early Country Music   202
   Charles K. Wolfe

Contributors   223

Introduction

Charles K. Wolfe and James E. Akenson

This third annual collection of new studies in country music reflects, as have the first two, the continuing diversity of approaches taken by scholars in dealing with this complex and influential commercial art form. Because of the rich variety of papers submitted for the volume, we have as a matter of policy avoided trying to create issues devoted to a particular topic or approach. At the same time, we have resisted the temptation to create issues that were tied too specifically to the musical events and developments of the current year. As with earlier issues, this volume spans the history of country music, from the earliest commercial recordings in the 1920s to the modern alt country of the 1990s. Along the way, we are treated to a number of subjects that have received their due attention: the scene of Australian country music (Andrew Smith), the application of cultural geography to the music (Carney), the development of trade organizations in the field (Pecknold), and the role of regional radio stations (Pruett).

One of the most notable trends in the country music scene in the last two years has been the rise in popularity of old-time country and bluegrass. The surprising commercial success of the soundtrack for the film *O Brother, Where Art Thou?*, filled with bluegrass, gospel, and old-time music, encouraged a number of mainstream country singers to do acoustic or tradition-based albums, and traditional performers like Ralph Stanley found themselves more popular than at any time in their careers. John Garst's study of the film's big hit song, "Man of Constant Sorrow," shows just how deeply the roots of this ballad extend into the American past. The year 2002 also saw the seventy-fifth anniversary of the pioneering recording sessions at Bristol, Tennessee, and a number of national and regional events designed to commemorate it. Charles Wolfe's article "The Bristol Syndrome" puts these sessions in historical perspective and explores the ways in which commercial record companies first documented the music.

Other topics explored in these articles include studies of specific artists (Conway Twitty, Tex Morton, the Drive-by Truckers), the way in which songs from a particular era reflect their time (the 1960s), and the way in which the music functions as an industry. An area of study that country scholars are just beginning to explore is historiography. Though we have had for some time studies of the historians and critics of fields like jazz, blues, and even rock (see, for example, Jim DeRogatis's 2001 book on critic Lester Bangs), little of this has been developed for country. Richard D. Smith's account of the history of his own award-winning biography of Bill Monroe is an early start in this direction.

We continue to invite ideas and submissions for later volumes of *Country Music Annual* and continue to invite scholars and general readers to sample the fare within.

CONWAY TWITTY
THE MAN AND HIS IMAGE

Jimmie N. Rogers

Conway Twitty is an icon in American culture. One way to know if someone has reached iconic status is to note how little must be said to identify the individual in a joke. Consider the following: A young man was assigned to a new church, and upon his arrival he thought he would canvass the neighborhood, introduce himself, and invite people to attend the church. When he knocks on the first door, a woman opens it and exclaims, "As I live and breathe, Conway Twitty!" The minister explains that he is not Conway Twitty; he is the new preacher at the local church out asking neighbors to visit on Sunday. The woman says she will think about it and once again comments on the minister's resemblance to Conway Twitty.

At the next door a man responds to the knock with an observation similar to the first greeting. Once again the minister admits that while he might resemble Conway Twitty, he is in fact the new preacher from the church down the street and asks the man to attend Sunday services.

He knocks and gets no immediate response at the third door. After knocking a second time, a young woman appears at the door with a towel draped around her, displaying evidence of having recently left a bath. She looks at the minister, drops her towel, extends her arms, and calls out "Conway!" The surprised preacher steps back and says, "Hello Darlin'."

"Looking Back"

Inclusion in the popular culture of the day offers other evidence of one's becoming an icon. Twitty is not mentioned in the first few minutes of Kris

Conway Twitty enjoyed a long and illustrious career in the music industry, recording numerous number-one hits.

Kristofferson's song "The Pilgrim," but does seem to fit a description found in its lyrics. Kristofferson is talking about some other contemporary picker when he sings, "He's a walking contradiction, partly truth and partly fiction."[1] Though written about someone else, the line aptly suits Twitty. Conway dedicated his life to creating a persona (partly true and partly fiction), which has allowed him to achieve great success as an entertainer.

Twitty's early life was not much different from those of other country pickers. He was named Harold Lloyd Jenkins at birth in Friars Point, Mississippi, on September 1, 1933. (This date must have been disagreeable to the star because it was not mentioned in the singer's authorized biography.)[2] His father was a ferryboat captain who ultimately settled his family on the west bank of the Mississippi River in Helena, Arkansas, when Harold was ten years old.[3]

Young Jenkins excelled in sports in school and front-porch music out of school. He organized a band called the Phillips Country Ramblers that played regularly on the local radio station by the time he was twelve.[4] His early performances were greatly influenced by the music he heard on the *Grand Ole Opry* and by some of the local bands he heard in Helena. KFFA, the radio station on which he began his career, was the home of the King Biscuit Boys, so Harold was able to hear some of the finest delta blues available anywhere.

Perhaps Jenkins was better at baseball than pickin' during his school years in Helena. During the early 1950s in Arkansas, professional baseball scouts were watching high school, American Legion, and semi-pro or town teams actively looking for talent. A scout from the Philadelphia Phillies told Harold that he would probably be offered a contract after finishing high school. This dangling offer allowed the young man to make plans for the future. He also considered serving as a preacher and gave some examples of his success as an amateur practitioner in his authorized biography.[5]

After becoming disillusioned with the ministry, Jenkins concentrated on a future in baseball. He finished school in Helena and went north to work while waiting for the baseball draft. After a brief stay in Chicago, he discovered that a girl in Helena was pregnant and he returned to Arkansas to marry her. The couple never lived together as man and wife, but he did what was considered to be the "right" thing in the fifties. The marriage resulted in divorce and a son named Mike. Before the Phillies were able to draft young Mr. Jenkins, the military did.

In March 1954, Jenkins reported to Camp Chaffee in Fort Smith, Arkansas, for his basic training. This is the same post that in March 1958 welcomed Elvis Presley into the armed services with great fanfare, but there was no such reception given to Harold. After basic he did advanced training and ended up serving most of his enlistment in Japan. During his stay in Yokohama, he played baseball and football and formed a band called The Cimarrons.

Returning from service in 1956, Jenkins discovered significant changes taking place in the music. A few miles up river from his hometown, Sam Phillips was creating a new genre of music. With Harold's background in and understanding of country, blues, and gospel, it was a natural step to follow the stars to Memphis. His short journey to Mecca was less than satisfactory, for he recorded eight sides for Sun and none was issued.[6]

Jenkins's experience with Phillips provided him an opportunity to get work, but it was through an army buddy that the young artist ultimately found a manager—located in New York—who displayed faith in him. Don Seats assured the singer that he could get him a new recording contract with a major label, but he suggested that "Harold Jenkins" was not a marquee name. Harold spent considerable time providing Seat a list of options, although they obviously varied in quality. Even Harold admits that "Kane Tucket" was a poor suggestion.[7] "Conway Twitty" was the final choice, marking the beginning of Harold Jenkins's alter ego in 1957. "Conway" was selected from a town in Arkansas and "Twitty" from a town in Texas. This was not the first use of geographic locations to provide stage names in the music industry. Marion T. Slaughter took the name of two towns from his home state of Texas to create the pseudonym "Vernon Dalhart."

"I Need Your Lovin'"

Conway's new manager arranged for a contract to record rockabilly at Mercury under his new name. Robert Oermann best described the fruits of that experience when he wrote that Conway's first release grazed the bottom of the charts,[8] and the second release was even less successful. Either because of or in spite of this early recording adventure, Seats sent Twitty out of the country by booking an appearance in Canada. The Canadian audience was probably as familiar with Conway and his music as they were with Conway, Arkansas, and Twitty, Texas.

After an initial hostile reaction to the music (even the bartenders left the building when the band started playing and emptied the room), the group gradually built a following and their engagement was extended. After playing clubs in Canada for more than a year, Conway returned to Nashville to record four sides on speculation for MGM. One of the songs from that session turned out to be Conway's first number-one song. "It's Only Make Believe" was not selected to be the "A" side of the first release, but the public disagreed, and on September 21, 1958, the song hit the top of the charts and remained on the lists for twenty-one weeks.[9] Considering Twitty's later propensity to select songs and song titles containing language with multiple meanings, it may not be coincidental that one of the songs recorded in that first session was entitled "I Vibrate."

Following Conway's first big hit with MGM, he made his way by redoing some old favorites and doing them well. It was also during this period that he appeared in films such as *Platinum High School* and *College Confidential* and "solidified his status as a teen idol."[10] His first step to becoming a pop culture icon was when a character named "Conrad Birdie" parodied Twitty in the musical *Bye Bye Birdie*.

Conway was improving at each step in his recording career, but he appeared to be more interested in country music than some of the things he was asked to record and expected to play on club dates. He wrote country songs during off times when he was performing in Canada, and—as evinced in his Mercury and MGM offerings—his work was clearly different from that of the other rockabillies. He may have been attracted to the music by the sound of Elvis, he may have sculpted his hair in the Elvis mold, but most of his self-penned material had more originality and sincerity than that displayed by the object of his mimicry.

After a series of well-received recordings, Conway waited out his contract with MGM and made the shift to country music. He received support and encouragement from Harlan Howard, one of Nashville's foremost songwriters, and obtained a contract with Decca in 1965. This shift in directions, as one might suspect, did not meet with overwhelming approval. Don Seats found giving up a steady source of revenue to launch a performer into a less profitable area of music decidedly unappealing. For their part, country-radio people did not readily accept an outsider who had previously performed the type of music that was doing them substantial harm. In addition, those close to Conway—as well as Conway himself—worried over the negative financial fallout this move could cause to a performer that was not in eclipse or dead on the vine. On the other hand, Twitty was able to move across genres from a fairly strong position, unlike those pickers who move to country because they failed in other areas of music. Conway made this move, as he would others in the future, because he wanted to sing country and he believed that he would be successful at it.

"The Image of Me"

It took three years to find initial success on Decca with "The Image of Me." Conway's switch to country in 1965 kicked off a flurry of chart happenings that is unparalleled in country music history. According to various sources, Twitty has had more number-one recordings than any other artist.[11] Yet the data to support this distinction vary for several reasons. Twitty recorded across genres, therefore his chart activity appears in different places. More importantly, a variety of charts exist, and any and all are used by the industry to present their product in the best light possible. If the Billboard charts are used, it is possible to see how active and popular Twitty was in his career. Ninety-seven of his recordings appeared on the Billboard charts from March 1966 to August 1993. This total includes fourteen duets with Loretta Lynn released from 1971 to 1981. Thirty-five of the songs he released as the primary performer went to number one, and five of the duets did the same.[12]

No matter the method for counting his chart totals, Twitty's success was greater than almost all other country artists when judged by popularity of releases. The 1970s were special for Conway and those who appreciate his music. He began the decade with the classic "Hello Darlin'." This song insured his place in country music and attracted a following from the pop world. Unlike today, a crossover hit was easy to identify in 1970. This song reached number one on the *Billboard* country charts (a position it retained for four weeks) and number fifty on the pop charts. From the spoken opening to the unstated plea for a lost lover to disregard his assurances that he is doing well without her, the song allows listeners to view a special slice of reality. The throb in Twitty's voice magnifies the futility of his plight. It takes great talent to open up inner feelings and state them in a way that does not disguise or muddle them for the listener. This technique was not original with Twitty, but he tuned it to a fine edge. The sentiment found in his early efforts on MGM was allowed to flow freely in the country mode.

While maintaining a cultivated view of what a "Conway Twitty" should be, the singer carefully maneuvered his way through the hazards of a career. His personal appearance evolved into a polished and almost worshipful ceremony that helped him to earn his reputation as "the high priest of country music." He began producing his own recordings in the late seventies, and more importantly to his fans—or at least more noticeably to them—he shaved his sideburns and curled his pompadour. Altering a hairstyle might not seem much to some, yet this act gave an outward confirmation that the carefully developed image was no longer the same. Conway retained his sartorial residue from the 1950s longer than all except a few amateur musicians and some television preachers did. Jimmy Bowen claimed credit for suggesting the new hairdo in a book published several years after Conway's death.[13]

At approximately the time of his fashion change, Twitty also began manipulating his musical image. He did a little rock in the late 1970s, but not enough to startle his fans or attract rock listeners, and he switched recording companies again. He moved to Warner/Electra in the early 1980s and began to remake some pop hits such as "Three Times a Lady" and "Slow Hand." He launched a project in 1981 that would have frightened a lesser or more private soul. Conway opened Twitty City, a $3 million place for his fans to honor him outside the concert hall. His business ventures, his home—and the homes of those closely related to him—and places to shop for all types of Twitty memorabilia were made available to the fans there. One motivation for this project may have been Twitty's displeasure at the image Nashville was presenting to the country music audience.

Conway returned to MCA in 1987 and produced some of his finest

The change from a straight pompadour to a curly hairdo showed the audience that they could expect a new Conway.

work. "Desperado Love" and other songs he did at this time continued to demonstrate his mastery of the language of love that can be found in a carefully crafted country song. He released other songs in this period that reinforced his reputation for speaking to women and men about their private feelings. He did "Saturday Night Special," which on its face would seem poorly chosen considering the common stereotype of the country audience. In other songs he played on words and delighted both women and men with "Something Strange Got into Her Last Night" and "Don't Call Him a Cowboy."

Twitty's last recording was another interesting step for him. In 1994, MCA released a compilation entitled *Rhythm Country & Blues*. "Rainy Night in Georgia," Conway's duet with Sam Moore, offered a bit of nostalgia and, at least figuratively, moved him back toward the blues of Helena.

Conway became ill following a show in Branson in 1993 as he was preparing to travel by bus for Nashville and Fan Fair. He died in Springfield, Missouri, as a result of a stomach aneurysm.

"What a Dream"

Many have offered their views on the reasons for Conway Twitty's success. Although she may not have tickled the performer's fancy, Alanna Nash did place Conway in perspective when she wrote: "Never handsome, and never a dynamic stage performer. Twitty can credit his longevity to primarily two factors—an uncanny ability to understand the psychology of the country music fan, and the knowledge that it is the song—and not the singer—that really matters."[14]

Michael Banes noted that the "Gospel" according to Conway was a tough one and outlined it in the picker's own words.

> On television: I stay away from it mostly. It's so powerful—it can eat you alive.
> On Vegas: Playing Vegas just doesn't do you any good as a performer and recording artist. It adds nothing. In fact, it takes away.
> On publicity companies: These people will use you right up. . . .
> On songs and songwriting: Without the song, you can hang it up. All the other things don't matter. . . .
> On songs: I don't make deals. I don't say, well, I'm not going to record this song unless I get part of the publishing on it or all of the publishing on it or any other political deal—nothing. The song stands on its own. I don't care who writes it. I don't care who publishes it. It doesn't matter. The song flat stands on its own.[15]

Robert Oermann summarized Twitty's on- and near-stage customs as: "Twitty did not speak onstage, do interviews, attend music-business parties, appear on TV shows, or perform encores."[16]

There is no doubt that the traits mentioned above helped ensure the success of Conway Twitty. For the most part, he understood his abilities as a singer, songwriter, recording artist, live performer, and business executive. More importantly, he was able to use his talents to achieve maximum and sustained results. In analyzing his talents and the use of those talents, it appears that some additional elements may be added to those identified by the three writers above.

"What Am I Living For?"

Twitty's ability to separate his professional life from his personal life allowed him to create, analyze, and hone the role of "Conway Twitty" while retaining the stability of being Harold Jenkins. He often spoke of Conway in the third person. He could work on Conway's image and not become obsessed with living an unnatural life. He knew the value of maintaining a consistent and understandable persona that the people would accept and support. The persona was not used to mislead or misinform the public. In fact, he became agitated when other entertainers would speak despairingly of their public image.[17] He carefully considered the wishes of his audience and did not betray its trust.

Successful country singers, especially from the 1950s through the 1980s, attracted and kept an audience by magnifying traits that are important in our interpersonal relationships.[18] We tend to support, appreciate, and understand our friends depending upon their and our needs and wishes. We are also more forgiving and less apt to question a friend's motives than we are those of acquaintances. We are less critical of people we know and care about. One of the ways this can help an entertainer is in the realization that a friend cares little about another friend's voice quality. We can and will forgive the behavior of a friend until it is obvious that the relationship is no longer beneficial or worthwhile. To improve relationships one must provide continuing reinforcement and justification for increasing the strength of the bond.

In order for a performer to enjoy special relationships with individual members of an audience, he or she must spend time and effort building and maintaining them. The effort given to meeting, greeting, and caring for fans before, during, and after concerts is one of the most important means to develop, keep, and solidify the important bond between singer and audience. Designing and delivering a live show of high quality demonstrates the faith and respect a performer has for the audience. Conway's stage shows were a masterful use of time and material.[19] He met the expectations of the audience by recreating the same songs night after night with enthusiasm and sincerity, a task that some pickers are unable to master. Little, however, turns a concertgoer off more than the casual or offhanded treatment of a well-liked song. They want to hear the material as they know it, and they want to feel the pain in the song and not the pain of the singer who must be tired of singing it.

Twitty knew his audience and they knew him. He treated them with respect through his songwriting, in his performing, and by not allowing his personal life to obscure his public persona. When he made changes in his personal appearance—such as adapting his hairstyle and moving toward less formal stage costuming—he did it gradually and always when he was on top of his game. In other words, he did not wait until he lost popularity to change his public presence. This gave the impression that he was tweaking a good thing rather than groping about in search of a way to stay afloat.

"I'd Love to Lay You Down"

The keen understanding of Twitty's audience allowed one of the most interesting and unique qualities of his music to become a staple of his style. Twitty wrote and sang about subjects that many performers would find impossible to include in their repertoires. Women in the audience were the primary targets for most of his messages. Alanna Nash said he was "a performer with an almost 'religious hold' on housewives . . . [because he] understands what women want." She goes on to say: "His lyrics manage to do what most other country songs don't, which is to acknowledge a woman's sensuality and her desire to be treated with respect."[20] In addition to the lyrics, Twitty had the nerve and the ability to use language with multiple meanings and the fortitude to say things that lesser (or more prudent) performers would be unable to say with any credibility at all. He would respond to questions about some line or word in a song that might be considered risqué by assuring the questioner that he never thought of the phrase or word in that way. Even if that assurance were heartfelt and sincere, Conway's fans would never believe it for a minute. Conway used a private language that connected to both women and men in his audience. They knew and understood what he was saying, and they appreciated the saying of it.

It is the ability to express some of these "inside" sentiments that separates Twitty from the rest. Many country songwriters and singers have considered it a personal challenge to say something in a song that might titillate the audience, and some were successful in this ploy before country became a widespread phenomena. Twitty was able to do this in modern times with ease and aplomb. Songs such as "You've Never Been This Far Before" contains several threads of meaning, and all are excellent. The title "I Can't Believe She Gives It All to Me" can and does mean different things to different folks. However, it is one of Twitty's last releases that best displays this marvelous ability to talk around, above, and below gatekeepers to deliver an intended message to the listener. "Something Strange Got into Her Last Night" features a linguistic turn through the use of a fairly well known cliché. The sincerity in Conway's voice and the serious, if naive, view he relays makes the song special because it diverts attention from the story line itself, until the last moments of the tune.

After veering off the path carved by Elvis, Twitty held his life to a fairly straight course and allowed his audience to keep up with and approve the various moves. After leaving Memphis, he gradually took control of his professional life and career. He made careful choices in the songs he wrote and those, written by others, he selected to record. He decided not to follow the glow of the TV camera (although he did drop by Hollywood for a spell) in order to preserve his exposure, which he thought might be a finite resource. He did turn to television and became more accessible for interviews when it became necessary to promote Twitty City. He studiously applied techniques for enhancing all that was attractive about "Conway Twitty" without losing control of his life off the stage.

Finally, he took over the various business matters related to his career and locked them in like Exxon. He wrote many of his songs, owned the publication rights, produced most of the recordings, and owned a part of the talent agency that handled his tours and personal appearances. When a person controls a product from conception to fruition, he or she must live by the results. Conway could survey his professional life with pride and a sense of accomplishment, knowing that he did it his way.

Conway Twitty may have been partly truth and partly fiction, but his capacity to know the difference between truth and fiction—and stick to it—was at least one key to why his career flourished. His ability and desire to personally communicate to a large audience made it possible to see what he was living for and how that aim was accepted and appreciated by country music fans everywhere.

Notes

1. Kris Kristofferson, "The Pilgrim-Chapter 33," *The Silver Tongued Devil and I* (Monument PZ 30679, 1971).

2. Robert Cochran, *Our Own Sweet Sounds: A Celebration of Popular Music in Arkansas* (Fayetteville, Arkansas: The University of Arkansas Press, 1996), 96.

3. Wilbur Cross and Michael Kosser, *The Conway Twitty Story: An Authorized Biography* (Garden City, New York: Doubleday & Company, Inc., 1986), 25.

4. Alanna Nash, *Behind Closed Doors: Talking with the Legends of Country Music* (New York: Alfred A. Knopf, 1988), 486.

5. Cross and Kosser, *The Conway Twitty Story,* 39–41.

6. Robert Palmer, "Get Rhythm: Elvis Presley, Johnny Cash, and the Rockabillies," in *Country: The Music and the Musicians,* ed. Paul Kingsbury and Alan Axelrod (New York: Abbeville Press, 1988), 321.

7. Cross and Kosser, *The Conway Twitty Story,* 67.

8. Robert K. Oermann, "Reinventing Conway Twitty," in *The Journal of Traditional Country Music* (June/July 2001): J4.

9. Richard Oliver, jacket notes, *20 Great Hits by Conway Twitty,* MGM 2-SES-4884, 1972.

10. Robert K. Oermann, "Conway Twitty," in *The Encyclopedia of Country Music,* ed. Paul Kingsbury (New York: Oxford University Press, 1998), 553.

11. Ken Tucker, "9 to 5: How Willie Nelson and Dolly Parton Qualified for 'Lifestyles of the Rich and Famous,'" in *Country: The Music and the Musicians,* ed. Paul Kingsbury and Alan Axelrod (New York: Abbeville Press, 1988), 382; and Oermann, "Conway Twitty," 553.

12. Joel Whitburn, *Top Country Singles: 1944–1993* (Menomonee Falls, Wisconsin: Record Research Inc., 1994), 389–91.

13. Jimmy Bowen and Jim Jerome, *Rough Mix: An Unapologetic Look at the Music Business and How It Got That Way—A Lifetime in the World of Rock, Pop, and Country as Told by One of the Industry's Most Powerful Players* (New York: Simon & Schuster, 1997), 156–57.

14. Nash, *Behind Closed Doors,* 485.

15. Michael Banes, "The Gospel According to Conway Twitty," *Country Music,* (November/December 1984): 28.

16. Oermann, "Conway Twitty," 554.

17. Cross and Kosser, *The Conway Twitty Story,* 96–97.

18. For an expanded view of the communication techniques employed by successful country singer/songwriters, see Jimmie N. Rogers, *The Country Music Message: Revisited* (Fayetteville: Univ. of Arkansas Press, 1989).

19. For a wonderful description of a Conway Twitty live concert, see Curtis W. Ellison, *Country Music Culture: From Hard Times to Heaven* (Jackson: Univ. Press of Mississippi, 1995), 252–55.

20. Nash, *Behind Closed Doors,* 485.

The Bill Monroe Biography
Journalism Assisting Scholarship

Richard D. Smith

A motto that is reproduced on the front page masthead of every edition of the *New York Times* reads: "All the News That's Fit to Print." This famous phrase reflects the commitment of the Ochs and Sulzburger families, owners of the *Times,* to avoiding the tasteless excesses of sensation-mongering reporting, a commitment as praiseworthy in our day of tabloids and paparazzi as it was in the era of "yellow journalism."

But let us not lose sight of the first word of this motto—all. The *New York Times* remains committed to *all* the news that is fit to print. It has a proud history of being the newspaper of record, reporting evenhandedly and in depth, without fear or favor.

As an occasional regional stringer correspondent and bylined freelance writer for the *Times,* I have been greatly influenced by that newspaper's standards and philosophy, some of which, I hope, has proven beneficial in the writing of *Can't You Hear Me Callin'—The Life of Bill Monroe, Father of Bluegrass,* published in July 2000 by Little, Brown & Co. I come from a journalistic and not an academic background. As I share the attitudes and techniques that I used while doing primary research for my book, please note the carefully chosen subtitle of this paper—"Journalism Assisting Scholarship." This is not about journalism replacing scholarship, journalism triumphing over scholarship, or even journalism attempting in any way to rival scholarship. Indeed, journalism has much to learn from scholarship, especially in terms of doing accurate research and having solid sources. It's too bad that time and space do not permit footnoting and referencing in newspapers and magazines; reporting would be a different and better profession.

But I would suggest that there are two major areas in which journalism can assist music scholarship, particularly scholarship in bluegrass and country music. Techniques of information gathering is but one. The other vital area of concern—which must be addressed at the outset and to which I've already alluded—is that of attitude: attitude toward the research/writing process itself.

Thankfully, country music and bluegrass are not beset by the excesses of tabloid-style sensationalism. We have yet to be subjected, for example, to *National Inquirer* reporters paying Jimmy Martin's neighbors for information on that colorful character, nor have we seen paparazzi pursuing Alison Krauss's tour bus. But country and bluegrass journalism often swings to the opposite extreme, an extreme in which nothing potentially controversial may be written, where the otherwise admirable dictum "if you don't have anything nice to say, don't say it at all" can potentially stifle objective and illuminating writing about the music's stars—preventing all the news that's fit to print from seeing print.

The issue is vexing because of the very real moral dilemmas involved: For example, in the introduction to his book *Traveling the High Way Home— Ralph Stanley and the World of Traditional Bluegrass Music,* John Wright explains why this volume is not a personal biography. He states that "the culture from which Stanley comes assigns a very high value to personal privacy. I was sympathetic to this predilection from the first and in the course of my work I came to share it to such a great extent that I could not have violated it even if I had wanted to."[1] I applaud Wright's genuine sensitivities. But this example illustrates the potential for a subject and his culture to define and thus limit the boundaries of reporting. Certainly, Ralph Stanley himself never dictated nor even requested that Wright observe such boundaries: It was the writer's own choice.[2] But when taken to the extreme, a self-censorship can develop that is antithetical to both serious scholarship and journalism, that can prevent all that is historically noteworthy or newsworthy from being recorded and reported.

And the news *is* fit to print. Honest, in-depth reporting is essential to any writing of history, including the histories of major American music figures. Nowhere is this better illustrated than in the case of Bill Monroe. Much of Monroe's personal life has been considered off-limits, certainly during his life and even now, some four years after his death. But, ironically, this self-censoring respect for Bill Monroe's privacy has in practice disrespected and dishonored the man by preventing a true appreciation of his life and art. Prior to *Can't You Hear Me Callin'* there was virtually no serious examination of Bill's autobiographical compositions, what he termed his "true songs."[3] To date, this has been a persistent problem in Monroe scholarship. Analyses of his songs have ignored or misunderstood his autobiographical compositions. One analysis, for example, relegates such numbers as "Used to Be," a Monroe classic about a souring love affair, to a catch-all category "Home, Past, Rural Oriented Titles."[4]

Bill Monroe deserves to be ranked with Hank Williams as a true pioneer of autobiographical country singer-songwriting. Such Monroe "true songs" as "Along about Daybreak," "Letter from My Darlin'," and the number that inspired the title of my book, "Can't You Hear Me Callin'," predate such better-known Williams compositions as "Cold Cold Heart" and "Your Cheatin' Heart." The greater credit given to Williams as an early autobiographical composer is the result of much more than Hank's greater record sales: the influence of Williams's life on his songs has been well known, while the role that Monroe's experiences played in his music has heretofore remained largely hidden.

Lest my commitment to uncovering information about Bill's love affairs reinforce the current image of journalists as intrusive purveyors of tasteless voyeurism, let me note that journalism has had—and continues to have—an important activist/advocate function. One need only think of the number of crusading newspaper articles that have exposed unsafe consumer products, racial prejudice, miscarriages of justice, or ecological disasters. This advocacy function does not run counter to journalistic objectivity. It is wholly consistent with the principle of accurate reporting. And scholars know all too well how misinformation can arise and root itself deeply in the lore and mythos surrounding a topic. Indeed, an important function of primary scholarly research is to revise inaccurate histories.

In the course of writing the Bill Monroe biography, I have reported on aspects of Bill's private life that some critics within the bluegrass community deem too personal to be revealed, and I have been criticized for this. But I have also taken the role of advocate for Bill Monroe and disproved misconceptions and myths—some bordering on outright lies—which have become attached to the Monroe legend. For example, I have put to rest the story that the Monroe Brothers broke up due to a fight over a woman in which Bill supposedly slashed Charlie across the face with a knife; I have set the record straight on many aspects of the famous but highly misunderstood Monroe–Flatt & Scruggs feud; and I have assured my readers that—widely reported allegations to the contrary—Bill Monroe never beat up an old woman using a Bible.

Journalistic writing—particularly for newspapers—must succinctly answer the questions who, what, when, where, and why. In approaching the Monroe biography, I believed the "why" was immensely important. Unlike biographies of such musicians as Hank Williams, George Gershwin, Elvis Presley, and Louis Armstrong—figures whose significance is well established—it was vital in my book to make the case for Monroe as being more than "the Father of Bluegrass." He is perhaps the most broadly influential figure in American popular music, whose legacy was felt in early and modern country, the folk music revival, and early and recent rock 'n' roll. I believed I needed to make this case in parallel with my recounting of the events of his life.

When starting work on a story, journalists typically ask themselves: "Who has the story?" That is, what persons will know the things that are important? Who will be, as folklorists and field researchers call them, the informants?

Rarely does any person reveal themselves fully to just one other person. Invariably, it will require several persons to illuminate a life from varying perspectives and angles. This was especially true of the often guarded and taciturn Bill Monroe. Each of my best informants possessed a few pieces of the titanic jigsaw puzzle of this man.

For an enjoyable and surprisingly accurate tutorial on the process of discovering "who has the story," I highly recommend the classic film *Citizen Kane*. In the movie, reporters go from person to person seeking to solve the tantalizing mystery of the powerful publisher's last utterance: "Rosebud." As they do, the movie unfolds and new facets of the man are revealed.

In Monroe's case, there was no single "Rosebud." (As far as I know, Bill never owned a sled, or if he did it never came to symbolize the lost innocence of his youth.) But I knew there would be many people who would have his story or the pieces of it.

Information about Monroe has usually been sought among former members of his band, the Blue Grass Boys, and, indeed, Bill's sidemen were consistently illuminating. But I knew that I should also seek information from two surprisingly underutilized sources.

One was the papers and records of the late Ralph Rinzler, the folklorist and later Smithsonian undersecretary who in the 1960s linked Bill up with the folk music revival, helped revive his career, and began documenting his life for an unrealized major Monroe biography. In the archives of the Smithsonian's Division of Folklife Programs were recorded interviews, correspondence, and miscellaneous notes that provided astonishingly valuable information on a range of central issues, including Bill's childhood and the roots of his lifelong feelings of isolation and "lonesomeness"; feelings about his brothers Charlie and Birch and their music; his artistic philosophy, including his opinions on the esthetics of fiddle playing; his business dealings (or lack of attention to them); and his relationship with his longtime companion and muse, Bessie Lee Mauldin. Although some highly significant material from interviews with Monroe had previously appeared in album liner notes written by Rinzler, most of this primary source material had laid unexamined.[5]

If there was no single "Rosebud" in Bill's life, there were certainly many flowers. The second eminently important primary source of information was the women in his life, and there were many. It has been said that Bill Monroe had two just things on his mind—and one of them was music. Again, lest I be accused of sensationalizing my subject's private passions, I have examined his affairs with a kind heart and stressed in the book that much of Bill's womanizing was the result of deep-seated loneliness, a sense of psychological isolation, and fear of being deserted.

By far the most significant of these affairs was his three decade–long relationship with Bessie Lee Mauldin. Best known as the bass player in the Blue Grass Boys in the 1950s and early 1960s, I have documented that Ms. Mauldin was much more. She was Bill's muse and the inspiration for his greatest love songs; she was the mother of one of his children (a love child who inspired Bill's famous composition "My Little Georgia Rose"); and she was later the ally of Ralph Rinzler, Mike Seeger, Neil Rosenberg, and other young folk music devotees who helped the often recalcitrant Monroe during the 1960s.

I have also stressed in my book that Bill had numerous important relationships with women that were entirely platonic. These included his relationship with Sally Ann Forrester (who was a member of his band and his bookkeeper in the mid 1940s), Gladys Flatt (Lester Flatt's wife, who also toured with Bill as a tent show worker and was trusted with large sums of money), and his last secretary, Betty McInturff.

It was intuitively obvious to me that the aloof and supremely competitive Monroe would reveal himself to women in ways that he never would to men. So it is puzzling that the women in Bill's life have almost without exception never been interviewed in depth about their relationships with him. This neglect may have partly arisen as the result of sexism or self-censorship.[6] But the major cause has probably been unconscious and innocent: Many people who write about music automatically seek out musicians as their informants. They do not stop to consider that friends, lovers, spouses, even neighbors and employees, can often be extremely enlightening sources of information—not only about the artist's life but about the circumstances that gave rise to his or her art.

(If I am criticizing those who have come before me as chroniclers of Bill's life, let me most definitely indulge in some self-criticism. I too was aware in the 1970s that Bill Monroe had had, in the diplomatic words of Ralph Rinzler, a "bass player and long time companion" named Bessie Lee Mauldin. Yet although I was already contributing to bluegrass magazines in this period, it never occurred to me to seek Bessie out and interview her, an opportunity that was lost forever with her death in 1982.)

I am extraordinarily grateful to several women who were emotionally involved with Bill and who agreed to be interviewed, sharing their stories and insights. From platonic relationships came equally valuable information. For example, Gladys Stacey Flatt was there at the beginning of her husband's professional career (she performed along with Lester as a member of Charlie Monroe's Kentucky Pardners), and she was at Lester's side through his days with Monroe and the extraordinarily successful partnership of Flatt & Scruggs. Wives and husbands of course hear all about the joys and miseries of their spouses' work, and it was Mrs. Flatt who confirmed on the record that Lester and Earl did not coincidentally both leave the Blue Grass Boys within a short period in 1948, but instead talked over and planned their move together.[7]

In cases where an important informant has died or is unable to be interviewed, the next question is "Who now has their story?" This meant speaking with family members, friends, and acquaintances of Bessie Lee Mauldin and in the case of Sally Ann Forrester, who was suffering from Alzheimer's Disease and died during preparation of my book, interviewing her son Robert.

Networking is an important skill for journalists and scholars alike. When completing an interview, it is important to ask: "Whom else would you suggest I talk to?" or if an interesting line of inquiry arises, "Who else would know about that?" Ask the informant if you may say that he or she referred you. If permission is given, it is extremely helpful to mention the referral immediately when you contact this new source. This helps orient the new interviewee and establish your credibility in a genuine way. People skills are vital for the journalist: the quicker one can establish common ground with an interview subject, the better.

Of course, this process must absolutely be grounded in truth and a genuine spirit of good will. This is not just the morally right thing to do; it has a pragmatic value in close-knit communities like those of bluegrass and country music, where everyone knows everyone else. To be tagged as an insincere or untrustworthy character is fatal to the research process. Insensitive or scheming reporters will soon find themselves as thoroughly ostracized as a blundering anthropologist in a small tribal society. Contrary to the popular image of the muckraking investigative reporter, the successful journalist knows that professionalism, courtesy, and honesty open far more doors than pushiness or manipulative machinations. This was particularly true during my work in the South, where good manners and sincerity are the passports to wide interactions.

A word on journalistic procedures: As a matter of policy, professional journalists do not allow interviewees to review and edit the material. However, I did read back and confirm quotes for some informants who requested it. I also did not use unnamed sources as primary sources. All interviews were by name and on the record except for two cases where sources who spoke under condition of anonymity were used to confirm on-the-record sources.

In addition to interviews, there is of course the written word in the form of the public record. An examination of wills, deeds, divorce and other court filings, and census records is mandatory in providing a general background and context for the subject and in developing specific leads.

The public record is just that—public—and available to any citizen. Despite the stereotype of bureaucrats as grouchy, uncooperative creatures, I found personnel in public offices and repositories—particularly in the South—to be extremely helpful, especially if one presents oneself in a courteous, professional manner and comes prepared with as much information as possible by way of complete names, birth dates, addresses, etc. Not all this information is necessary to make a search—and you may not have it all at the outset—but the more you have the better. And if you inquire at the wrong office, the personnel will be happy to direct you.

Although a complete tutorial on public record searching is beyond the scope of this talk, here are some useful tips:

The town or city that serves as the seat of the county where your subject lived or owned property is the first place to start. Ask at the county clerk's office about deed records (which in small towns are often kept in the main courthouse but in larger towns and cities may be in an annex building). There are parallel sets of real estate records—the "grantor" books listing the sellers of real estate and the "grantee" books listing the purchasers of real estate—and both should be examined. Starting with the indexes will direct you to the main deed books. (The office personnel will show you how to look up names in the arcane indexing system, which can be daunting to a beginner.)

Sometimes there can be wonderful, unexpected finds in these books. For example, in the Sumner County deed books, I found entered a non-realty document. It was a prenuptial agreement between Bill Monroe and his second wife, Della Streeter, filed with the country clerk. To this was appended a detailed financial statement (which thus became part of the public record). This statement confirmed much anecdotal evidence about Monroe as a business person.

Divorce filings are listed in court records offices, usually in index books but in larger cities—such as Nashville, the seat of Davidson County—in a computerized, alphabetized database.

Divorce filings are made by persons who obviously have a vested interest in the outcome of their cases. But these statements—as well as other legal filings—are made under oath with potential penalties for perjury. Therefore they are certainly as accurate as statements made to a tape-recorder-carrying journalist or folklorist, and probably more so. And because they necessarily contain names, dates, and declarations about events—the legal equivalent of journalism's who, what, where, and when—they are exceptionally valuable sources of biographical background information in addition to means of shedding light on specific episodes in the subject's life.

Although most journalists have no qualms about delving into divorce case files, many scholars may shy away from examining these records of very personal and painful periods in their subjects' lives. But consider the fact that scholars routinely read, quote, and cite diaries, letters, and other private writings that were never intended for public dissemination. Why, then, should there be a reluctance to examine documents that are generated under legal authority, intended to be part of the public record?[8]

Some examples will illustrate how oral and public record sources intertwined during research for my book. Hazel Smith, a prominent country music journalist/publicist and close friend of Bill's, informed me that Bessie Lee Mauldin—who had never actually married Bill—had sued him for alimony under common law. Hazel estimated that this occurred sometime in the mid 1970s and added that a small item had appeared in the *Tennessean*. Scrolling through microfilm representing the span of several years would have been a daunting task, but fortunately during a visit to the *Tennessean* to examine the old clippings files (sometimes referred to as the "morgue" files), I discovered the article in the Bill Monroe folder.

The article was brief but noted that Bessie Lee's attorney had filed the suit in chancery court. (Regular divorce cases are usually brought in circuit court.) I visited the chancery court offices and was able to find the case records because I had the approximate date of filing and the name. I asked the clerk to search under both "Mauldin" and "Monroe," which proved wise because the plaintiff identified herself as Bessie Lee Mauldin Monroe for purposes of her suit.

The file of course provided the only direct statement we are likely to uncover by the late Bessie Mauldin about the history of her relationship with Bill Monroe. It was also was rich in primary biographical material, making it a very valuable find.

During my check of the general court records for material relating to Bill Monroe, I also checked for anything involving Bessie Lee Mauldin or Nelson Gann, her husband and Bill's great romantic rival, to shed more light on the Mauldin-Gann relationship and the estrangement from Bill which caused Monroe to write so many of his most famous autobiographical love songs. I discovered a Mauldin-Gann divorce file that was small but rich in information.

One of the most useful pieces of information in Bessie's deposition during her divorce from Gann was that she and Gann had previously married and divorced but had remarried on Feb. 7, 1948, in Franklin, Kentucky.

A friend in Kentucky located the license for this second marriage. It recorded not only the names of Bessie's parents and her place and date of birth, but those of Nelson as well. This absolutely invaluable information allowed me to begin researching Nelson Gann's background in census records for Lebanon, Wilson County, Tennessee, where he was born. While examining the census microfilms at the Tennessee State Archives in Nashville, I also examined the archives' collection of Nashville city directories.

The old directories contained not only names and addresses but occupations of the listees. There was a second Nelson Gann in Nashville during an overlapping period but with a different middle initial, so it was an easy matter to track our Gann's history right to the time of his death.

Knowing that I was looking for a Nelson Gann living in the Nashville suburb of Goodlettsville, I was able to get his month and year of death through on-line Social Security records. Admittedly, it might have been possible to find an exact day of death by going through microfilms of local newspapers, but by now I was facing writing deadlines. I tried to locate surviving relatives or survivors who might know something of the Mauldin-Monroe-Gann triangle by cold-calling Ganns in the Lebanon area phone listings—a journalistic technique of last resort only a few steps above telemarketing. The process was not specifically successful, but I was eventually referred to a Gann family genealogist in California who comforted me by saying that the central Tennessee Ganns are exceptionally difficult to research. He was happy to receive the information I had on Nelson C. Gann, and, naturally, I was happy to share it with him.

I felt I had done my best. Scholarship teaches completeness, but part of the wisdom of journalism comes in knowing when the point of diminishing returns has been reached and deadlines must be met.

As mentioned earlier, people skills are vital to the work of a journalist. As a journalist, and now as the author of a major biography, I have discovered that I need an entire roster of skills: not only those of a writer but of a historian, archivist, field researcher, detective, psychologist, and paralegal, not to mention functioning as my own secretary, travel agent, chauffeur, nutritionist, personal trainer, and chief of security on the road.

In a sense, the successful journalist is also like his or her own academic department: the chairman, professors of varying interests and specialties, grad students and teaching assistants, secretaries and support staff all rolled into one. The finest academic departments and the most successful journalists bring a wide range of knowledge and talents to their work for the same purpose—to provide all the history, all the learning, and all the news that's fit to print.

Notes

This paper was adapted from a presentation given by the author on June 3, 2000, at the International Country Music Conference, Nashville, Tennessee. My thanks to conference organizer James Akenson for his acceptance of my proposal; to Charles

Wolfe for his introduction (and the many professional courtesies he extended during the writing of my Monroe biography); and to my fellow conference attendees for their kind and sincere interest in my observations and suggestions.

1. John Wright, Traveling the High Way Home (Champaign, Ill.: Univ. of Illinois Press, 1993), p. xii.

2. John Wright was not only concerned about the propriety of revealing the private life of someone he greatly admires but also the issues involved in writing about a living subject. Ellen Wright, personal communication, n.d.

3. A forthcoming book on the music of Bill Monroe by Charles Wolfe with definitive discography by Neil Rosenberg will consider in depth the entire Monroe oeuvre and certainly shed even more light on the "true songs."

4. Tom Ayers, "I Feel It Down Through Music: World View in the Titles of Bill Monroe's Recordings," *Journal of Country Music* (fall 1975).

5. Some of the most interesting material was uncataloged: Among the eighty-five–some boxes of Rinzler books and papers kept in storage in the basement of the Division of Folklife Programs's L'Enfant Plaza headquarters were a few containing correspondence from the early to mid 1960s, the period of Ralph's direct involvement with Monroe as manager. These were discovered when the author asked if there might be any relevant material not in the upstairs files.

6. In the latter regard, many writers are probably less aware of—and less eloquent about—their ambivalence in examining the life of their subjects than John Wright was in approaching his book about Ralph Stanley.

7. I have also taken the occasion of my book to adopt an advocacy role in another area, giving long-overdue credit to Louise Certain Scruggs, Earl's wife, for her pioneering role—and extraordinarily successful career—as a country music manager and booking agent.

8. That divorce case files are a surprisingly underutilized resource in country music scholarship was illustrated by an exchange at the June 2000 International Country Music Conference. During a panel discussion on the Carter Family, the divorce of A.P. and Sara Carter and its impact on the group was brought up. There was discussion of the mystery behind the divorce, who in the surviving family might know about it, and who might be willing to talk about it. One panelist commented, "I guess it's time that someone went down and opened the divorce file." As a professional journalist, this writer was stunned to learn that the divorce has vexed Carter Family scholars for decades, yet no one had examined the public record in the matter.

"MAN OF CONSTANT SORROW"
ANTECEDENTS AND TRADITION

John Garst

Laws of Tradition:
  (1) Nothing is lost.
  (2) Nothing stays the same.

I am a man of constant sorrow,
  I've seen trouble all of my days,
I'll bid farewell to old Kentucky,
  The place where I was born and raised.
    Richard Daniel "Dick" Burnett (1883–1977)
    "Farewell Song" 1913

By August 3, 2001, its 227th day in release in the United States, the box-office gross of the Coen Brothers' film, *O Brother, Where Art Thou?*[1] was $46 million.[2] In comparison, *Rush Hour 2* grossed $199 million in 32 days ending September 3, 2001.[3] *O Brother* is a box-office success, but by no means a blockbuster.

The corresponding soundtrack CD is another matter.[4] An August 14, 2001, press release states that the soundtrack "has been certified double platinum with sales in excess of two million copies. The soundtrack is currently in its 16th week at No. 1 on Billboard's 'Country Album' chart and is the best-selling 'Country' album of 2001 and the 14th best-selling album of 2001 in all genres."[5] It achieved this despite a lack of play, at least initially, on mainstream country music radio stations.[6]

The stations are part of the apparatus that promotes industry ideas, and what the CD contains is definitely *not* the industry idea of mainstream country music today. Instead, much of the album is similar in style to 1920s and 1930s material that might be called the "original" country music. The rest is similar to blues, work song, religious song, and instrumental music of the same period.

In the film, set in about 1930, three white escaped convicts, along with a black bluesman they pick up, become the "five" "Soggy Bottom Boys" and record "I Am a Man of Constant Sorrow" ("Man of Constant Sorrow") at a rural Mississippi radio station. It is a smash hit. Later, when the disguised escapees perform this song at a political rally, they are recognized by their music and are squared with the law by a gubernatorial pardon. Surviving subsequent near disasters, they may live happily ever after.

The soundtrack CD contains four versions of "Man of Constant Sorrow," two by the Soggy Bottom Boys, featuring lead singer Dan Tyminski, with different backup instruments. A guitar solo by Norman Blake and a fiddle solo by the late John Hartford, patterned after the version of famous fiddler Ed Haley, are the other two. The Soggy Bottom Boys' "Man of Constant Sorrow" has received several honors, including nominations for the

Dan Tyminski, lead singer of the Soggy Bottom Boys, whose recording of "Man of Constant Sorrow" for the film *O Brother, Where Art Thou?* became one of country music's most acclaimed releases in 2001

Country Music Association's 2001 "Single of the Year"[7] and the International Bluegrass Music Association's 2001 "Song of the Year."[8]

With the release of *O Brother* and its soundtrack CD, "Man of Constant Sorrow" has become an icon representing old-time and bluegrass music in the modern country-music world. It was already venerable. For over seventy years, it has been a staple of bluegrass and old-time string bands, having endured, as Charles Wolfe put it, "through the years as one of Kentucky's most famous lyric laments."[9]

Just how far back aspects of the text and tune can be traced may be surprising. With some features dating back nearly two hundred years, the story of the song well illustrates the workings of tradition. In addition, the style of an 1846 musical setting of a religious hymn, which was a probable antecedent of "Man of Constant Sorrow," may have had an influence on the harmonies of singers such as Bill Monroe, providing another link to the musical past (see Appendix E).

The best known version, that of Ralph Stanley, comes from Kentucky musicians Dick Burnett and Emry Arthur, friends and neighbors in Wayne County.[10] Arthur's 1928 recording was issued as "I'm a Man of Constant Sorrow."[11] Earlier, in 1913, Burnett had published a songbook containing the text, entitled "Farewell Song" (see Appendix A).[12]

When Burnett was asked if he wrote "Farewell Song," he replied, "No, I think I got the ballet from somebody—I dunno. It may be my song."[13] He probably tailored a preexisting song to fit his blindness.

> Oh, six long year I've been blind, friends,
>   My pleasures here on earth are done,
> In this world I have to ramble,
>   For I have no parents to help me now.

Burnett's song turns religious in the sixth and last verse,

> But there's a promise that is given,
>   Where we can meet on that beautiful shore.

suggesting the possibility of an antecedent hymn. Indeed, the term "man of sorrows" is biblical, appearing in Isaiah 53:3.

Charles Wolfe writes that "Burnett apparently based his melody on an old Baptist hymn called 'Wandering Boy.'"[14] While I have seen and heard songs with this or a similar title, none had a tune that I could identify with CONSTANT SORROW, the tune used by Burnett and Arthur.[15] (A name in capital letters represents a tune. A poem, hymn, or song lyric is denoted by a first line in quotation marks, e.g., "I am a man of constant sorrow," while a song, a tune-lyrics combination, is given a capitalized title in quotation marks, "Man of Constant Sorrow." An exception to the hymn and song rules is "Christ Suffering," a hymn that is so entitled in the original source.)

With minor variations, Arthur's lyrics are the same as Burnett's. "In trouble" is substituted for "blind, friends" ("For six long years, I've been in trouble"), "friends" for "parents" ("no friends to help me now"), etc. Arthur told Dock Boggs that he had written it, so perhaps Burnett got it from him.[16]

Arthur's recording can be regarded as seminal because it was the earliest commercial sound recording. Its text and tune have become standard in country, folk revival, and rock music, while texts and tunes of versions from other lines of transmission differ substantially. "Man of Constant Sorrow" is commonly performed as Arthur sang it, with minor variations ("Maid of Constant Sorrow"),[17] substantial modification,[18] or major textual changes ("Girl of Constant Sorrow," a coal-mining protest song).[19]

Another version was sung by Frances Richards for Cecil Sharp in Callaway, Virginia, in 1918.[20] Richards' song overlaps with "In Old Virginny" ("East Virginia"), which mourns the parting of lovers, one of the themes of Burnett/Arthur as well.

Other informants tell of versions that substantially predate Burnett/Arthur. In 1957, Norman Lee Vass sang a "Constant Sorrow"[21] that emphasizes parted lovers and overlaps somewhat with "East Virginia" but more strongly with "Come All You Fair and Tender Ladies" ("Little Sparrow"), of which Sharp prints no less than eighteen versions.[22] Vass said that his brother Mat wrote "Constant Sorrow" in the 1890s, after he lost his sweetheart. (When her husband died shortly thereafter, she married Mat, who then died. She was luckier on her third try.)

An even older origin is described by Almeda Riddle of Mena, Arkansas, whose handwritten "ballit" was given to her grandfather by a friend around 1850 (see Appendix B).[23] In language very different from Burnett/Arthur, it tells of a jilted lover who joined the California gold rush.

> I am a man of constant sorrow,
>   And many troubles I've gone through . . .

> I have some friends who have proved unfaithful,
>   But one to me's been most unkind . . .
>
> I will bow my head like an humble Christian,
>   To California I'll go on. . . .

Richards includes a line similar to one of Riddle's

> I'll hang my head like a humble Christian

but no similar religious reference is present in Burnett/Arthur or Vass.

Riddle opined, "Maybe this man that gave this to my grandfather had heard an older ballad on 'Constant Sorrow' and had just written his song from that. That's what I think." She was surely correct. The antecedent was a religious ballad that dates back to 1807, at least.

While digging into "Wayfaring Stranger,"[24] I examined Stith Mead's hymnal.[25] Here are the first two lines from the second verse of hymn 54, "Christ Suffering" (see Appendix C).

> He was a man of constant sorrow,
>   He went a mourner all his days

Later verses describe Christ being taken to Pilate by soldiers; being condemned; wearing a crown of thorns and bleeding; being nailed to the cross, whipped, and spit upon; giving up the ghost as huge massy rocks burst asunder; being laid in a new sepulchre; bursting the bonds of death; and bringing salvation to the poor.

The couplet quoted above is a clear model for the opening lines of "I am a man of constant sorrow." Further, in each poem the "man of constant sorrow" suffers "all his days." Each gives a detailed description of the suffering and each ends with a reference to heavenly salvation. By paraphrasing "Christ Suffering," the author of "I am a man of constant sorrow" invites others to liken his own suffering with Christ's.

Continued printings of "Christ Suffering" into the mid-nineteenth century, often in altered forms, imply that it was well known and popular. It appears in an 1829 edition of Mercer's *Cluster*[26] with a remarkable first line, "Come all ye skilful souls in weeping," and in Thompson's 1844 *Baptist Hymn-book*.[27]

The popularity of "Christ Suffering," or of Bible verses on which it is based, is also indicated by the appearance of a fragment as a Negro spiritual in *Slave Songs of the United States*.[28] Song number two, "Jehovah, Hallelujah," includes the second half of Mead's second verse: "De foxes have a hole, an' de birdies have a nest, De Son of Man he dunno where to lay de weary head" (see Matthew 8:20 and Luke 9:58). The meter and tune are both different from CONSTANT SORROW, however.

Similarly, an undated (probably circa 1960) booklet of the Phipps Family's "old time songs, hymns, and pictures"[29] contains "The Broken Heart," arranged by A.L. Phipps, which could be a three-verse (and chorus) recomposition of "Christ Suffering." The first verse tells of the Lord's coming to earth and people's apathy; the chorus tells of the crown of thorns and the beating, crucifixion, and heartbreak; and the third verse appeals to sinners not to turn Him away. The second verse echoes "Christ Suffering."

> The foxes have holes, the birds have their nest;
>   He had no place for His head.
> A pallet of stone, on the cold mountain side,
>   Was all that He had for His bed.

None of the hymnals cited above contains a tune for "Christ Suffering." William Walker's 1846 *Southern and Western Pocket Harmonist* does, however, in a tune entitled TENDER-HEARTED CHRISTIAN. (see Appendix D).[30]

TENDER-HEARTED CHRISTIAN is a variant of CONSTANT SORROW. It has an AABA form (or, in more detail, abab.cc'a'b, where A = ab or a'b and B = cc'), while CONSTANT SORROW is AAAA (abab.abab). Part A of CONSTANT SORROW compares well to part A of TENDER-HEARTED CHRISTIAN, both noted here with tonic G.

CONSTANT SORROW (Part A)

I am a man of con-stant sor-row I have seen trou-bles all my days

The tune CONSTANT SORROW, as sung by Emry Arthur.[a] Based on a transcription by Hally Wood.[b] Arthur uses part A only. This version is in the mixolydian mode.

Notes:
[a] Arthur 1928
[b] Cohen, Seeger, and Wood 1964

TENDER-HEARTED CHRISTIAN (Part A)

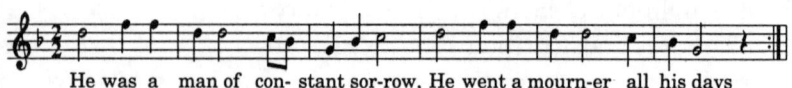

He was a man of con- stant sor-row, He went a mourn-er all his days

The tune TENDER-HEARTED CHRISTIAN,[a] part A. The rhythmic notation is awkward. Traditionally, singers follow the poetry, not the musical notation, in placing accents.
Note:
[a] Walker 1846

CONSTANT SORROW is heptatonic and mixolydian, with a minor (underline) seventh, 123456$\underline{7}$; TENDER-HEARTED CHRISTIAN, part A, is pentatonic with a minor third and seventh, 1$\underline{3}$45$\underline{7}$. To emphasize the parallels with "Man of Constant Sorrow," TENDER-HEARTED CHRISTIAN is set in Appendix D with lines from "Christ Suffering."[31] The text used by Walker is a variant of Mead's.

In the first phrase of each tune, an initial D is followed by a drop to F or G and a rise to an ending C. In the second phrases, a rise from C or D to F is followed by a drop to D and another to a terminal G. Details differ, but the melodies are similar.

A pitch versus syllable comparison filters out rhythmic differences. In this diagram, degrees of the scale, in half steps, are plotted on the vertical axis and successive syllables of the poetry are plotted horizontally. The horizontal dashed line represents the pitch of the tonic. The vertical dashed lines lie to the left of the most heavily accented syllables (4 and 8 in each phrase). A close similarity between CONSTANT SORROW and TENDER-HEARTED CHRISTIAN is evident.

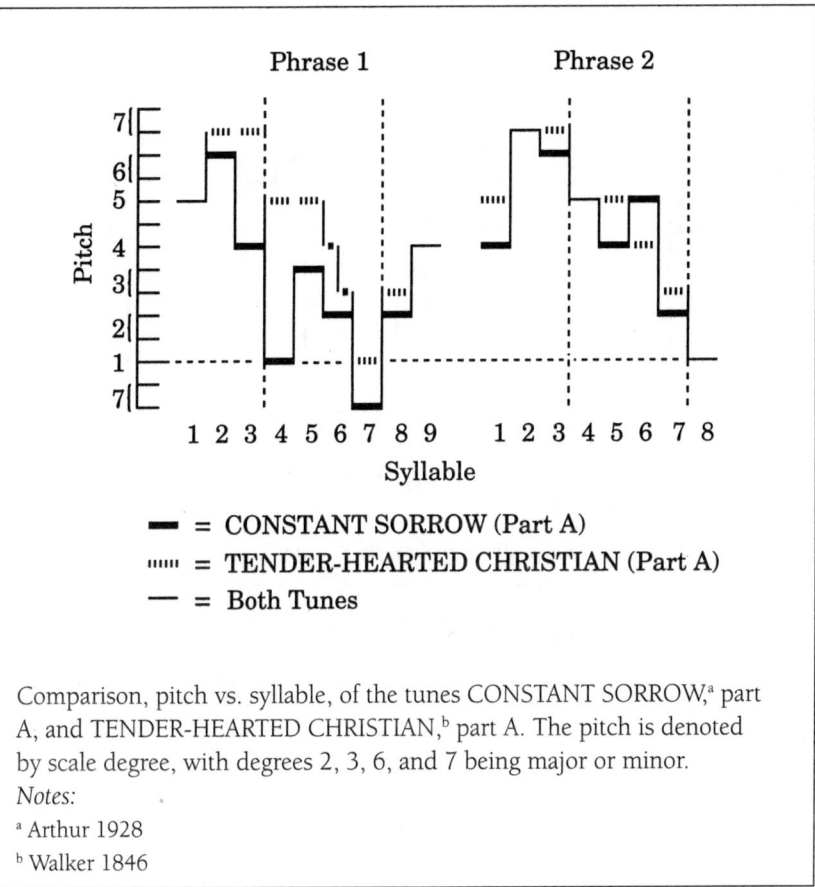

Comparison, pitch vs. syllable, of the tunes CONSTANT SORROW,[a] part A, and TENDER-HEARTED CHRISTIAN,[b] part A. The pitch is denoted by scale degree, with degrees 2, 3, 6, and 7 being major or minor.
Notes:
[a] Arthur 1928
[b] Walker 1846

There is additional evidence that CONSTANT SORROW derives from TENDER-HEARTED CHRISTIAN.[32] At least twice, CONSTANT SORROW has been recovered with a B part, having the same AABA form as TENDER-HEARTED CHRISTIAN. Fiddler Ed Haley played and Riddle sang it this way.[33] A pitch-syllable diagram of the B parts of Riddle's CONSTANT SORROW and TENDER-HEARTED CHRISTIAN shows great similarity between the first phrases and contour similarity between the second phrases, which end a fifth apart. Haley's B part resembles that of TENDER-HEARTED CHRISTIAN even more closely—both second phrases end on the fifth.

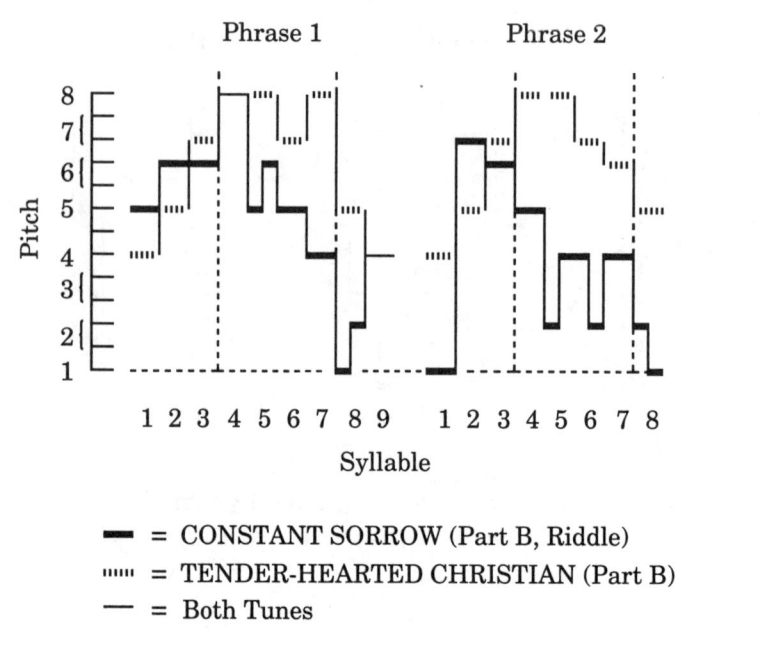

Comparison, pitch vs. syllable, of the tunes CONSTANT SORROW, part B, as sung by Almeda Riddle,[a] and TENDER-HEARTED CHRISTIAN,[b] part B.
Notes:
[a] Riddle, Abrahams, and Foss 1970
[b] Walker 1846

The meter of "Christ Suffering" and "I am a man of constant sorrow" is 9898 (doubled in "Christ Suffering"). The first line consists of nine syllables, 4 ½ iambs (-/, where "/" is a stress and "-" is not), and the second line eight syllables, 4 iambs. TENDER-HEARTED CHRISTIAN and CONSTANT SORROW also have the same meter, that is, they accommodate any lyrics with this type of 9898 meter. In hymns, this meter is uncommon ("I am a poor, wayfaring stranger" is one example). In Anglo-American folksong, it is more frequent, and is present in examples such as "Awake, awake, you drowsy sleeper"[34] and "Come all you fair and tender ladies."[35]

The commonality of "Come all you" and "tender" in the first lines of "Come all you fair and tender ladies" and "Come all you tender hearted Christians" (see "Christ Suffering," Appendix C) suggests that one may have inspired the other. This is reinforced by an astonishing similarity between part B of TENDER-HEARTED CHRISTIAN and the first two phrases of FAIR AND TENDER LADIES, the tune commonly used with "Come all you fair and tender ladies" (Sharp's "A" tune).[36]

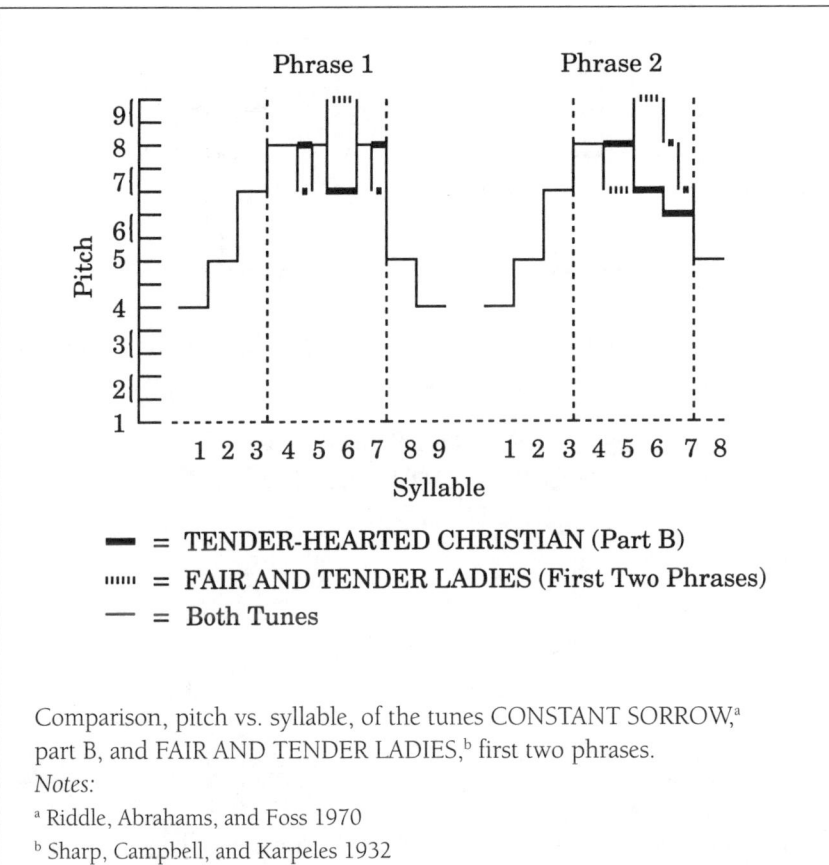

Comparison, pitch vs. syllable, of the tunes CONSTANT SORROW,[a] part B, and FAIR AND TENDER LADIES,[b] first two phrases.
Notes:
[a] Riddle, Abrahams, and Foss 1970
[b] Sharp, Campbell, and Karpeles 1932

These and related tunes can be regarded as a family. Included with CONSTANT SORROW, TENDER-HEARTED CHRISTIAN, and FAIR AND TENDER LADIES are WAYFARING STRANGER ("I am a poor, wayfaring stranger," circa 1870),[37] FULFILLMENT ("See how the scriptures are fulfilling," 1844),[38] PARTING FRIENDS ("Farewell, my friends, I'm bound for Canaan," 1829–30),[39] JUDGMENT HYMN ("The great tremendous day's approaching," 1805),[40] and numerous tunes for British secular songs.

Part A of JUDGMENT HYMN (form: AABB) is close to part A of CON-

STANT SORROW or TENDER-HEARTED CHRISTIAN. This pushes antecedent tunes for CONSTANT SORROW back to 1805.

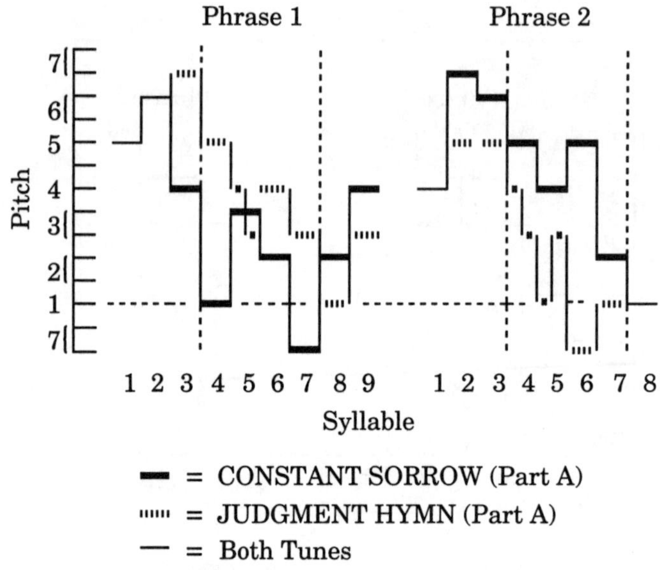

Comparison, pitch vs. syllable, of the tunes CONSTANT SORROW,[a] part A, and JUDGMENT HYMN,[b] part A.
Notes:
[a] Arthur 1928
[b] Ingalls 1805

Although the rhythms of these tunes vary considerably, they can all be regarded as basically that shown below.

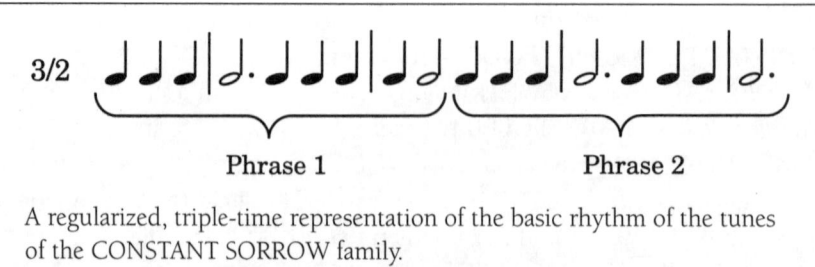

A regularized, triple-time representation of the basic rhythm of the tunes of the CONSTANT SORROW family.

The archaic nature of CONSTANT SORROW is demonstrated by its long initial note. In the period around 1800, it was a customary practice to sing hymn tunes this way, as is seen in *The Sacred Harp*.[41]

In summary, part of the path of "Man of Constant Sorrow" in tradition is clear. The hymn "Christ Suffering" and the tune JUDGMENT HYMN go back nearly two hundred years in American music history. The tune has antecedents in British folk song that are probably much older. In 1846, "Christ Suffering" was printed with TENDER-HEARTED CHRISTIAN, a variant of JUDGMENT HYMN, but they were probably used together earlier. TENDER-HEARTED CHRISTIAN was arranged in the style of the "good old songs," the musical tradition of which dates back to at least A.D. 1200. Today, echoes of the ancient harmonic style of the good old songs are found in bluegrass vocals, especially duets (see Appendix E).

Around 1850 someone wrote a 9898 song of a jilted lover's flight to the California gold rush. They altered a line from "Christ Suffering" ("He was a man of constant sorrow") to make the first line of a new ballad ("I am a man of constant sorrow"), which has been sung to CONSTANT SORROW, a variant of TENDER-HEARTED CHRISTIAN. The resulting song, "Man of Constant Sorrow," was frequently recomposed and mixed with other songs related by theme and meter. Emry Arthur's 1928 recording set a pattern for subsequent versions, which tend to adhere closely to it. Even so, recomposition has continued; see, for example, versions of Gunning and Dylan.

This typical folk-song story well illustrates the "Laws of Tradition." The ancient hymn text and tune survive ("Nothing is lost") in altered forms ("Nothing stays the same").

Should we be surprised at the success of "Man of Constant Sorrow" in 2001? I suppose that we should be—ancient traditional songs aren't smash hits every year. Even so, we can't ignore "Banjer" Bob's aphorism: "It isn't good because it's traditional, it's traditional because it's good."[42] Coupling this with the adage that "the cream rises to the top" gives an adequate explanation of the song's positive reception.

Still, the Coen brothers had to bring it about. Ethan Coen said of this kind of music, "We have always liked it. The mountain music, the delta blues, gospel, the chain-gang chants, would later evolve into bluegrass, commercial country music and rock 'n' roll. But it is compelling music in its own right, harking back to a time when music was a part of everyday life and not something performed by celebrities. That folk aspect of the music both accounts for its vitality and makes it fold naturally into our story without feeling forced or theatrical."[43]

Joel Coen called the film "a valentine to the music."[44] We are grateful.

Acknowledgments

The University of Georgia and the Department of Chemistry provided an office, supplies, and computational facilities. Helpful comments came from James Akenson, Joel Cordle, Jocelyn Neal, Neil Rossi, Charles Wolfe, Johnny Wright, and a number of newsgroup correspondents,[45] none of whom necessarily endorse opinions expressed here.

Appendix A

Dick Burnett's "Farewell Song"

From Wolfe 1973

> I am a man of constant sorrow,
>   I've seen trouble all of my days;
> I'll bid farewell to old Kentucky,
>   The place where I was born and raised.
>
> Oh, six long year I've been blind, friends.
>   My pleasures here on earth are done,
> In this world I have to ramble,
>   For I have no parents to help me now.
>
> So fare you well my own true lover,
>   I fear I never see you again,
> For I'm bound to ride the Northern railroad,
>   Perhaps I'll die upon the train.
>
> Oh, you may bury me in some deep valley,
>   For many year there I may lay.
> Oh, when you're dreaming while you're slumbering
>   While I am sleeping in the clay.
>
> Oh, fare you well to my native country,
>   The place where I have loved so well,

For I have all kinds of trouble,
  In this vain world no tongue can tell.

Dear friends, although I may be a stranger,
  My face you may never see no more;
But there's a promise that is given,
  Where we can meet on that beautiful shore.

Appendix B

Almeda Riddle's "Man of Constant Sorrow"

From Riddle, Abrahams, and Foss 1970.

I am a man of constant sorrow,
  And many troubles I've gone through,
But the thing that bows my heart in sorrow
  I will shortly tell to you.

I have some friends who have proved faithful,
  But one to me's been most unkind.
I'll bow my head like an humble Christian
  And leave my troubles all behind.

I will bow my head like an humble Christian,
  To California I'll go on.
When I am traveling through the mountains
  I'll cast a wishful look behind.

Yes, when I'm traveling o'er the Rockies
  I'll cast a longing look behind.
I will pray for the friends who have been faithful
  And forgive the one who's been unkind.

So, fare you well my loving comrade,
  The days I spent with you have been good.
I'll think of you often by the campfires
  While I am traveling my lonely road.

When I am traveling down the mountain
   I'll think of you whom I've left behind,
For though some friends have proved unfaithful,
   To me you ever have been kind.

Appendix C

"Christ Suffering"

From Mead 1807

Come all you tender hearted Christians,
   O Come and help me for to mourn,
To see the son of God a bleeding,
   And his precious body torn,
To see him in the garden lying,
   And his body bowed down,
To see the bloody sweat a running,
   In drops a falling to the ground.

He was a man of constant sorrow,
   He went a mourner all his days,
And with grief was well acquainted,
   He never went in sinful ways,
The foxes they have holes provided,
   And the fowls of th' air have nests,
But the son of God had no where,
   For to lay his head to rest.

Behold the soldiers when they took him,
   And led him unto Pilate's bar,
Come all you broken hearted mourners,
   O Come and view your Saviour here,
Behold him when he was condemned,
   A wearing of his thorny crown,
And his tender temples pierced,
   Until the blood came trickling down.

See the soldiers, now they take him,
   And nail him to the rugged tree,
With their knotted whips they scourge him,
   Until the bones by-standers see,
He gave his back up to the smiters,
   Who made long furrows in the same,
And his visage was more marred,
   Than any of the sons of men.

He did not hide his face from spitting,
   Nor his cheeks from cruel hands,
You persecuting sinners view him,
   For you he spreads his bleeding hands,
O Who is that that comes from BOZRAH,
   With his garments dyed red,
And his vesture with crimson stained,
   Like one who in the wine press tread?

Behold him on the cross a bleeding,
   And his soul in agony,
The glittering sun withdraws his shining,
   All this was done for sinful me,
Huge massy rocks were burst asunder,
   When the lamb gave up the ghost,
The pond'rous earth did quake and tremble,
   And many of the dead came forth.

They laid him in a new sepulchre,
   Where never man was laid before,
He burst the bands of death asunder,
   And brought salvation to the poor,
Behold him pleading for poor sinners,
   At his heavenly father's side,
And when justice cries against him,
   Says, father spare them I have died.

Appendix D

Tender-Hearted Christian

From Walker 1846

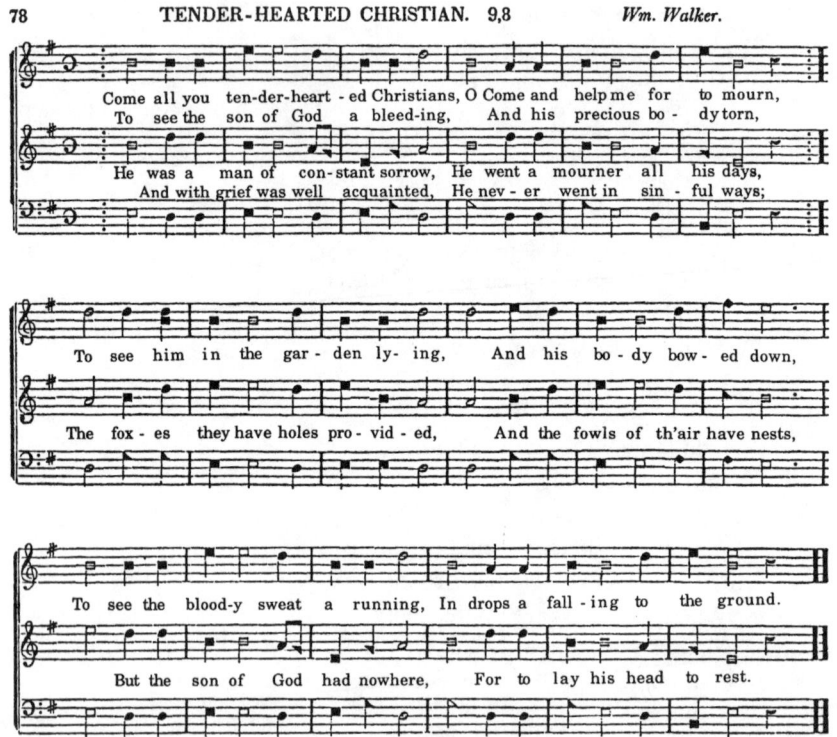

The music shown here is from Walker,[a] the words are from Mead.[b]
Walker sets a variant of the same hymn to his music.
Notes:
[a] Walker 1846
[b] Mead 1807

Appendix E

"Man of Constant Sorrow" and Bluegrass Vocal Harmony

The text ("I am a man of constant sorrow") and tune (CONSTANT SORROW) of the song "Man of Constant Sorrow" are derived from two-hundred-year-old antecedents. One of these is part of a tradition that may have influenced recent and current performances in another way. The 1846 tune TENDER-HEARTED CHRISTIAN, a close variant and probable precursor of CONSTANT SORROW, is arranged in three vocal parts in the distinctive style of the "good old songs." Characteristics of the good old songs, discussed below, are found in the bluegrass vocal harmony of Bill Monroe and others.

Many authors have commented that bluegrass singing is rooted in old church music. According to John Cohen, "One can hear more of the old church sounds in Bluegrass singing than in Charlie Poole's style."[46] Here, "old" is taken to mean, roughly, extant in the first half of the twentieth century. Which old music is relevant? Possibilities from white song traditions include "new works" (southern gospel songs);[47] other holiness songs;[48] singing in the "old way";[49] and the good old songs.[50]

Surely all influenced bluegrass. Bluegrass bands commonly perform gospel songs from the new works tradition, often in vocal quartets; Ralph Stanley's slow, ornamented singing illustrates the old way, with which he is very familiar from church; and the energy of holiness singing is often heard. But the focus here is on the good old songs, their contrasts with new works, and their residues in bluegrass.

The good old songs are alive today in singings from shaped-note singing-school manuals such as *The Sacred Harp*,[51] *The Christian Harmony*,[52] *The Southern Harmony*,[53] *The New Harp of Columbia*,[54] and *The Good Old Songs*.[55] The first four, which are oblong, are commonly known in the south as "old harp" books. *The Good Old Songs*, an upright Primitive Baptist hymn and tune book, is the source of the name chosen here to designate this music. (It should be noted that none of these books contains good old songs exclusively.)

Some of the good old songs were written by New England and British composers, mostly from the period between 1750 and 1810. Here, however, we are more interested in the folk hymns that were arranged by singing-school masters and their friends beginning in the 1790s. TENDER-HEARTED CHRISTIAN is a folk hymn and good old song found in *The Southern and Western Pocket Harmonist*,[56] an old harp book.

New works are found in upright books, published mostly in paperback by R.E. Winsett, James D. Vaughn, Stamps-Baxter, and many others. They trace to early-nineteenth-century Americans led by what Gilbert Chase called the "better music boys,"[57] Lowell Mason, Thomas Hastings, William B. Bradbury, etc., to whom the good old songs were anathema because they did not conform to their ideas of "modern" principles of harmony. B.C. Unseld, Ephraim Ruebush, and Aldine S. Kieffer were important post–Civil War figures in the development of new works.[58] In the term "southern gospel song," "southern" serves to distinguish the genre from black gospel song, but it is misleading, as plenty of Yankees were involved from the very beginning. "New works," "new book," and "little book" are terms commonly used in the South to distinguish this music from the good old songs of "old harp" books.

There are great differences between new works and the good old songs. Eight specific points are noted here.

(1) The good old songs are arranged in two to four vocal parts, with three being common, but not universal, in the nineteenth century, while most twentieth-century editions have four parts. New works have always been in four parts.

(2) Many of the melodies of the folk hymns are pentatonic or basically so. The melody of TENDER-HEARTED CHRISTIAN (middle staff) is basically pentatonic (EGABD)—C occurs once (measure 12). (F# occurs once or twice in each harmony part but not in the melody.) Most new works' melodies are heptatonic.

(3) There are differences in modality. In the tradition of the good old songs, music is classified as "major" (major third degree) or "minor" (minor third). About half is "minor." In "major" music, the seventh degree is sometimes minor (as in the mixolydian mode) or there may be other variations from the conventional major scale. Almost exclusively, new works are in conventional major keys (ionian mode).[59] Minor keys and other modes are very rare.

Where the sixth is present in good-old-songs "minor" music, it is sung major (as in the dorian mode, a half-tone higher than in a natural minor scale), following a long tradition of *musica ficta,* in which accidentals are supplied in performance but not printed in the score. In measure twelve of TENDER-HEARTED CHRISTIAN, the printed note C in the melody (second staff) would be raised to C# by singers. New works are intended to be sung as written.

(4) In the original arrangements of the good old songs, the melody lies in an inner voice (see, for example, *The Sacred Harp*). This was commonplace around 1800. It survives today in barbershop singing as well in the good old songs. In old harp books, the parts are written on separate staves, forming a brace (see Appendix D). From bottom to top, the parts are bass, tenor, alto (if four parts are present), and treble. The melody is in the tenor part.

The "better music boys" placed the melody in the highest part (soprano), as do new-works books, which are issued regularly. When women are included among new-works singers, sopranos sing the melody. When there are no women, the parts may be rearranged. One common method places the soprano part in the male tenor vocal range and the alto part higher, in the female alto vocal range,[60] thereby shifting the melody to an inner voice, as in the good old songs.

Professional male and mixed quartets and other groups in southern gospel song do not always represent the grassroots new works tradition very well. They often use elaborate arrangements, different from the ones printed in the song books, which show off their virtuosity. The characteristics of new works considered here are those found in "class" singing. A "class" denotes either a singing-school class or a group of men and women gathered for a singing that follows the arrangements printed in new-works books.

(5) New works use conventional harmony, with triads and related chords in conventional progressions. The good old songs do not. They belong to a tradition, dating back as far as A.D. 1200 in Europe,[61] in which the parts have nearly equal importance and each is a good tune on its own. This kind of polyphony[62] may be termed "melodism." Although jarring dissonances tend to be avoided, there is no insistence on triads or chord progressions in the usual sense. A small degree of melodism may be found in some new works, despite the restrictions imposed by harmonic requirements, but in the good old songs melodism is paramount. This can be seen in TENDER-HEARTED CHRISTIAN, even though it is misbarred and noted in a rhythmically awkward manner.

(6) Many of the "chords" of the good old songs are dyads, or two pitches, often with octave doubling.[63] Fourths and open fifths abound and wide intervals such as octaves and tenths occur frequently. (Horn analyzes the music in terms of quartal harmony, based on fourths).[64] In contrast, new works use complete chords and close harmony,[65] where "close harmony" denotes the use of adjacent pitches of the chord, spanning no more than an

interval of about a twelfth for the entire chord in four parts.⁶⁶ In the "open harmony" of the good old songs, the span can be greater and inner pitches are missing. In TENDER-HEARTED CHRISTIAN all of the "chords" are dyads except for E-minor triads (in various inversions) in measures six, ten, and eighteen and G-major triads in measure seven.

(7) Rules of conventional harmony proscribe parallel fifths, voice crossing, and other things. New works tend to follow these rules; the good old songs do not.⁶⁷ Several sequences of parallel fifths are found in TENDER-HEARTED CHRISTIAN. See, for example, measure two.

(8) New works often use "backfire" (also known as "Arkansas counterpoint"), in which vocal responses to the lead fit mostly between the moving parts of the lead. This is absent from the good old songs, some of which instead have fuging sections, where imitative parts enter successively, wind up together, and fight it out in between. Fuging is absent from new works.

Where does bluegrass fit in? According to Daniel Gore, "the mountain sound one can hear in the Stanleys' and Delmores' singing can be traced to the singing schools of B.F. White and Billy Walker,"⁶⁸ compilers of old harp books and composers and arrangers of good old songs.

When I consulted news groups (alt.music.bluegrass, rec.music.country.old-time) and other contacts about the extent to which bluegrass singing follows conventional harmony, I got two opinions. The universal opinion from the newsgroups, which are heavily populated with musicians, is that bluegrass singing does not follow conventional harmony.⁶⁹ A contrary opinion came from an employee of an institution that teaches vocal harmony—including bluegrass—who believes that bluegrass harmony is strictly conventional.

A few newsgroup readers figured out that I was really interested in the possible influence of the good old songs on bluegrass and initiated private correspondence. The common opinion among this group is that such an influence is beyond doubt and that to reach this conclusion all one has to do is listen to some *Sacred Harp* and bluegrass singing. Neil Rossi wrote, "In fact, it was from having heard bluegrass gospel that I was struck so strongly the first time I heard Sacred Harp sung at the '63 Newport Folk Festival. I didn't know enough about Sacred Harp to know what I was hearing; I thought they were a bluegrass group without the instruments because the tunes and harmonies were so similar!"⁷⁰

Bluegrass singing frequently uses harmony parts higher than the melody. In bluegrass terminology, "tenor" and "baritone" do not denote vocal ranges but instead specify harmonic roles.[71] ("Tenor" originally denoted the part carrying the melody, rather than a vocal range,[72] a terminology that is still used with the good old songs, where women as well as men sing the tenor and treble parts.[73] In bluegrass, "tenor," "high tenor," and "high baritone" parts are all higher than the melody. The bluegrass "tenor" could be the counterpart of the new-works alto, sung in the female range, in a male quartet in which the soprano is sung in the male tenor range,[74] as described earlier; it could have been patterned after the tenor (melody) and treble (soprano) parts of the good old songs; or it might trace to both sources, which reinforce one another in having a high harmony part.

Bluegrass bands use chording instruments, typically rhythm guitar or mandolin and sometimes banjo. The chords and progressions played by the instruments are conventional except, possibly, for adaptations to modality. Tunes in modes other than ionian (conventional major) are much more frequent in bluegrass and good old songs than new works.

Elements of bluegrass harmony that are characteristic of the good old songs, rather than new works, have been recognized in classic recordings by Bill Monroe, the Stanley Brothers, Jim and Jesse, and others.[75] Raim and Dunson comment on open harmony, stating that "in a good deal of bluegrass harmony . . . the sweetness of the major third is cut by the octave separation," which produces a tenth.[76] Melodism is noted by Rosenberg: "Basically these are harmony parts, but there is a tendency—particularly in duets—toward vocal polyphony."[77] Both open harmony and melodism caught Seeger's attention: "Harmony in parallel thirds, popular in more formal music, is rarely used and Monroe's tenor harmony often seems to be a separate and superior melody"[78]

The following elements of the good old songs flavor bluegrass singing: (1) vocal duets and trios; (2) pentatonic melodies, drawn from the same folk sources as the good old songs; (3) modality, also from shared folk sources; (4) high harmony parts; (5) melodism; (6) open harmony; and (7) voice-crossing.

Tendencies toward open harmony and melodism are strongest in bluegrass duets.[79] As more voices are added, the chord structure may mold the parts more effectively. This point was emphasized to me by Joel Cordle, an old-time and bluegrass musician from Athens, Georgia. When I asked if he believed that the good old songs influenced bluegrass singing, he said, "It's in the duets. You can have wide open harmony. With more voices you fill in the chords."[80]

How can there be much melodism against an instrumental background of conventional chords? In a tradition that allows minor melodies to be sung against major chords, background chords might not be strongly restrictive. Further, when open harmony is allowed, as in much bluegrass duet singing, then a judicious selection of notes from the chords, together with some non-chord notes, permits effective melodism.

The good old songs are well known in southern states where many bluegrass musicians were born and raised. Old-timers attended singing schools in their youths, and while it is likely that most of these taught new works, some surely taught good old songs.

For example, the Louvin Brothers grew up attending *Sacred Harp* singings in northeastern Alabama. According to Charlie Louvin, "If anyone really wants to hear where Louvin Brothers' harmony came from, all they have to do is listen to a session of *Sacred Harp* singing."[81] In my opinion, the Louvin Brothers' music fits comfortably into the bluegrass tradition.

Given that distinctive features are shared by the good old songs and bluegrass singing, especially bluegrass duets, and that early bluegrass musicians were probably familiar with the good old songs, it would be difficult to argue against the influence of good old songs on bluegrass. Serving as another noteworthy example of the ties between good old songs and bluegrass, the Universal Pickers, an innovative bluegrass gospel group based in Waco, Georgia,[82] recently issued an album of *Sacred Harp* singing.[83]

Notes

1. bventertainment.go.com
2. the-numbers.com/movies
3. the-numbers.com/charts
4. Burnett 2000
5. georgeclooney.org
6. Ahrens 2001
7. cmaawards.com
8. ibma.org
9. Wolfe 1982
10. Ibid.
11. Arthur 1928
12. Wolfe 1973
13. Ibid.
14. Wolfe 1982

15. Arthur 1928; Wolfe 2000
16. Cohen, Seeger, and Wood 1964
17. Collins 1961
18. Dylan 1962
19. Gunning 1965
20. Sharp, Campbell, and Karpeles 1932
21. Shellans 1968
22. Sharp, Campbell, and Karpeles 1932
23. Riddle, Abrahams, and Foss 1970
24. Garst 1980
25. Mead 1807
26. Mercer 1829
27. Thompson 1844
28. Allen, Ware, and Garrison 1867
29. Anonymous; no date
30. Walker 1846
31. Mead 1807
32. Walker 1846
33. Haley 1997; Riddle, Abrahams, and Foss 1970
34. Sharp, Campbell, and Karpeles 1932
35. Ibid.
36. Ibid.
37. Garst 1980
38. McGraw 1991
39. McCurry 1855
40. Ingalls 1805
41. McGraw 1991
42. Woodcock 2001
43. Oermann 2000
44. Ibid.
45. Garst and others 2000
46. Cohen, Seeger, and Wood 1964
47. Vaughn 1922
48. Ely 1993
49. Titon 1997
50. Lomax 1998; Lomax 1998a
51. McGraw 1991
52. Walker 1866
53. Walker 1835
54. Swan 1867
55. Cayce 1964

56. Walker 1846
57. Chase 1966
58. Jackson 1933; Wolfe 1996
59. Jackson 1933
60. Wright 2000
61. Horn 1970; Seeger 1977
62. Ammer 1972
63. Horn 1970; Seeger 1977
64. Horn 1970
65. Jackson 1933
66. Ammer 1972
67. Horn 1970; Seeger 1977
68. Gore 1993
69. Garst and others 2000
70. Rossi 2000
71. Wernick 1976
72. Ammer 1972
73. McGraw 1991
74. Wright 2000
75. Cantwell 1992; Wernick 1976
76. Raim and Dunson 1968
77. Rosenberg 1985
78. Seeger 1991
79. Rosenberg 1985
80. Cordle 2000
81. Wolfe 1996
82. The address of the Universal Pickers is 5950 Mt. Zion Road, Waco, GA 30182.
83. Wright 2000

References

Ahrens, Frank. "Brother, Where Art Thou?: Country Stations Shun Best-Selling Movie Soundtrack," *Washington Post*, January 23, 2001, http://www.washingtonpost.com (Accessed September 6, 2001).

Allen, William Francis, Charles Pickard Ware, and Lucy McKim Garrison, eds. 1867. *Slave Songs of the United States*. New York: A. Simpson and Company. Reprints by Peter Smith: 1929 and 1951.

Ammer, Christine. 1972. *Harper's Dictionary of Music*. New York: Harper and Row.

Anonymous. No date. *The Phipps Family—Kathleen, Hester and A. L.—Present Their Album of Old Time Songs, Hymns and Pictures*. No place. "The Phipps family unto this day are entertaining thousands over Southeastern Kentucky's most powerful Radio Station, W.C.T.T., Corbin, Kentucky." Possibly written by A.L. Phipps and published circa 1960, this paperback booklet of sixteen pages, plus covers of heavier stock, includes twenty-four songs, four photographs of the Phipps Family, and a brief biographical sketch of the group that contains no dates.

Arthur, Emry. 1928. *I'm a Man of Constant Sorrow:* Paramount 3289, Vocalion 5208. 78-rpm phonograph record.

Burnett, T-Bone. 2000. *O Brother, Where Art Thou?* Mercury 088 170–069–2. CD. Produced by Burnett, featuring various artists.

bventertainment.go.com. http://bventertainment.go.com/movies/obrother/html/index.html (September 6, 2001). "Touchstone Pictures and Universal Pictures present, in association with Studio Canal, a Working Title Production, 'O Brother, Where Art Thou?' Directed by Joel Coen, the screenplay is written by Ethan Coen & Joel Coen, based upon 'The Odyssey' by Homer. Ethan Coen produces the film. Executive producers are Tim Bevan and Eric Fellner. Coproducer is John Cameron. Buena Vista Pictures distributes domestically and Universal Pictures distributes internationally."

Cantwell, Robert. 1992. *Bluegrass Breakdown: The Making of the Old Southern Sound.* New York: Da Capo Press. Pages 212–13. First published 1984; Urbana: University of Illinois Press.

Cayce, C.H. 1964. *The Good Old Songs.* 26th ed. Thornton, Arkansas: Cayce Publishing Company. First edition: 1913.

Chase, Gilbert. 1966. *America's Music.* 2nd ed. New York: McGraw-Hill. 1st ed.: 1955.

cmaawards.com. http://www.cmaawards.com/2001/press/press_082801_2.asp (September 6, 2001). Article dated August 28, 2001.

Cohen, John, Mike Seeger, and Hally Wood. 1964. *The New Lost City Ramblers Song Book.* New York: Oak Publications. The quotation about church music is from John Cohen's "Introduction to Styles in Old Time Music," p. 21.

Collins, Judy. 1961. *Maid of Constant Sorrow.* New York: Elektra Records EKL-209.

Cordle, Joel. May 2000. Personal communication. Cordle is now executive director of the Folkways Center of the Georgia Mountains, Inc., Dahlonega, Ga.

Dylan, Bob. 1962. *Bob Dylan.* New York: Columbia Records LP CS-8579. Recorded 1961.

Ely, Brother Claude. 1993. *Satan Get Back!* London: Ace Records Ltd, CDCHD 456. Notes by Tony Russell. These recordings of white holiness singing in Kentucky were made between 1953 and 1962. Those that were issued prior to Ace CDCHD 456 appeared on the King label.

Garst, John, and others. 2000. *Bluegrass Harmony* (thread title). The posted messages can be accessed with a WWW browser by searching "bluegrass harmony" at http://groups.google.com/.

Garst, John F. 1980. "Poor Wayfaring Stranger"—Early Publications. *The Hymn* 31 (2):97–101.

georgeclooney.com. http://www.georgeclooney.org/html/OBWATsoundtrack.html (September 5, 2001). Article dated August 14, 2001.

Gore, Daniel. 1993. The Shape-Note Tradition in Bluegrass Songs. *Bluegrass Unlimited* (April):42–44.

Gunning, Sara Ogan. 1965. *Girl of Constant Sorrow*. Sharon, Connecticut: Folk-Legacy Records, Inc., Cassette C-26. Issued as an LP record in 1965.

Haley, Ed. 1997. *Forked Deer (Ed Haley Vol. 1)*. Cambridge, Mass.: Rounder Records Corp., Rounder CD 1131/1132. Recorded 1946–1947.

Horn, Dorothy D. 1970. *Sing to Me of Heaven*. Gainesville: Univ. of Florida Press.

ibma.org. http://www.ibma.org/awards/index.html (September 6, 2001).

Ingalls, Jeremiah. 1805. *The Christian Harmony*. Exeter, N.H.: Henry Ranlet, Printer.

Jackson, George Pullen. 1933. *White Spirituals in the Southern Uplands*. Chapel Hill: Univ. of North Carolina Press. Chapters 26–34 treat the history and attributes of southern gospel song.

Lomax, Alan. 1998. *Southern Journey Vol 9: Harp of a Thousand Strings*. Cambridge, Mass.: Rounder Records Corp., Rounder CD 1709. Recorded 1959 at a *Sacred Harp* singing in Alabama.

Lomax, Alan. 1998a. *Southern Journey Vol 10: And Glory Shone Around*. Cambridge, Mass.: Rounder Records Corp., Rounder CD 1710. Recorded 1959 at a *Sacred Harp* singing in Alabama.

McCurry, John G. 1855. *The Social Harp*. Philadelphia: T.K. Collins, Jr. Reprint edition edited by Daniel W. Patterson and John F. Garst: Univ. of Georgia Press, 1973.

McGraw, Hugh, ed. 1991. *The Sacred Harp*. Bremen, Ga.: Sacred Harp Publishing Company, Inc. First edition: 1844.

Mead, Stith. 1807. *A General Selection of the Newest and Most Admired Hymns (and Spiritual Songs)*. Richmond. Shaw-Shoemaker 13045.

Mercer, Jesse. 1829. *The Cluster of Spiritual Songs, Divine Hymns, and Sacred Poems*. 5th ed. Philadelphia: J.J. Woodward.

the-numbers.com. http://www.the-numbers.com/movies/2000/BTHOU.html (September 5, 2001).

the numbers.com. http://www.the-numbers.com/charts/today.html (September 6, 2001).

Oermann, Robert K. 2000. Liner notes (Burnett 2000).

Raim, Ethel, and Josh Dunson. 1968. *Grass Roots Harmony*. New York: Oak Publications.

Riddle, Almeda, Roger D. Abrahams, and George Foss. 1970. *A Singer and Her Songs—Almeda Riddle's Book of Ballads*. Baton Rouge: Louisiana State Univ. Press.

Rosenberg, Neil V. 1985. *Bluegrass: A History*. Urbana: Univ. of Illinois Press. Page 7.

Rossi, Neil. 7 March 2000. Personal communication.

Seeger, Charles. 1977. *Studies in Musicology, 1935–1975*. Berkeley: Univ. of California Press. Chapter 13, "Contrapuntal Style in the Three-Voice Shape-Note Hymns of the United States," was published originally in *The Musical Quarterly,* 1940.

Seeger, Mike. 1991. *Mountain Music, Bluegrass Style.* Washington, D.C.: Smithsonian/Folkways. CD SF 40038. Originally issued in 1959 (Folkways). Notes by Mike Seeger.

Sharp, Cecil J., Olive Dame Campbell, and Maud Karpeles. 1932. *English Folk Songs from the Southern Appalachians.* London: Oxford Univ. Press.

Shellans, Herbert. 1968. *Folk Songs of the Blue Ridge Mountains.* New York: Oak Publications.

Swan, M.L. 1867. *The New Harp of Columbia.* Bellefonte, Alabama.

Thompson, Wilson. 1844. *A Baptist Hymn-book.* Greenfield, Ind.: D.H. Goble.

Titon, Jeff Todd. 1997. *Old Regular Baptists: Lined-Out Hymnody from Southeastern Kentucky.* Washington, D.C.: Smithsonian Folkways Records SF CD 40106. Recorded 1992–1993 at Defeated Creek Old Regular Baptist Church, Linefork, Kentucky. Singing by members of the Indian Bottom Association of Old Regular Baptists.

Vaughn, James D. 1922. *Hallelujahs: For Sunday-Schools, Singing-Schools, Revivals, Conventions and General Use in Christian Work and Worship.* Lawrenceburg, Tenn.: James D. Vaughn. This is a representative example of a stream of small, paperback gospel song books that have been issued annually or semiannually for years by many publishers. The "conventions" referred to in the subtitle are singing gatherings, usually held on regular schedules at church meeting houses or other appropriate locations.

Walker, William. 1835. *The Southern Harmony and Musical Companion.* New Haven.

Walker, William. 1846. *The Southern and Western Pocket Harmonist.* Philadelphia. TENDER-HEARTED CHRISTIAN is on pp. 78–79.

Walker, William. 1866. *The Christian Harmony.* Spartanburg, S.C.

Wernick, Peter. 1976. *Bluegrass Songbook.* New York: Oak Publications. Page 102.

Wolfe, Charles K. 1973. Man of Constant Sorrow—Richard Burnett's Story. *Old Time Music* 10 (August):8.

Wolfe, Charles K. 1982. *Kentucky Country.* Lexington, Ky.: Univ. Press of Kentucky.

Wolfe, Charles K. 1996. *In Close Harmony: The Story of the Louvin Brothers.* Jackson: Univ. Press of Mississippi.

Wolfe, Charles K. 22 Feb. 2000. Personal communication. Burnett's recording of "Man of Constant Sorrow" for Columbia was never issued, but he and Arthur used the same tune.

Woodcock, "Banjer" Bob. 2001. "Re: The Problem with self-produced CDs;" rec.music.country.old-time; 2001–08–30 04:24:23 PST; and other postings. Woodcock uses this aphorism in his signature file.

Wright, Johnny. 6 Apr. 2000. Personal communication.

The Selling Sound of Country Music

Class, Culture, and Early Radio Marketing Strategy of the Country Music Association

Diane Pecknold

In 1957, Columbia Records president Goddard Lieberson wrote an article for the *New York Times Magazine* that described, for the presumably shocked residents of Manhattan, country music's development into a $50 million-a-year business. The article dwelt at length on the simultaneous increase in country's profitability and respectability and concluded its exploration of the subject with a quote from Minnie Pearl. Asked when hillbilly music became country music, the comedienne reportedly pulled her blue mink stole around her shoulders and laughed, "Hillbilly gets to be country when you can buy one of these!" Country music scholarship since the early 1970s has tended to assume, with a similarly knowing wink, that it's all about the money. Studies by Richard Peterson, Charles K. Wolfe, and others have demonstrated conclusively that, even as early as the 1920s, country music was a carefully manufactured product aimed at pleasing advertisers as much as audiences. William Ivey and Don Cusic have elaborated on the impact that the economy of the recording industry has had on Nashville and the production of country music. And Minnie Pearl's equation of country with cash has been more often and more famously echoed in Chet Atkins's description of the Nashville Sound as the jingle of coins.[1]

Having discovered that commercial interests of various kinds have dominated the development of country music from the outset, many scholars have tended to assume as a corollary that if country's authenticity is fabricated—if it really is all about the money—then it cannot also be about the audience. This belief has been particularly apparent in historical assessments of the Nashville Sound and the efforts to promote country music that were undertaken by the Country Music Association (CMA) in the early 1960s. Even writers who seem ultimately sympathetic to the desire of Nashville Sound–era producers and businessmen to broaden country's appeal seem to view the stylistic changes and marketing strategies of that period as a cynical hoax perpetrated against an unsuspecting audience. Joli Jensen, for instance, has argued that the truth or untruth of charges that country music "sold out" are less important than the role the debate itself plays in helping us to recognize the unresolvable dilemmas of modern life: the payoffs and losses associated with waged work, cheap consumer goods, and intense individualism. But she also describes the Nashville Sound as a set of "economically based changes" that had to be retrospectively "justified as necessary and, ultimately, worthwhile." Bill Malone describes the Country Music Association as "a facet of the music's counterattack against the threats posed by rock-and-roll in the late fifties" and credits the organization with increasing the genre's popularity and securing its position on radio dials across the country. But he also frets about the fact that the organization's "yearly conventions remind one of a meeting of businessmen," symbolizing how much country music "has succumbed to the middle-class ethic of respectability and success."[2]

As Jensen suggests, the debate over commercialism in country music can never be resolved. But our understanding of how country (and popular music more generally) is produced and received can be enriched by exploring how commercialism itself may become a way of expressing deeper emotions and hopes harbored by many country listeners. In clutching her mink stole, Minnie Pearl was making a comment not only about her own success as an entertainer, but also about how country music and its audience were perceived and labeled by outsiders, and how commercial success affected that labeling process. In the late 1950s and early 1960s, the Nashville Sound and the Country Music Association remade the image of country music and its audience. During these years, the last great rural-to-urban migration of southern whites was coming to a close. While some migrants remained mired in poverty in ports of entry like Chicago's Uptown, the vast majority moved up and out, finding in the suburbs the economic success they sought, even if a deeper sense of well-being and belonging often proved elusive. For these migrants, the persistent stereotype of illiterate, poverty-stricken, promiscuous mountaineers was a source of continuing frustration. At the same time, proving to advertisers that its audience was not composed of skid-row down-and-outers was critical to the country industry's economic survival. Country music had always relied on radio airplay for its popularity, and in the absence of sponsor support, stations would continue to cut country songs from their increasingly narrow play schedules. The Country Music Association's marketing campaign was, in part, undeniably an attempt to broaden the audience and perhaps even to "appeal to people who had long denigrated country music and country fans." But at the heart of the campaign was an effort to recast the popular image of the southern migrants who had always been the music's core audience. When examined in its historical context, the CMA's public relations program must also be viewed as an effort to make the commercial power of country music a way of acknowledging the dignity of its audience.[3]

Country Music and the Politics of Trash

Like commercialism, notions of respectability and success have been woven into country music culture since at least the 1930s. Rural-to-urban migrants in North Carolina's Piedmont insisted that musicians on the *Crazy Water Crystals Barn Dance* express the same decency, religiosity, and moral rectitude that listeners wished to project in their own lives. Artists who ran afoul of audience definitions of respectability could easily find themselves without the local performance bookings that constituted the majority of any hillbilly musician's income. As one musician recalled, "Word gets around . . . and brother, you was in bad shape. They always looked at you up there as a bunch of nice people, you see." Bradley Kincaid discovered a similar phenomenon when he appeared at a southern Ohio engagement in rustic dress rather than a suit. Shortly after the concert, he received a letter from one of his fans explaining how disappointed she was that he would betray "the very thing we [Kentuckians] stand for aristocratsy [sic], dignity, honesty." Rural southerners who left familiar communities for unknown towns and cities hoped that their music, like their religion, might continue to help them identify themselves as members of a proud, respectable community. But in the wake of World War II, just the opposite appeared to be happening. Rural-to-urban migrants during the late 1950s bore all of the stereotypes that had been associated with earlier migrations, but a new wrinkle had been added. The hillbilly became threatening not only by virtue of the violence and recklessness that had always been attributed to him, but also because of his troubled relationship to the organizations and, especially, the media technologies that seemed to dominate American life during the Cold War.[4]

Though not as well known or understood as the dust-bowl migrations of the 1930s or the dislocations of World War II, the post-war migration from the Upland South to the industrial cities of the Midwest that peaked in the 1950s was no less significant. The dust-bowl migration had given rise to stereotypes of "Okies"; the movement of rural dwellers to the textile towns of North Carolina had created the image of the "lint-head"; and wartime population shifts had popularized the hillbilly archetype. So, too, did a host of negative associations follow postwar migrants northward, this time propagated by popular media as well as local prejudice. Those unsympathetic to the newcomers were likely to view them as lazy, illiterate, and promiscuous. Even the social activists and scholars who worked to help the new arrivals adjust to urban life too often focused on those among them who had fared the worst, thereby unintentionally reinforcing the stereotype of poverty and ignorance. Country music was an easily recognizable component of this modern hillbilly stereotype. Sociologist Lewis Killian, in his 1949 study of Chicago's southern migrant community, even suggested that the "indiscriminate application of the term [hillbilly] to all southern white laborers" could be attributed to "the influence of 'hillbilly music,' heard on radio programs featuring southern white performers and in taverns frequented by southern white migrants."[5]

By the late 1950s, the country music industry had nearly succeeded in jettisoning the hillbilly label, but the hillbilly stereotype attached to much of its audience still retained currency. A 1958 article on Chicago's migrant population in *Harper's Magazine* ran through the familiar elements of the hillbilly caricature. The new migrants, like the old, were "proud, poor, primitive, and fast with a knife," "fecund," "anti-social," unable to maintain an orderly home or watch over their rampaging children—"on the streets of Chicago [southern migrants] seem to be the American dream gone berserk." The article echoed an earlier exposé in the *Chicago Tribune* that spoke of the migrants in similarly degrading terms. "The Southern hillbilly migrants, who have descended like a plague of locusts in the last few years, have the lowest standard of living and moral code (if any), the biggest capacity for liquor, and the most savage tactics when drunk, which is most of the time." Opinion in other northern cities was hardly more favorable. A 1956 poll in Detroit showed that citizens objected more to the presence of "poor southern whites and hillbillies" in their city than they did to "transients, drifters, dole types."[6]

The hillbilly's inability, or unwillingness, to adjust to modern life had always been a key element in the popular stereotype, but cultural images of the southern migrant in the 1950s were updated for the nuclear age in a way that made his relationship to popular culture particularly important. Even when he was outwardly successful, the new media hillbilly was a savage underneath, lurking behind a mask of suburban respectability and technological sophistication. This, at least, was the story told by the best-selling novel *No Down Payment,* which was adapted for the screen in 1957. Part of a spate of suburban potboilers that reflected America's fascination with its newest consumer lifestyle, *No Down Payment* was a melodramatic reflection on America's evolution from benighted ruralism to sleek suburbanization. The novel warned of what could happen if the primitive hillbilly were not kept in check on the long march of progress. In the climactic scene, anti-hero Troy Noon (Boone in the film), a World War II veteran from the hills of Tennessee who has been relegated to a job as a gas station attendant in the California suburb of Sunrise Hills, self-immolates in a frenzy of violence aimed at the symbols of suburban gentility and class immobility. Consumed by envy at the ease with which his college-educated neighbors manage the modern order while his own southern accent and lack of organization-man social skills brand him an outsider, he assaults his neighbor's wife and dies trying to escape the scene of the crime. Like most treatments of suburbia in the 1950s, the book is critical of suburban conformity and pretense. But while the novel encourages a degree of sympathy for Noon's plight as a symbol of obsolete frontier independence (and lawlessness), in the end it is clear that hillbillies like Troy Noon must go the way of all creatures that have been passed by in the course of evolution. In the nuclear age, Americans needed to reject the rural past and join the brave new world of consumerism and technology.[7]

The image of the hillbilly in the modern world was nowhere better captured than in Elia Kazan's 1957 film *A Face in the Crowd.* A dark satire that fused fears about the effects of the mass media with the urbanite's traditional disdain for country music, the screenplay by Budd Schulberg cast the hillbilly as a symbol of social and political decay in a classic denunciation of the totalitarian potential inherent in mass communications that called attention not only to the demagogic potential of television, but also to the artifice of the down-home country music image. The film tells the story of an uneducated but wily hillbilly singer named Lonesome Rhodes, played by Andy Griffith, who is molded into a popular icon by the broadcasting and advertising industries. When the television cameras focus on Rhodes for the first time, his handlers slap a cowboy hat on his head and a straw in his mouth and instruct him to "be perfectly natural, easy, and relaxed—and real country." Moving from Pickett, Arkansas, to Memphis to New York, Rhodes begins as a singer, becomes a musical spokesman for a do-nothing patent pill, and winds up as a mouthpiece for right-wing political interests. He is ultimately ruined when he inadvertently calls his loyal fans "a bunch of trained seals" and "stupid idiots" on the air. But the film confirms Rhodes's impression of his audience, alternating between close-ups of hysterical fans and anonymous mass audience shots to convey the gullibility and irrationality of the rural crowd from which the hillbilly singer has sprung. In *A Face in the Crowd,* the danger of the mass media lies in the ignorance of the audience that believes in the just-plain-folks hokum being peddled by advertisers and the country music industry.[8]

Ironically, the film reflected, in its production as well as its message, the humiliation born of many Americans' personal experience with the hillbilly stereotype. Kazan discovered early in production that Griffith still agonized over the insults he had suffered as a child growing up in North Carolina, where he had been taunted as white trash. Throughout filming, whenever Kazan wanted to transform Griffith into the deranged hillbilly demagogue, he would whisper "white trash" to the actor before rolling the cameras. This meshing of Griffith's own experience with the biography of his character reached sadistic proportions as production progressed. Kazan encouraged the cast and crew to ostracize Griffith and, on one occasion, to openly ridicule him for the "dumb-hick ignorance" of art and literature he had displayed at a cast party the night before. Griffith barely survived the filming with his marriage and psyche intact.[9]

The same blurring between fiction and reality took place when the figure of the unlettered hillbilly manipulating, and being manipulated by, the despotic machinery of mass media migrated from Hollywood to Washington. Kazan's story of media deception was perfectly echoed in arguments presented at the 1958 congressional hearings on the Smathers Bill, legislation that proposed to make it illegal for broadcasting interests to own stock in music licensing, publishing, or recording firms. At heart, the hearings were merely another installment in the prolonged battle between the two titans of the music licensing business—the American Society of Composers, Authors, and Publishers (ASCAP) and Broadcast Music, Inc. (BMI). The same dispute had already generated a much-publicized round of hearings led by Congressman Emanuel Celler of New York, which produced a string of vituperations against BMI-licensed country, rhythm and blues, and rock and roll music by well-known pop entertainers such as Frank Sinatra, Bing Crosby, and Billy Rose. Though predicated on antitrust concerns, the Celler and Smathers hearings served as a venue for discussion of some of the most controversial cultural issues of the day, including the erosion of traditional hierarchies, the "youth problem," and the potential dangers of mass media.[10]

In addition to revealing a great deal about race and class hostilities in the 1950s, the hearings reaffirmed the image of an ignorant hillbilly audience embracing whatever broadcasters chose to place before them. Vance Packard, author of *The Hidden Persuaders,* the best-selling exposé on the coercive potential of advertising psychology, made an appearance to testify about the "fantastic machinery" that BMI had created to "manipulate the public into accepting cheap music," especially country, rock and roll, and Latin American music. Though Packard conceded that not all BMI music was "necessarily trashy," politicians agreed with outraged country music supporters that his testimony, which claimed that "the public was manipulated . . . into liking hillbilly," implied that country music was culturally inferior to the music produced by urbane Tin Pan Alley composers. Senator Al Gore Sr. read before the committee a statement from Tennessee governor Frank Clement that protested Packard's testimony as "a gratuitous insult to thousands of our fellow Tennesseans both in and out of the field of country music." But it fell to Little Jimmy Dickens to point out the broader social implications of Packard's statements. "I think that when they [ASCAP supporters] refer to country and western music as trash they are referring to the American people as trash," Dickens wrote to the committee. "My folks and their neighbors love country and western music. They are simple, everyday, hard-working, God-fearing people and they certainly are not trash . . . . This isn't the kind of music that you have to force down the public's throat."[11]

Unlike the later stock-character rubes that would populate sixties television shows like *The Beverly Hillbillies* and *Green Acres,* the hillbilly in the late 1950s was a contemporary figure, capable of arousing real fear and deep anger. The hillbilly served much the same function that the stereotype of European and Asian immigrants had fulfilled at the turn of the century. A symbol of cultural, social, and political degradation, he represented everything that could not be digested by the modern body politic. This image was not merely a persistent holdover from earlier prejudices. In significant part, it was a new creation pieced together over the course of the decade from scraps of personal experience, sociological study, popular culture, and political conflict. And, as we have seen, country music played an important role in that image, both as an audible identity marker and as a metaphor for the hillbilly's inferiority.[12]

A Chamber of Commerce for Country Music

In November 1958, as Congress began to turn its attention away from broadcasters and toward disc jockeys in its search for a conspiracy against the public taste, the country music business converged on Nashville for the seventh annual WSM Disc Jockey Convention. On Thursday evening, just as the convention got underway, Jack Stapp, who had recently left his position as program manager for WSM to open his own publishing firm, delivered a keynote address and organizing speech for the newly chartered Country Music Association. The country music industry, Stapp warned, was in a dangerous position "created by bad publicity we cannot fight as a group" and "by inroads on the taste of people." Executives in New York and Los Angeles and radio programmers around the country were woefully ignorant of the country field, he said, and viewed the country artist as "an uncouth, unintelligent, no talent, no appeal individual." The chief goal of the CMA would be to "educate the people behind the closed doors" of the television networks and radio stations, to help them understand what country music could do for their ratings and for their sponsors. This educational campaign would need to be extended to the public as well, Stapp pointed out, for without attention to exposure, the country business would be "relying to a dangerous extent on the tastes of [its] loyal followers." And while Stapp spoke of the need to get country music into markets that were still "virgin territory," he explained that this effort was aimed particularly at keeping country music before its existing audience. Without "constant reminders" the loyal country audience would simply vanish. "If country music does not become more accepted nationally . . . if we do not saturate the country with good publicity, if we do not educate the public," he told the crowd, "we must be prepared to suffer the consequences."[13]

The evident alarm in Stapp's speech attested to the difficulties the country music business faced in the late 1950s. He almost certainly had in mind the recent congressional hearings when he spoke of "bad publicity and other mud that has been thrown at our business." Combating allegations of corruption and underhanded tactics in the music business would continue to be a part of the CMA's role over the next several years. The more important educational campaign, though, was aimed at the radio industry itself. As the 1950s progressed, Top Forty formatting had progressively overtaken the more eclectic block programming principle that had dominated broadcasting from radio's inception as an entertainment medium. The results for styles, like country music, that aimed for a relatively targeted audience appeal were devastating. In 1953, 65 percent of the nation's radio stations played country music on at least one show, and 236 offered their listeners twenty or more hours of country. By 1961, when the CMA conducted its first survey of AM radio stations, it estimated that only 36 percent were programming country music, and only 112 played even eight or more hours of the genre.[14]

In addition to addressing the condition of the industry, Stapp spoke to the personal histories of the individuals gathered before him. Like many people in the country audience, most of those who convened for the DJ convention had direct personal experience with the hillbilly stereotype. The cultural condescension in evidence at the 1958 congressional hearings had its roots not in the committee itself but in the popular music industry, and nearly everyone in the country field had endured ridicule at one time or another. By addressing his audience first as individuals deserving of the same dignity that so many other rural-to-urban migrants sought in the 1950s, Stapp put the assembled group in the shoes of country music listeners. "Country music," he said, "has helped to house you and your family, it has medicated your children, it has furnished you with the automobile you are driving. It's helping you to utilize your American heritage to progress and gather for yourself not only the necessities of life, but some of its luxuries." Deliberately or unconsciously, Stapp had hit on the same connection between personal experience and cultural representations that had proven so powerful for Elia Kazan. Underlying the educational mission of the CMA was the belief that country music could become a symbol of success rather than inferiority, for its practitioners as well as its audience.[15]

The CMA had actually been in existence for several months by the time Jack Stapp made his plea to the industry to insure its future by pooling resources, and the organization's nonprofit charter from the State of Tennessee made its central purpose clear. The new association would be dedicated to the "fostering, publicizing and promoting of country music, by bringing the commercial possibilities of country music to the attention of advertisers, advertising agencies, station managers, and radio and TV networks." The specific means by which this goal would be accomplished were less clear, however, and the CMA struggled to define its mission and strategy for several years.[16]

In January 1959, the CMA board elected Harry Stone, former station manager of WSM, to be the association's executive director. Stone's past experience suggested something of what the CMA hoped to accomplish. Working with the *Grand Ole Opry* from 1928 to 1950, Stone had been instrumental in transforming the show from a regional phenomenon into a national institution. His strategy had involved not only the selection of artists with a more modern sound than that which had previously characterized the roster, but also the restructuring of the show to make time slots more appealing to advertising sponsors. When R.J. Reynolds picked up the *Prince Albert Show* for national network sponsorship, it was Stone who helped develop a program that would retain its dedicated listeners throughout the South and appeal to a new audience unfamiliar with the *Opry* tradition. Few men in the industry in the late 1950s could point to a more impressive record of shepherding country music to success before a national audience, or of convincing advertisers of the genre's commercial potential. Wesley Rose announced on behalf of the board of directors that the CMA's new executive director would "expound [country music's] commercial advantages . . . through personal contacts with advertising agencies and supplying a steady flow of information to station managers and program directors."[17]

Unfortunately, the fledgling association was in no position to take advantage of either Stone's expertise in broadcasting or his personal contacts in the advertising industry. Instead, he quickly found himself occupied almost exclusively with fundraising. At the outset, the CMA's organizers imagined that only about a third of the money to support the group would come from the $10-a-year membership dues, with the remainder to be raised through benefit spectaculars and other fundraisers. Stone accepted the directorship under the mistaken impression that the major record labels had already committed to financial support of the association. He must have been considerably dismayed to discover, when he took up his post on February 1, that his treasury consisted of a few thousand dollars in individual membership dues, plus $1,200 that had been carried over from the treasury of the defunct Country Music Disc Jockey Association. The sum would not even cover the organization's most basic expenses—his own salary and that of his assistant and office manager, Jo Walker. Faced with the desperate need for funds, Stone set about arranging a series of benefit concerts. The first spectacular was planned for March 8 at the Kentucky State Fair Coliseum in Louisville. Showering city and county newspapers throughout Kentucky and Indiana with promotional material, Stone hoped to attract small-towners from miles around for "the biggest influx of visitors since the running of the Derby." But in spite of a scheduled lineup that included Johnny Cash, Ray Price, and Ernest Tubb, the show attracted only about ten thousand people, filling just over half of the coliseum. A second benefit in June at the Jimmie Rodgers Day festival drew about seven thousand fans, less than a third of the number who had attended the first festival concert in 1953. Between the two benefits, the association raised less than fifteen thousand dollars.[18]

In addition to raising money, the shows had been meant to generate media exposure for country music by demonstrating the size and devotion of its audience. As recently as 1957, Jim Denny's Philip Morris package shows had brought in crowds of thirty thousand to forty thousand weekly throughout the South, frequently with the same talent that donated services for the CMA benefits. The Philip Morris shows had been free, but they had set the attendance standard for package extravaganzas. Thus, the comparative size of the crowds at the benefits was discouraging and could not have been considered newsworthy except at the local level. The CMA also found itself at cross-purposes in relying on performances for income. First, the arrangement demanded a disproportionate contribution from artists, who donated their time and paid their own expenses to get to the shows. The organization could not long rely on a single category of the membership for support before resentment began to surface. Moreover, in arranging the benefits, the CMA had to avoid competing with the regular engagements upon which artists and booking agents relied for income. As a result, locations for benefits were selected in part precisely because they were less likely to produce large crowds and were therefore less desirable for commercial shows. Ironically, rural areas had always been a challenge for promoters of large-scale country shows, and as the countryside was progressively depopulated between 1945 and 1960, the challenge became even greater. It soon became apparent that benefit shows were not particularly well-suited to any of the purposes for which they had been intended: publicity, fund-raising, or audience development.[19]

The addition of institutional members in July 1959, the largest of which paid one thousand dollars annually, afforded the CMA a temporary reprieve, but not a permanent solution to its financial woes. By the time the general membership met at the WSM Disc Jockey Convention in November 1959, the fledgling organization could point to only a few specific steps toward its central goal of promoting the commercial potential of country music among the public, advertisers, and broadcasters. Stone had presented the board with a number of proposals for projects, including an idea for a greatest-hits promotional album like the one that would eventually fund construction of the Hall of Fame, but they were deemed unworkable with the existing staff and funds. The most notable achievements for the year had been the institution of a regular newsletter, *Close-Up;* the creation and distribution of a logo for the association; the mailing of five thousand copies of a promotional brochure titled "Country Music—Approved Everywhere"; and Mississippi senator James Eastland's motion to declare National Country Music Day in conjunction with the Jimmie Rodgers Day celebration. As participants arrived for the WSM event, a meeting of the officers and directors of the CMA focused on financial issues and on how to salvage ticket sales for the first annual CMA banquet to be held on Friday evening at the Brentwood Country Club. The same tone dominated the full membership meeting the following day. "Money is what we need and what we have very little of," Treasurer Hubert Long told the members after outlining the costs involved in running the organization. Harry Stone made an urgent plea for support, telling those assembled that "Country music has its best chance in a long time to sell itself to the American people." In spite of these appeals, the financial situation had already reached a critical pass. When the newly elected board met at the end of the WSM festival a few days later, the directors voted to remove the executive director and cut the association's staff back to its secretary, Jo Walker. Stone, frustrated by the lack of support and unhappy with the way his position had evolved, readily agreed to resign. As Walker later explained, "We just didn't have the money to pay both of our salaries. Mine was a lot less and, besides, I could type."[20]

In February 1960, the officers and board of the CMA convened in Shreveport for the first quarterly meeting since Stone's departure. The night before the business meeting, Jo Walker met with President Connie B. Gay to discuss the state of the organization. The CMA's two bank accounts, she told him, contained only about $735. If the gathering the following day were not opened on a positive note, Walker feared the directors would vote to disband. When the directors arrived for the meeting, Connie Gay began the meeting with a few comments. He had just finished a cross-country trip, he said, and was pleased to report that their efforts were having an effect. More stations were playing country music, a few had even started a full-time country schedule and they were meeting with success. RCA-Victor vice-president Steve Sholes remarked that his company's country record sales had improved. As the discussion continued, optimism grew, and by the time the finances were discussed, all agreed that they had made enough headway to justify continued effort. D Kilpatrick, who headed the Acuff-Rose Artists booking agency, one of the CMA's first institutional members, suggested that in order to keep the association afloat the institutional members might be persuaded to pay their annual dues right away, rather than waiting until they came due in July. The representatives of the institutional members who were present agreed. Jo Walker remembers this as the turning point for the organization. "It just grew from there, but not by leaps and bounds for quite some time. But the people were dedicated and they were determined. And of course that was an inspiration to me. It made me work longer hours and work harder than I'd ever worked in my life." In June, the board reported that the treasury was on firm footing.[21]

Changes in broadcasting had been at the root of the country industry's problems in the late 1950s, and the rebirth of country radio provided the foundation for the CMA's promotional efforts, and for the organization's success. Measuring and publicizing the growth of country radio, both as an argument for the music's essential appeal and as an index of the association's impact, became one of the CMA's central concerns. *Close-Up* provided the most obvious vehicle for drawing attention to the nascent trend. The same issue that reported the results of the pivotal Shreveport meeting listed four stations that had switched to an all-country format, and announcements of stations that had recently increased country programming became a regular feature in the newsletter. The announcements not only created an impression of country music's popularity, but also helped record companies, booking agents, and concert promoters to identify DJs for their promotional lists. But it was not until August 1960 that the association formalized its radio campaign. At the quarterly meeting, the board appointed Capitol executive Ken Nelson to head a committee that would conduct "an educational campaign at the ad agency level . . . to acquaint time-buyers and other agency executives with the full facts relative to the mass popularity" of country music. Within a month, the committee had sent its first mailing to three hundred agents and buyers, a reprint of an article in *Sponsor,* one of the largest trade magazines in the broadcast advertising field, that had run under the title "Country Music: A Gold Mine for City Broadcasters."[22]

Like the larger radio campaign it initiated, the mailing was aimed at helping advertisers understand the audience for country music in new terms: as average, middle-class, urban and suburban adults, not listeners who had been lured away from the pop audience, but country music fans who would otherwise not be reached by radio. The country music audience, the article from *Sponsor* said, was composed of "the every-day working people of any city, large or small—the housewife, mill worker, fisherman, truck driver—in short, the people the advertiser wants to reach." And while the article suggested that this was where the advertiser would "find the immensity of the middle class," the audience it described was clearly affluent blue-collar workers rather than the stereotypical suburban middle class. The article argued that a properly run country music station in any of the large metropolitan areas of the Northeast or Midwest could reach "a listening audience never dreamed of in a general market format," "a vast untouched audience" commanding "many, many thousands of consumer dollars." In September, Charles Bernard, a New York advertising representative who had long specialized in country music, announced the results of a national survey of the country radio audience he had commissioned from a leading ratings firm. The survey reaffirmed the growing consensus on the nature of the country audience. Country listeners were loyal to country stations; they could not be reached by contemporary format radio. They were adults, "the man who works for the dollar and the woman who spends it." And perhaps most surprising to sponsors, their median income was actually higher than the national average. It was an image in sharp contrast to the white trash stereotype that dominated popular culture.[23]

The Selling Sound of Country Music

The CMA tried to communicate its message about the country music audience at every opportunity: in press releases about concerts (such as the one that referred to the first *Grand Ole Opry* appearance at Carnegie Hall as "a great meeting of the white collars and the blue denims"); in sales materials for radio time-sellers; in the comments of CMA directors and officers in the trade press; in programming guidelines distributed by mail and in the press; and in personal correspondence between the CMA and station managers around the country. But one of the most notable vehicles for promulgating the image of the prosperous, working middle-class country listener was the CMA sales presentation entitled "The Selling Sound of Country Music." In the four-year span between 1963 and 1967, the show was presented to several thousand potential sponsors and advertising executives in New York, Chicago, and Detroit. The basic text was also modified for smaller presentations to groups in Norfolk, Virginia; Nashville; and San Diego, among other cities. The scripts for these sales shows offer a unique perspective on the message of the CMA, a rare record of the face-to-face interaction between the country industry and the people the industry perceived as being "behind the closed doors" of the broadcasting and advertising industries. Perhaps because the relatively informal atmosphere of the live performance allowed for directness without offense, the scripts dealt head-on with the stereotyping and class divisions that characterized images of the country audience and the country industry. In addition to being an effort to sell country airtime, the shows were clearly meant to disprove what the CMA felt to be "the widespread feeling in New York that country is a medium run by hillbillies for hillbillies." Though the content of the scripts varied slightly from performance to performance, the basic message was always the same: country listeners were consumers, and therefore deserved to be treated as respectable, intelligent citizens, not ignorant hayseeds; and country artists, like their audience, had become reputable, successful craftsmen.[24]

The concept for the sales shows developed over the course of several years between 1960 and 1963. In the fall of 1960, Connie Gay told the CMA membership that potential sponsors should be the association's main focus. "Country music's most urgent, immediate need is a 'crash program' on Madison Avenue and elsewhere," he urged, "to place the sales story of country music in the hands of large commercial sponsors and advertising agency decision makers." The first step was taken in January 1961, when the board and officers of the CMA met in New York and sponsored a luncheon for advertising agency representatives. After lunch, Gay delivered a brief speech on the commercial potential of country music and the mission of the CMA. Though the agency guests expressed interest, the lunch seemed to produce little in the way of concrete results. But at the quarterly meeting a year later, Charles Bernard reported that the Radio and Television Execu-

Emcee Tex Ritter joins the audience in applauding the performers at the 1965 Chicago staging of the CMA's "Selling Sound of Country Music" show. The show was presented to the Sales-Marketing Executives of Chicago as part of the CMA's effort to improve the image of the country audience. *Sponsor,* August 8, 1966.

tives Society of New York had contacted him about the possibility of presenting a show for the society's annual newsmaker luncheon.[25]

The luncheon took place in February 1962, with Ferlin Husky appearing before five hundred of the society's members as the emcee and star of a show titled "A Salute to Country Music." The choice of Husky as presenter suggests that, from the beginning, class was a central theme of the presentations. Husky was a well-known star, and his 1957 hit, "Gone," had ushered in the big, smooth sound that characterized Nashville production for the next decade. But Husky's stage act had always relied on the presence of his comic alter-ego, Simon Crum. Crum started out as a standard hick

Ferlin Husky/Simon Crum appears on stage with the president of the Radio and Television Executives Society of New York during "A Salute to Country Music," a promotional presentation that prefigured the CMA's "Selling Sound of Country Music" campaign. *Courtesy of the Country Music Foundation Library and Media Center.*

rube, but in the mid-1950s, Husky inverted the joke and became the country fool who fools the city slickers. Rather than aiming at the uneducated mountaineer, the traditional target of rube comedy, the new Crum—a well-dressed, pretentious fop whose ignorance betrays him as a hick on the inside—satirized the class snobbery of upwardly mobile middle-income

America. In 1958, Husky took his character to the big screen in *Country Music Holiday*. An unexpected box-office success, the film featured Husky/Crum as a gullible Tennessee boy transplanted to Manhattan, where he manages to charm a beautiful, high-society knockout (Zsa-Zsa Gabor) and is whisked away to a world of fox hunts and country mansions. Husky spent much of the New York luncheon in his Crum persona, dressed in white slacks and loafers, a dinner jacket, and a cummerbund. The inversion of clever hick and ignorant snob was completed when Crum crowned the society's staid president with a white Stetson, as if to suggest that broaching the class distinctions surrounding country music was as easy as a quick costume change. Bernard announced that the event had been a success and that the society was considering making it an annual affair.[26]

Whatever the use of humorous stereotypes in "A Salute to Country Music," familiarizing New York advertising executives with the sales potential of country music was a particularly serious issue for the CMA. The association estimated that 75 percent of the advertising campaigns that bought time on country stations had to be cleared through New York offices. The lack of country music programming in the city meant that the executives who made decisions about time purchases had little opportunity to familiarize themselves with the sound or style of a country station. The problem was eased somewhat when WJRZ in Newark, New Jersey, added an hour of country programming to its weeknight schedule, but a single show could not approximate the results a full-time country station would produce. The connection between the show for the Radio and Television Executives Society and the addition of country to the WJRZ schedule was probably tenuous at best, but letting the music speak for itself seemed to be an effective strategy. In December, the directors of the CMA announced that it had formed a committee to plan for a country show to be presented to the Sales Executives Club of New York the following May.[27]

Unlike the earlier presentation to the Radio and Television Executives Society, the Sales Executives performance in its very execution would demonstrate that country music was serious business. The show was to be a scripted stage production featuring half a dozen artists, and in addition to the presentation itself, the committee planned to produce a souvenir program and to record the show and press a promotional album to distribute to those not in attendance. The talents and resources of the entire industry would be on display. Early in planning, the CMA contacted Joe Allison and asked him to prepare the script for the show. A native of Texas who split his time between California and Tennessee, Allison had already been involved for several years with developing the full-time country radio format at some of the biggest stations on the West Coast. His experience as a disc jockey, radio consultant, master of ceremonies, television producer, and songwriter all influenced his approach to the script, though he had never worked on a trade show. In this first show, Allison sought not so much to demonstrate the demographics of the audience as to familiarize the ad men with country music itself. "You couldn't tell them anything about demographics," he later recalled. "They had the numbers. They could tell you [who] would listen to country music [and when]. . . . But what they didn't know was anything about country music." Allison designed the show to include a broad range of styles and to demonstrate for the executives the country influences in music they heard every day, from Ray Charles to Flatt & Scruggs.[28]

His work in radio consulting had made Allison acutely aware of the misconceptions and very personal emotions that surfaced in connection with country music. A few months earlier he had been invited to Sacramento station KRAK to help implement a new country format. When he arrived to meet the sales staff, he discovered that the station manager had outfitted each salesman with a bright red cowboy hat and a walking stick. The mortified team was delighted to hear Allison suggest that the hats and sticks would have to go, but it was a graphic demonstration of why many executives loathed the idea of being associated with country music. One of Allison's goals in the New York presentation was to convince the advertisers that they would be dealing with professionals, and indeed "not just [with] professionals, but top professionals."[29]

The goal of portraying country musicians as top professionals was achieved in part by the choice of Tex Ritter as master of ceremonies. In addition to being a well-known star, Ritter was himself a successful businessman and an outstanding speaker. "When Tex spoke you thought God was talking to you. He was like Franklin Roosevelt . . . when he was in a room and he talked, everybody listened." Between songs by Leon McAuliff, Don Gibson, and the Anita Kerr Singers, Ritter emphasized again and again that the modern country artist was an everyday businessperson. Country artists in the 1960s had to be sure to leave time to "confer with their brokers, tally their oil stock dividends, buy and sell real estate, send out the laundry, and regulate their highly successful lives in general." In other words, they behaved like any successful entrepreneur. The status-conscious executives of the broadcasting business, Allison felt, "were trying to find something that their wives could talk about at the country club and not be ashamed of it." The sales show supplied that something by emphasizing the professionalism and profitability of the country field.[30]

By the time the show was presented to the Adcraft Club of Detroit the following year, Allison had widened his focus to include the audience as well as the professionals of the country industry. The sophistication of the country entertainer was still an important point, but it was treated with a more delicate touch. "The songwriter who once tended stock on his daddy's farm is now consulting his broker regarding another kind of stock," Ritter told the audience, and like other affluent Americans, wise to the ways of the consumer world, he "[did] not consider his Cadillac a luxury but a commodity." In this second presentation, the country audience took center stage, with a narrative that explicitly contradicted the popular image of the destitute, ignorant hillbilly migrant. Using survey and sales account data collected by KFOX in Los Angeles, Ritter demonstrated that the all-country station was the most successful sales vehicle for new cars in the Los Angeles area. "Who are the people who enable the country music station to sell more cars than any other radio station?" Ritter asked. "Metropolitan population influx figures show that the largest percentages have their roots in the middle-west and south. Craftsmen, technicians, laborers, and home folks who are the working force." The audience the CMA was selling was not a new, more middle-class audience attracted by the modern sound of Nashville production. On the contrary, the country listener that potential advertisers were encouraged to envision was the same rural-to-urban migrant who had always made up the bulk of country's fans. The goal of the marketing campaign was to cast this traditional audience in a new light: as citizens, workers, and consumers. "The fans of our music elect the presidents, run the factories, grow the food, transport our goods and in general manipulate the gears of this country every day," Ritter told the Detroit advertisers. The "pseudo-intellectual" sponsor who overlooked the country audience "while searching for more so-called intellectual advertising pursuits might very well be cutting off his nose to spite his own face."[31]

By 1965, the tide had clearly turned for country radio programming, in part because of the CMA's success in advertising the format's achievements. A handful of stations along the West Coast—KFOX in Los Angeles, KSON in San Diego, KAYO in Seattle, and KRAK in Sacramento—had proven that a full-time country music format could capture a significant share of the audience market in metropolitan areas. In February 1965, the market that would soon be identified as containing the largest number of "country-western music households" got its first full-time country format radio station. Within weeks, Chicago's WJJD was broadcasting to nearly five hundred thousand households and pulling in a full 25 percent of the city's radio audience. The CMA was aware of the possibility that the station might change its format when, in the fall of 1964, the organization decided to make its sales presentation to the Sales-Marketing Executives of Chicago. In addition to inviting representatives from key ad agencies throughout the Midwest, the association invited country station managers from around the U.S. to discuss their success with the country format and offer advice to potential sponsors. The purpose of the show would be "to sell country music to advertisers and their agencies with emphasis on the responsiveness of audiences to radio programming of country music."[32]

In the Chicago script, the themes of cultural snobbery and audience respectability were fully developed, particularly in a segment that dramatized the interaction between the country station salesman and the advertising time-buyer. "If all the sales managers of the Country Music radio stations could collect and print their experiences connected with the objections of retail advertisers, media directors, and time buyers, the resulting work would have to be classified as a study in snobbery," Tex Ritter told the admen. He pointed out that country music offered an acceptable outlet for class derision that was otherwise inappropriate in a pluralistic society. "What a capital opportunity existed when the buyer of advertising used to open the door to a country music salesman! If the buyer happened to be in need of therapy, how good it was to say, 'You don't expect me to advertise with that (cuckoo) hillbilly music, do you?' . . . We simply do not feel that your (cuckoo) music is right for our product. Our marketing objective is the middle income consumer, and your gravy-sopping, hog-calling, barefoot itinerant hardly fits the image!'" Again using survey data from stations in major metropolitan areas, the script went on to sketch a very different profile of the country audience. The country listener was an educated adult homeowner, but was also clearly part of the working class, not the white-collar world. Country listeners were "bricklayers and plumbers, carpenters, truck drivers and stevedores . . . electricians, machinists, electronic specialists, technicians, and craftsmen." Though migrants from country to city, they were "*not* from some other planet," but ordinary, respectable folk. The advertising executive who looked down on the country music audi-

In this ad from *Broadcasting* magazine, WJJD portrays its DJ staff as thoroughly at home in the modern city by posing them in front of Chicago's Marina Towers, then a brand-new experiment in modern architecture. The image contrasted sharply with prevailing views of southern migrants in the city. *Broadcasting*, October 18, 1965.

ence could only be described as a class snob, "an otherwise bright person . . . so eager to display his 'status quotient' that he becomes a victim of his own propaganda."[33]

Such open attacks across class lines revealed what one historian has called the "stylistic war between plebian and patrician" that remained mostly obscured in the 1950s but found new voice in the 1960s. Yet, if the tone of the sales presentations echoed the emerging reaction against liberalism, it was inspired by the same pluralistic values that animated other social movements of the 1960s. Joe Allison remembers that "almost everything we did back in those days was very defensive . . . because we still had people hacking at us and calling us hillbillies and all that kind of thing," and he specifically compares the effort to recast the country audience with other, contemporaneous struggles for equality. "Being country was like being a Jew or being black or being any other ethnic derivation that had to fight its way out of the criticism into the light," he maintains, "It was the same thing. I don't know if it socially was as important, but we felt that way." The CMA was not alone in this perception, as a *Sponsor* feature on country programming acknowledged in 1966. The days of programming country music as "almost 'ethnic' stations" were passing, the magazine declared. "Now these same 'limited appeal' outlets are pulling in healthy shares of markets and turning up an audience that is a far cry from the Yokum-family image so long associated with the country idiom."[34]

By the end of 1965, the cultural redemption of the country audience was well underway. In October, *Broadcasting* published a special report on programming the country format. While the sound of country music had become more sophisticated, the key change the magazine cited for country's resurgence as a programming choice was "the awareness by broadcasters that their country music audience isn't limited to hayseeds, Okies, rubes, or Jed Clampetts." The magazine listed the healthy economic characteristics of the country listener along with a list of sponsors that included airlines and Cadillac dealers. Some station managers reported that they still had to deploy "great sales effort and unlimited patience" to overcome the "*Grapes of Wrath* stigma," but advertisers seemed to relinquish the stereotype with naive good humor. When WJJD encouraged one of its sponsors to attend a country music concert and actually see the audience first-hand, she told *Sponsor*, "I never believed I would see so many sophisticated and affluent people at a Country show." "They may not all show up in Cadillacs

A far cry from his role as a hillbilly demagogue in *A Face in the Crowd,* special guest star Andy Griffith awaits the start of the CMA show in Chicago. Seated with him are RCA Victor executive Jack Burgess and BMI Nashville head Frances Preston. *Courtesy of the Country Music Foundation Library and Media Center.*

and minks but neither do they qualify for aid from the poverty program," *Broadcasting* told its readers.[35]

There are many reasons to wish that the country music industry and the country music audience had clung more tightly to an alternative vision of respectability—one that did not rely so heavily on consumerism and commercialism—but the terms of value were set in cultural dialogues that transcended the world of country music. In Cold War America, prosperity was a resonant political and cultural language. It was invoked to illustrate the ideological superiority of democracy over communism and the cultural superiority of the urban North over the rural South. Perhaps to a greater extent than in any previous era, consumer culture became one with the American Way in the 1950s and 1960s. And the thousands of rural-to-urban migrants—country music professionals among them—who left small towns and family farms for work in the city were motivated by the pursuit of more affluent lives. Their identity as consumers, symbolized partly by the commercial success of country music, was the measure of their success as they themselves defined it.[36]

It was ironically fitting that the CMA show for the Sales-Marketing Executives of Chicago should culminate with a special guest appearance by Andy Griffith.

Like Minnie Pearl before him, Griffith had gone from hillbilly to country as he was transformed from the backwoods demagogue of A Face in the Crowd to the homespun respectability of a small-town sheriff. In his personal success as well as in the roles he played, Griffith symbolized the rehabilitation of rural America. In Chicago, he stood before an audience of hundreds of urbane white-collar professionals neither as poor white trash, nor as a representative of a threatening hillbilly mob, but as a country boy made good.

Notes

1. Goddard Lieberson, "'Country Sweeps the Country," *New York Times Magazine,* July 28, 1957, reprinted in Linell Gentry, *A History and Encyclopedia of Country, Western, and Gospel Music* (St. Clair Shores, Mich.: Scholarly Press, 1972), 165; Richard A. Peterson, *Creating Country Music: Fabricating Authenticity* (Chicago: Univ. of Chicago Press, 1997); Charles K. Wolfe, *A Good-Natured Riot: The Birth of the Grand Ole Opry* (Nashville: Country Music Foundation and Vanderbilt Univ. Press, 1999); William Ivey, "The Bottom Line: Business Practices That Shaped Country Music," in Paul Kingsbury and Alan Axelrod, eds., *Country: The Music and the Musicians* (New York: Abbeville Press, 1988), 407; Don Cusic, "Country Green: The Money in Country Music," *South Atlantic Quarterly* 94 (winter 1995): 231–41; Nicholas Davidoff, *In the Country of Country: A Journey to the Roots of American Music* (New York: Vintage, 1998).

2. Joli Jensen, *The Nashville Sound: Authenticity, Commercialization, and Country Music* (Nashville: Country Music Foundation and Vanderbilt Univ. Press, 1998), 160, 84; Bill C. Malone, *Country Music USA,* Revised Edition (Austin: Univ. of Texas Press, 1985), 265–66.

3. Jensen, *The Nashville Sound,* 160, 168–69; Chad Berry, *Southern Migrants, Northern Exiles* (Urbana: Univ. of Illinois Press, 2000); John Morthland, *The Best of Country Music* (Garden City: Doubleday, 1984), 282; John Morthland, "Changing Methods, Changing Sounds: An Overview," *Journal of Country Music* 7.2 (1976).

4. Pamela Grundy, "'We Always Tried to Be Good People': Respectability, Crazy Water Crystals, and Hillbilly Music on the Air, 1933–1935," *Journal of American History* 81 (March 1995): 1614; Kristine M. McCusker, "'Dear Radio Friend': Listener Mail and the National Barn Dance, 1931–1941," *American Studies* 39 (summer 1998); Curtis W. Ellison, *Country Music Culture: From Hard Times to Heaven* (Jackson: Univ. Press of Mississippi, 1995), 161–216.

5. Berry, *Southern Migrants, Northern Exiles,* 172–200; Lewis M. Killian, "Southern White Laborers in Chicago's Local Communities" (Ph.D. diss., University of Chicago, 1949), 123, 126.

6. Albert N. Votaw, "The Hillbillies Invade Chicago," *Harper's* 216 (February 1958): 64–66; Berry, *Southern Migrants, Northern Exiles,* 176.

7. John McPartland, *No Down Payment* (New York: Simon and Schuster, 1957); Emanuel Levy, *Small-Town America in Film* (New York: Continuum, 1991), 111–15.

8. *A Face in the Crowd,* dir. Elia Kazan (Newtown, 1957); Michael Denning, *The Cultural Front: The Laboring of American Culture in the Twentieth Century* (New York: Verso, 1997), 469.

9. J.W. Williamson, *Hillbillyland: What the Movies Did to the Mountains and What the Mountains Did to the Movies* (Chapel Hill: Univ. of North Carolina Press, 1995), 168–69.

10. Russell Sanjek, *Pennies from Heaven: The American Popular Music Business in the Twentieth Century* (New York: Da Capo Press, 1996), 404–6, 422–27.

11. U.S. Congress, Senate, Subcommittee on Communications of the Committee on Interstate and Foreign Commerce, *Hearings on S. 2834,* 85 Cong., 2 sess., March 11–13, 19–20, April 15–17, May 6–7, 20–21, July 15, 23, 1958, pp. 107, 109, 124–25, 141, 418, 490.

12. Several scholars have argued that the image of the hillbilly (now more commonly labeled as redneck or white trash) remains one of the nation's most potent, and politically acceptable, ethnic stereotypes. See Matt Wray and Annalee Newitz, eds., *White Trash: Race and Class in America* (New York: Routledge, 1997).

13. "A Prophetic View of CMA," *Billboard,* March 18, 1978, pp. 18, 20; "CMA Organizes for C&W's Biggest Era; Directors Elected," *Music Reporter,* Nov. 24, 1958, pp. 1, 4; Jack Stapp, typescript speech, pp. 4, 9, 11, Country Music Association Sales and Marketing Programs (microfiche: fiche 2 of 3), CMA Papers (Country Music Foundation Library, Nashville).

14. Stapp, typescript speech, 3; Richard Price Stockdell, "The Development of the Country Music Radio Format" (M.A. thesis, Kansas State University, 1979), 24; "36% of U.S. AM Stations Carry C&W," *Billboard,* Sept. 4, 1961, p. 2. In fact, the 1961 figures probably represent an improvement over 1958, since the development of the country format was already underway and a number of stations had increased the amount of time they devoted to country music in 1960 and early 1961. See "All Country," *Close-Up,* Jan. 21, 1960, p. 2; "60 Stations Expand C&W Output," *Music Reporter,* Oct. 31, 1961, p. 18; and Bill Sachs, "21 More Stations Add More Country Music or Go 100% Country Music in One Month," *Close-Up,* March 1961, p. 2.

15. Stapp, typescript speech, 1.

16. "Country Music Assn. Gets State Charter" *Music Reporter* 3 (Sept. 29, 1958): 14.

17. Wolfe, *A Good-Natured Riot,* 179–80, 261–65; John Rumble, "Harry Stone,"

in Paul Kingsbury, ed., *The Encyclopedia of Country Music* (New York: Oxford Univ. Press, 1998), 511; "CMA Taps Stone to Lead C&W into Greatest Era," *Music Reporter,* Jan. 19, 1959, p. 15.

18. Jo Walker-Meador interview by Diane Pecknold, Aug. 2, 1999, audiotape (in Diane Pecknold's possession), side 1, tape 1; "Stone Floods Ky.-Ind. with Come-Ons for CMA Spec," *Music Reporter,* Feb. 9, 1959, p. 16; "CMA Spec Grosses $8,100—'Bigness' Potential Seen," *Music Reporter,* March 16, 1959, pp. 16, 18; "Impressive Jimmie Rodgers Fete Re-Stresses C&W Power," *Music Reporter,* June 22, 1959, pp. 16–17; *Country Music Association Special Newsletter,* July 2, 1959.

19. "C&W Personal Appearances Cure 1957 Gold Bonanza," *Billboard,* March 23, 1957, pp. 79, 86.

20. *Close-Up,* July 2, 1959, p. 1; Ibid., Aug. 24, 1959, p. 1; Ibid., Oct. 7, 1959; Minutes of the CMA Board of Directors, Nov. 11, 1959 (microfilm: reel 1), Joe Allison Papers (Country Music Foundation Library); "CMA Sponsors First Anniversary Banquet, Salutes Grand Ole Opry 34th Birthday," *Music Reporter,* October 17, 1959, p. 16; "CMA Stresses Need for $$, New Members," *Billboard,* Nov. 16, 1959, pp. 2, 14; "Harry Stone Leaves CMA Executive Post," *Billboard,* Nov. 23, 1959, p. 4; "Jo Walker: CMA's Lucky Accident," *Billboard,* March 18, 1978, p. 8.

21. "Just Plain Jo Is a Dynamo," *Billboard World of Country Music,* Oct. 28, 1967, p. 74; Walker-Meador interview by Pecknold, tape 1, side 2; *Close-Up,* Feb. 26, 1960, p. 1.

22. "Optimism Pervades C&W Music Fete," *Billboard,* Aug. 22, 1960, p. 2; *Close-Up,* Feb. 26, 1960, pp. 1-2; Ibid., June 10, 1960; Ibid., August 11, 1960, p. 4; "CMA Committee Works on Second Mailing," *Music Reporter,* Oct. 31, 1960, p. 40.

23. "CMA Committee Works on Second Mailing," 40; "Country Music: A Gold Mine for City Broadcasters," *Sponsor,* Aug. 8, 1960, p. 76; Charles Bernard, "The Madison Avenue Report," *Close-Up,* July 1961, pp. 1, 3.

24. "Country Stations: Fatter and Happier," *Sponsor,* Aug. 8, 1966, p. 43.

25. "Sponsor Crash-Plan Held Country Music 1st Need," *Music Reporter,* Nov. 7, 1960, p. 16; *Close-Up,* Feb. 6, 1961, p. 1.

26. "Crum vs. Husky? Audiences Won't Decide in Advance," *(Country) Music Reporter,* Oct. 20, 1956, p. 6; Williamson, *Hillbillyland,* 50–51; "C&W Salute Wins N.Y. Radio Execs," *Music Reporter,* March 31, 1962, p. 37.

27. "C&W Salute Wins N.Y. Radio Execs," 37; "C&W Crashes Air Time in Sophisticated New York," *Music Reporter,* July 28, 1962, p. 24; "CMA Sets Museum & Show," *Music Vendor,* Dec. 1, 1962, n.p.

28. "CMA Steps Up Bid for Status," *Billboard,* April 6, 1963, p. 8; Hal B. Cook, "CMA Sings a Message," *Billboard,* May 18, 1963; John Rumble, "Joe Allison," in Kingsbury, ed., *Encyclopedia of Country Music,* 11; "Allison: Sincerity, Simplicity—Acceptance," *Billboard World of Country Music,* Oct. 18, 1965, p. 112; "Allison Sees

C&W as Source of Today's Music," *Billboard World of Country Music,* Nov. 2, 1963, p. 133.

29. Joe Allison interview by Diane Pecknold, March 26, 1999, audiotape (in Diane Pecknold's possession), tape 2, side 1.

30. Ibid.; Joe Allison, Presentation to the Sales Executives Club of New York, Country Music Association Sales and Marketing Programs (microfilm: reel 1), CMA Papers.

31. Joe Allison, "The Sound of Country Music, Presented for the Adcraft Club of Detroit on Friday, April 17, 1964," pp. 4, 11, 14, 15, Country Music Association Sales and Marketing Programs (microfilm: reel 1), CMA Papers.

32. "C&W Pulse Published for 24 U.S. Markets," *Close-Up,* September 1965, p. 1; "CMA's 'The Sound of Country Music'—Smash!" *Music City News,* 3 (July 1965): 1, 6; Hal Cook to Frances Preston et al, Nov. 12, 1964, Chicago Show 1965 (microfiche: 1 of 1), CMA Papers.

33. Joe Allison, "The Sound of Country Music, Presented for the Sales-Marketing Executives of Chicago, Monday, June 7, 1965," pp. 8, 13–17, Country Music Association Sales and Marketing Programs (microfilm: reels 1 and 2), CMA Papers.

34. Jonathan Rieder, "The Rise of the 'Silent Majority,'" in Steve Fraser and Gary Gerstle, eds., *The Rise and Fall of the New Deal Order, 1930–1980* (Princeton: Princeton Univ. Press, 1989), 248; Allison interview by Pecknold, tape 1, side 1; "Country Stations: Fatter and Happier," 42.

35. "Growing Sound of Country Music," *Broadcasting,* Oct. 18, 1965, pp. 70, 75; "Numbers Mean Dollars on Madison Avenue," *Sponsor,* Aug. 8, 1966, p. 44; "The New Appeal of Country Music," *Broadcasting,* Aug. 1, 1966, p. 56.

36. Elaine Tyler May, "Cold War—Warm Hearth: Politics and the Family in Postwar America," in Fraser and Gerstle, eds., *The Rise and Fall of the New Deal Order,* 153–81; Karal Ann Marling, *As Seen on TV: The Visual Culture of Everyday Life in the 1950s* (Cambridge: Harvard Univ. Press, 1994), 243–83; Meg Jacobs, "'Democracy's Third Estate': New Deal Politics and the Construction of a 'Consuming Public,'" *International Labor and Working-Class History,* 55 (spring 1999), 45–47.

Tex Morton and His Influence on Country Music in Australia During the 1930s and 1940s

Andrew Smith

Tex Morton was a skinny, pasty-faced nineteen-year-old when he stepped in front of the solitary microphone of the Columbia Graphophone Company in Sydney, Australia, on Tuesday, 25 February 1936. Accompanying himself with his battered guitar, he cut four songs: two about faraway Texas, a place he had never seen ("Texas in the Spring" and "Goin' Back to Texas"), and two compositions of his own ("Happy Yodeller"[1] and "Swiss Sweetheart"). His style leaned heavily on American country music of the day—his slightly nasal voice, with traces of an American accent, resembled the vocal style of Jimmie Rodgers; his guitar playing was simple but effective; and his yodeling owed much to the style of Goebel Reeves. Although an outsider might have considered these recordings as derivative of country music from the United States, they projected a vitality and energy that would mark the recording session as a watershed in the fledgling Australian country music industry.

Tex Morton was not the first person to record country music in Australia, but by 1940 he was already the most influential Australian "western" singer, and his early recordings, released on the well-known red-and-green Regal Zonophone label, inspired fellow Australian artists like Slim Dusty, Australia's best-known bush balladeer, who remarked that Tex's early songs laid a foundation for others to follow. In 1949, Ralph Peer purportedly paid Morton this tribute during a visit to Australia: "Tex has created and pioneered in Australia a country and western industry which compares

Tex Morton and His Influence on Country Music 83

Australian country music legend Tex Morton as he appeared early in his career, performing in the late 1930s.

more than favorably with some of our best areas in America. He achieved in five years what it took us in the States more than twenty years to do. The people of Australia should be forever grateful to him. He is the Jimmie Rodgers of Australia."[2]

The origins of recorded country music in Australia, however, predate Morton's first Columbia session. Before 1927 there was a steady influx of American hillbilly music into Australia on labels such as Edison, Banner, Lincoln, and Domino. Australian entertainers were quick to capitalize on this new music, though at first they merely imitated the styles and sounds they heard on imported and locally released American recordings. Harry Cash, a relatively obscure singer, recorded "The Black Yodel" in 1927, but his song, like Grace Quine's "The Faded Coat of Blue," had little in common with American hillbilly stylings of the time. During the late 1920s and early 1930s, Vince Courtney recorded popular sentimental songs such as "Bird in a Gilded Cage" and "Through the Sin of a Son," his own composition. Morton later recorded both songs for Columbia, so it is possible that he had listened to Courtney's discs as a youngster.

Some collectors argue that the honor of being labeled Australia's first country music recording artist belongs to Len Maurice, who recorded as "Art Leonard." Leonard was a popular baritone of the day and his discs had a "citybilly" style, like those of the prolific American artist Vernon Dalhart. Between 1929 and 1932, Leonard recorded American standards such as "The Big Rock Candy Mountains,"[3] "The Red River Valley," "Can I Sleep in Your Barn Mister," and "A Picture from Life's Other Side." In 1933 the Two Barnstormers, Vic Massey and Tom Stevenson, covered a Kessinger Brothers disc when they recorded "Mary Jane Waltz" and "Wildflower Waltz" playing fiddle and guitar. In the same year, the Hillbilly Singers, a male-female duet, cut "When I Get to the End of the Way," but these discs had all the trappings of professional locals copying the then-new American sounds that were permeating the country during the Depression.

After 1927, songs by American country artists continued to be heard in Australia, mainly on Columbia Graphophone's Regal Zonophone label, which had more country music releases than any other label outside the United States. About 950 records, comprising local talent and material from American labels Columbia, Brunswick, Vocalion, and Bluebird as well as British labels Columbia and Regal, were released between 1927 and 1958, when the Regal Zonophone label was discontinued. Jimmie Rodgers's "Away Out on the Mountain," coupled with "Never No Mo' Blues," the first of a plethora of Australian releases by the Singing Brakeman, was issued on the Zonophone label in early 1929. A year later, the Carter Family's disc "River of Jordan" coupled with "Keep on the Sunnyside" was released in Australia. Rodgers made an immediate impact on Australians. Norm Scott, an early Australian country singer, sang his songs at live performances as early as 1929, and there was even a Jimmie Rodgers Club in the state of Tasmania in 1934 (predating the Jimmie Rodgers Society in the United States). Jimmie's widow, Carrie, gave the club one of Jimmie's polka-dot ties in 1935.

The popularity of American country music did much to submerge Australia's own folk music. Unlike much traditional American music that found its way, in one form or another, onto hillbilly discs, the traditional music of Australia was virtually ignored by local record company executives, who showed much more enthusiasm for the American product. The plaintive music of American hillbilly artists struck a responsive chord among Australian farm workers, many of whom experienced a harsh existence eking a living from the bush during the tough Depression years. Rodgers, the Carter Family, Vernon Dalhart, Carson Robison, Bill Carlisle, Bradley Kincaid, Gene Autry, and the Girls of the Golden West were merely some of the well-known Americans whose records sold in Australia. "The older songs that came from America had that rural aspect, the same as a lot of our songs still have,"[4] Slim Dusty recalled. To the Australian public at large, though, country music was an unknown quantity. Very few radio stations played the music, and the average listener was apt to confuse hillbilly music with Bing Crosby or orchestral versions of "Springtime in the Rockies."

By 1928, in the New Zealand town of Nelson, early country music from the United States was attracting the interest of young Robert Lane (later known as "Tex Morton") and his friends, two of whom were Bill Homan, an itinerant worker who later became a seaman, and Alan Howatt. Homan was a boarder in the Gear household in Nelson. Both Homan and Howatt were interested in American country music, and every Sunday morning the pair practiced their singing and playing in the Gear's lounge room. Soon afterward, Robert Lane joined them. "Bob was definitely the leader and dominant character," recalled Bob Gear, who was about twelve years old when he first met Lane. "He was an intelligent, lively, likeable character who, given an opportunity, would be assessed as 'most likely to succeed.' He was certainly the best guitar player and singer of the three at our place."[5]

Lane also played and sang with Paddy McLaren, Benny Morgan, and others in his grandfather's house in Nelson while he was still a teenager.[6] At one stage, he had a group of musicians playing fiddle, guitar, and accordion.[7] One of the participants at these get-togethers was Gil Harris, who later traveled to Sydney and recorded four tracks as "The Whispering Yodeller" before vanishing into obscurity. Lane and Harris learned the guitar together and exchanged records.

We do not know the titles of songs Lane played, but it seems likely that much of his music came from hillbilly records and from American seamen whom he met on the wharves in New Zealand. Later in his career, he recalled sailors coming ashore in Auckland and singing genuine American songs about cowboys and the West.[8] Almost certainly, the young Lane listened to American country music on 78-rpm records. Early on, Carson Robison and his novelty songs such as "Peg Leg Jack" and "Barnacle Bill the Sailor" inspired him. Later, he copied the songs and styles of recording stars such as Goebel Reeves ("The Texas Drifter"), Jimmie Rodgers, the English yodeler Harry Torrani, and possibly some Alpine-style yodeling discs from Europe. He seemed to be particularly impressed with the yodeling of Rodgers, Reeves, and Torrani. Both Lane and Harris learned to yodel in the distinctive style of Goebel Reeves, and Lane recalled that he and his friends considered Torrani to be "the greatest singer that ever came down the pike, and the best yodeller we'd ever heard."[9]

In the 1930s, yodeling on country music records was guaranteed to intrigue Australian listeners. Most of Australia's early country music artists were capable yodelers, and in the mid 1940s, Arch Kerr, who produced most of Australia's recorded country music at the time, told Slim Dusty that the record company "couldn't sell this country stuff without a yodel."[10] An English group called "The Hillbillies" (Ted Ford, Ezra Sirett, Ben Evans, and Lefty Calnan) also influenced Lane, who used their "Roll Along Covered Wagon" as the theme of a series of radio programs he made in 1938.

Lane had a turbulent adolescence. Although he was a talented student at the prestigious Nelson College, he left just after he turned fifteen. For the next five years most of his life was spent away from home, working in a variety of show-business roles and singing in the streets of New Zealand towns for money ("busking"). He later recalled busking in the streets of Waihi and being apprehended by a policeman, who asked him his name. The young runaway glanced nervously over the policeman's shoulder and, spotting a sign that read "Morton's Garage," blurted out "Robert Morton, sir." Like many of Morton's recollections, however, this story is probably apocryphal. "Morton" was probably the name of a family that he stayed with while running away from home. Later, Jack Davey, a star of early Australian radio, gave him the sobriquet "Tex." Thus, sometime in the 1930s, Robert Lane became "Tex Morton."

Morton recalled recording about twenty songs on aluminum discs in 1932 in Wellington, New Zealand. These songs, he said, were played on local radio, paving the way for artists such as Jimmie Rodgers to be played over the airwaves. If the story is true, it is probable that either Morton made the discs at Bob Bothamley's[11] house, where Bothamley had built a recording device that cut aluminum masters, or they were one-off "vanity" recordings made at special booths where people could record messages on discs. Rex Franklin, a New Zealand country singer, recalled that he once saw three such discs at Morton's home in Sydney. One disc may have been titled "Happy Cowboy," but Franklin stated that the other titles were unfamiliar and not obviously "country" songs.[12] As with other early Tex Morton stories, this has to be treated with caution. Morton later claimed, for example, that he had lived in the United States as a boy and had once met Jimmie Rodgers—a story that was most likely pure fancy, since there is no evidence of his visiting America prior to 1949.

Tex Morton sailed across the Tasman Sea to Sydney, Australia, some time in the early 1930s (the usual date given is 1932, but this cannot be verified independently, and the year may have been 1934).[13] He probably busked in Sydney for a few months before traveling north to Queensland, riding trains and sleeping under bridges. Morton later stated that he had led a rough-and-tumble life during those years and had been willing to try anything, including riding motorcycles around the "wall of death" at traveling shows. He relied on his singing to survive, and it was presumably during this period that he learned the basics of showmanship that would prove invaluable later in his career. By the 1940s he was generally regarded as one of Australia's most innovative and effective traveling showmen.

On his return to Sydney, Morton mingled with the entertainment set—the famous Skuthorpe Family of roughriders, with whom he later toured, and actors such as Peter Finch and a young Errol Flynn, who had not yet moved to Hollywood. He learned sharpshooting skills from Lionel Bibby, a crack police marksman. "Tex was the best shot of all the singing cowboys," wrote Smoky Dawson, his compatriot. "He could put a bullet down the barrel of the other fellow's gun if ever he had a mind to."[14] Morton eventually incorporated trick shooting and hypnotism into his act.

Around 1935 Morton made contact with Tim Tyler, at the Columbia Graphophone Company, for an audition. By this time, Morton had already won first prize in a talent quest that was broadcast on Radio Station 2KY. Tyler, an Englishman, was probably aware that American country artists were selling well in rural Australia, and he approved Morton's first commercial recording session in February 1936.[15] Although Tyler suggested that Morton sing in a Jimmie Rodgers style, Morton's selections at that first Columbia Graphophone session seem to be a combination of "cowboy"

Tex Morton in the early 1940s or 1950s, sporting his trademark cowboy hat and western gear.

songs ("Texas in the Spring" and "Goin' Back to Texas") and showcases for Swiss-style yodeling ("Happy Yodeller" and "Swiss Sweetheart"). His subsequent recordings, however, were more "hillbilly" based, suggesting that feedback from listeners favored these types of songs over "Alpine"-style material.

The unprecedented popularity of these discs rocketed Tex Morton to instant stardom in Australia. "When he started it was just like when the Beatles came out. He was a complete sensation. The country just went crazy," recalled Smoky Dawson.[16] Morton attributed his success partly to the fact that he was, as he put it, "such a darn novelty," with his cowboy hat, fancy western clothes, yodeling, and guitar. According to some accounts, by the 1940s in Australia, Tex's records outsold those of international artists such as Bing Crosby and his sales exceeded the total of those for all country singers—Australian and American—Down Under. He was mobbed in the streets; he regularly drew large crowds to his live shows (including a reported fifty thousand people at a show in Brisbane, Queensland); and he clearly beat Bing Crosby in a Melbourne charity group's competition to see who was the more popular singer.[17]

But not everyone was taken with the latest Australian cowboy singing sensation. Some radio station announcers treated his recordings with disdain and ridiculed his record-label moniker, "The Yodelling Boundary Rider." Actually, Tex didn't much like the title either, but he was content to let Columbia use the "bloody silly name" if it might boost record sales. In later years, Morton claimed that it was the popularity of his music that paved the way for American country music to be played on Australian radio stations. Moreover, because country music sales effectively subsidized the recording of other types of music released on Columbia's expensive labels, even avowed haters of yodeling cowboys had reason to thank Morton and his ilk. "We reckoned that the income derived from our country recordings made it possible to record a great deal of the music for the full-priced labels," commented ex-Columbia executive Ron Wills.[18]

By 1939, Morton had recorded some fifty sides for Columbia, including standards such as "Rocking Alone in an Old Rocking Chair," "The Letter Edged in Black," and "Red River Valley," as well as original compositions such as "The Yodelling Bagman," "On the Gundagai Line," and "Sergeant Small"—a song about a railway policeman, who threatened to sue Morton after the tune was released. He had also put together a large traveling show that featured roughriding, whip cracking, and his own blend of singing, hypnotism, and fancy shooting. The immense popularity of these shows and his phenomenal record sales clearly established Morton's reputation as the first star of Australian country music. Tex's traveling companion at the time was Dorothy Ricketts ("Sister Dorrie"). Morton recorded some duets with her in 1941, thus establishing her as Australia's first female recording artist. Prior to his duetting with "Sister Dorrie," Morton had recorded four songs with harmonica player Harry Thompson (in 1938) and two tracks with Pat Fraley, an American wrestler and folk singer (in 1939).

Tex Morton poses here with one of his horses in the early 1940s. Horses played an integral part in Morton's traveling show and were the subjects of several of his hit songs.

Although he was clearly influenced by recordings from the United States, Morton also wrote much of his own material, increasingly emphasizing local motifs in his music. "Wrap Me Up in My Stockwhip and Blanket" (1936) was his first recorded song set in Australia. He followed this course with numbers such as "Wandering Stockman" (1936), "The Yodelling Bagman" (1936)—which, according to Eric Watson, was perhaps the first thoroughly authentic Australian song in the new idiom—and his trio of roughriding classics: "Rocky Ned" (1939), "Aristocrat" (1940), and "Mandrake" (1941), all songs about horses in his traveling shows.

A key factor in Morton's popularity was his manager, Bill Scott. An American, Scott had traveled to Australia with the Marcus Show in 1937. "He was the great organizer and the first from overseas with American know-how," said Smoky Dawson. "We were so naive in those days, but he knew exactly how to promote our music. He knew the effect it would have on the ordinary bloke in the bush. He'd smoke on his big fat cigar: 'Aah got the big American know-how. I'll show you how to do it!'" When the Marcus Show folded, Scott became Morton's manager.[19]

In 1939 Morton met the talented guitarist Dick Carr at a coffee lounge on Sydney's Darlinghurst Road. At the time, Morton was earning an average of about fifty pounds a week busking in Kings Cross, a suburb of Sydney. Carr recalled that this was "big money for those days." (By way of comparison, a farm laborer's wage in 1939 was about three pounds a week, plus keep, and a shirt was worth five shillings.)[20] Over a cup of coffee, Morton invited Carr to accompany him on his tours around Australia as a musician in his band. At first Carr was reluctant: "You'll have me sleeping in the trucks in no time," he said. Yet Morton persisted and offered not only to buy Carr a new Ford van, but to allow him to hire two more musicians as an incentive. Thinking he was kidding, Carr agreed to the deal. Then, to his astonishment, Morton took him to the local Ford agent, pulled out a wad of notes "that would choke a horse," and bought a new van on the spot. Carr toured with Morton and Sister Dorrie for a little over a year before quitting due to the frenetic pace of traveling with Morton and his troupe.

Carr remembered that Morton had a huge tent that was capable of seating two thousand people and a fleet of vehicles that included a pole truck, a tent truck, a seat truck, and a truck for the cook. Morton's car was a Buick with speakers wired into two extra headlights on the bumper. When he arrived at a new town, Morton would drive slowly through the streets and announce the show's location and starting time through the speakers on the Buick's bumper.[21] Often, Morton would drum up interest in his shows by going on local radio, claiming that one of his horses had escaped and offering a reward for its return.

The arrival of the Tex Morton show was a significant event in the lives of small country towns of the 1930s and 1940s, and Morton's presence nearly always guaranteed large crowds. He made an immediate impact on a young Slim Dusty, who recalled his tours during this period:

> I first met Tex Morton when I was about 10 or 11 years of age. He came through with the Skuthorpe Family, and he sang in their rodeo arena on the showgrounds. Tex was very flamboyant back in those days. He drove down the mid way in the morning through the sideshow tents and caused a complete traffic jam, and a complete people jam. Nobody could move. Tex

was sitting in his car, trying to get his car down to the rodeo tent. Shorty Ranger and myself were only kids. . . . When I eventually got up near Tex's door, I remarked to Shorty "She [meaning Morton] looks a bit stuck up." And I'll never forget Tex, leaning down, and saying "Do you think so son?" Well, you could have knocked Shorty and I over with a feather. We certainly attended a few sessions where he sang "I'm Gonna Yodel My Way To Heaven," and we saw Tex periodically through the day, around some of the sideshows and the shooting galleries. Wherever he went, there were people following him. He was a very flamboyant character.

The next time I remember Tex he came through Kempsey in '38 or '39 with this huge rodeo and a sort of three-in-one show: circus, rodeo and Dick Carr and a band, with Sister Dorrie. That was a really big show—the biggest show of its kind that travelled in those days. Tex was very flamboyant once again.

I never saw Tex again until the war years, and that was after I'd made my first private [process] record, which was in 1943. Tex had lost all his gear then. All his trucks had been taken over by the authorities and Tex was actually travelling his buckjumpers by road and had only one old truck for the gear. But he still did a great show—he did all the compering [acting as master of ceremonies, introducing the acts] himself. I fronted up with my process record and he gave me a good reception. He played it on the speaker system before the show and said "This is your own local boy, Slim Dusty." I travelled with the show for about two weeks. . . . I even did a few songs in the tent, in his show. He was very cooperative, gave me a lot of tips in his own professional way, and said you've got to be with the people, with your fans, but always be that little bit aloof—something which I've never ever forgotten.[22]

Morton's traveling shows and records did much to popularize country music in Australia. "The country people worshipped Tex and travelled hundreds of miles to see and hear him," Carr remembered. Morton regularly drew two thousand to three thousand people a night, six nights a week.[23] When the seats were filled, people would sit on tarpaulins around the ring to see the show, and children would often sneak into the tent by crawling underneath the canvas, away from the tent's entrance.[24]

One youngster who saw Tex Morton's show in Queensland recalled the event fifty years later:

I still have vivid recollections of my first and only experience with Tex Morton, when . . . I went to the Charters Towers Show in July 1939, and paid a shilling to get in. There was just an area perhaps 30 feet [10 meters] in diameter roped off, and the . . . paying customers stood to see the show. Being all bush boys in the group, Tex was our idol. A "wild" horse which "had never been held" was brought in, a bag thrown over its head and, amid patter from Tex, a stockman took up his position to hold it. The bag was [removed], the man was pulled about the enclosure for a few seconds, and finally [he] held the horse still. It was many years before I came to realise that the horse had been trained to pull away for a bit, then stand still! Tex then cracked the lighted end [from] a cigarette held in the mouth of an attractive cowgirl. He produced a highly polished item which looked like a revolver, but must have been a toy only, and, after twirling it around, told us the police would not give permission for him to fire it. [He] returned it to its holster, amid groans of disappointment from the onlookers. Finally the "piece de resistance": Tex was given his guitar, put his foot on some sort of rest to assume, a "standing-at-the-campfire" pose, and yodelled and sang "The Big Rock Candy Mountain."[25]

Morton sometimes had an abrupt, if humorous, manner with the people who came to see him. One night, a performer who specialized in fancy rope tricks had drunk too much before his part of the show. With characteristic flair, Morton introduced him as "Australia's greatest performer with a lasso." When the inebriated man stumbled onto the stage and repeatedly fell over while attempting to spin his ropes, the audience at first chuckled and then burst out laughing. Seizing the moment, Morton walked out on stage and announced, "Ladies and gentlemen, the reason I previously introduced this artist as 'Australia's greatest performer with a rope' was to gain your attention. He is, in fact, Australia's greatest comedian."[26]

By 1940, however, Morton was having trouble with Columbia's new record sales manager, Arch Kerr. Kerr was born 5 August 1907 in the north Queensland town of Charters Towers, and his lifelong interest in music and recording was sparked upon hearing an Edison phonograph when he was four years old. Two years later, in 1913, his parents bought him a piano. Inspired, he commenced a serious study of music that persisted throughout his life. His family moved first to Ipswich in 1914 and then, in 1917, to Brisbane, where he worked as an office boy in Harrold's Music Warehouse. Later, he was promoted to manager of the warehouse's record section. By 1928, this position had assumed a greater importance because Harrold's was appointed the Queensland distributor for Columbia and Regal Records.

Kerr was a professionally trained musician. During the Depression he headed his own dance band, "Arch Kerr's Nitelites." By the late 1930s, the

Nitelites had appeared at such prestigious Brisbane venues as Lennons, the Bellevue Hotel, and the Brisbane City Hall. In 1934 the band even played for the Duke of Gloucester at a royal ball.

After he married in February 1938, Kerr decided that he should give up playing music professionally in favor of a "regular" job. So, while he was on his honeymoon in Sydney, he stopped off at Columbia Graphophone's studio in Homebush and applied for a position. On 4 July 1938 he was appointed assistant sales manager. When war broke out in 1939, Tim Tyler returned to England to enlist in the Royal Navy and Arch Kerr took over as Record Sales Manager.

By 1939, the Columbia Graphophone Company was run along the strict lines of its British parent company. It had a monopoly on country music records in Australia, and Kerr's position as the newly appointed record sales manager gave him enormous power. One of Kerr's tasks was to listen to country music discs from the United States and decide which songs would be released locally. Kerr's other responsibilities included auditioning local artists and, if they were good enough, signing them to Columbia and even supervising their recording sessions. Perhaps no one has ever held as much power and influence in Australia's country music industry as Arch Kerr.

Auditioning for Kerr was a daunting experience, even for seasoned performers, as Smoky Dawson remembered:

> We all had to go through this audition behind a partition at Homebush Studios. First of all, you arrived in the early hours of the morning. Saturday was the day of recording but prior to that you'd make an appointment.
>
> You were met at the door by a commissioner, who looked more like a cop ready to make an arrest, with all his heavy braid on. He looked at you as if you were guilty of something, and as if there was a war on, before you could even get inside the door. And then he'd phone through to see if Mr Kerr would receive you, and you made your way up to go to him.
>
> You had to pass through this room with about thirty or forty typists going for their lives, all looking up at the next victim getting ready for his gruelling experience of having to audition just behind a partition. And that was the one time that the typewriters all stopped. All the typists waited to see if he would get thrown out.[27]

To his credit, Arch Kerr had a professional attitude toward country music, even if he may not have liked it. In 1981, when Australia's country music fraternity "rediscovered" him, Kerr told a television interviewer: "I was perhaps tough but I was a perfectionist, and I treated country music seriously. There were a lot of people who treated it very badly, and the result is that they've got bad results in their recordings. But I treated it as seriously as any other kind of music, because I knew I had a big audience that I was catering for, and I contended that just because it was country music it didn't have to be rubbish or badly done. It had to be as well done as anything else."[28]

Slim Dusty described Arch Kerr as "a tough bloke" who had complete say in what was recorded and released on Columbia in Australia. "If he said 'no,' it was no," said Dusty in 1991. "He was very arrogant and dogmatic." Dusty believed that Kerr saw country music only as a means of making money. "He didn't really want us."[29] In contrast, Bernie Burnett, who recorded for Kerr in 1941 and 1943, described him as "a fantastic, understanding person, kind and most pleasant in every way."[30]

Kerr's attitude to country music was somewhat condescending, particularly when recording local artists. He believed that solo singers and yodelers who recorded with just guitar accompaniment were more likely to achieve popularity in rural areas than singers who recorded with full "hillbilly" bands. This view clashed with Morton's opinion that a band would improve his recordings. By the 1940s, Morton had a group called The Roughriders, but Kerr was averse to recording with them. Morton also claimed that Kerr was reluctant to allow him to record his own songs and that he tried to tell Morton how to sing and yodel. Consequently, the two argued frequently. Morton told Kerr that he would record when he was ready, and—when he did turn up—Kerr recalled that they had "fun and games—all sorts of difficulties." Once, Morton had to be recorded sitting on a platform so that he did not stomp his feet. "He got a bit independent at times," said Kerr.[31]

By 1940, however, there were other local singing cowboys that Kerr could use as leverage to motivate the recalcitrant Morton. One of these was Billy Blinkhorn, a Canadian who had migrated to Australia around 1939. Blinkhorn had been the star of a hillbilly-style radio program in Vancouver, where he had built a reputation among local audiences with his horse "Silver," his yodeling, and his cowboy and folk songs. But when he asked his sponsors, Dad's Cookies, for a salary raise, a company executive advised him to try his luck in Australia.

In Australia, Blinkhorn had his own radio show on 2GB. It wasn't long before he started performing in vaudeville theaters in and around Sydney.

A record contract followed, and in October 1939 he cut six sides for Columbia, including his own song, "Poor Ned Kelly," about an infamous Australian bushranger who was hanged in 1880.

A more serious threat to Tex Morton was Buddy Williams. Born Harold Taylor, the son of Annie Taylor, Williams spent the first seven years of his life at Sydney's Glebe Point Orphanage, where, he recalled, life was lonely and difficult. "Instilled on my memory was the fact that I had no people on my side to visit me," he said. "When visitors would come to visit the kids, I'd be in the background, and it always hurt me to see them getting little presents."[32] Once, Williams escaped from the orphanage. With a small dog he befriended, he spent a night rummaging through garbage cans, searching for food. The next day, a man found the sleeping boy and his canine companion in the back seat of a car and returned them both to the orphanage. This experience was the basis for his 1946 recording "The Orphan Boy and His Dog."[33]

When he was seven, Harry Taylor was sent to live with Mr. and Mrs. Bandy McFarland, who owned a dairy farm in Dorrigo. They renamed him Harry McFarland and put him to work at the homestead. "Harry had a very hard life on the farm," Cleve McCarthy, a school friend, remembered.[34] "He had to help milk fifty cows by hand morning and night, seven days a week, do all his chores six days a week, and attend church on Sundays. His school lunch was damper and golden syrup, with no butter."

Life on the property was miserable. The McFarlands were looking for an unpaid farm hand, and treated Williams cruelly. "Mr. and Mrs. McFarland would never let him play. They'd say he had too many chores to do," McCarthy recalled. "One Christmas, we were having a Christmas tree at school. The ladies were bringing cakes and sandwiches on trays, and offered some to Harry. But his foster mother said, 'Don't give Harry sandwiches. I've got some crusts out back. That's all he'll be getting.'"

A keen shooter, Williams nearly always carried a rifle to school, and would hide the weapon in bushes near the classroom. On the way home, he would shoot rabbits, birds, and telephone poles. Music was another of his interests. He frequently took the leads in school musical productions, and when Ted Lorromier, his teacher, organized a school production of *Old Man River*, Williams, made up in blackface, played a leading role. Musically, though, his major influences were the recordings of American country music singers. He'd listen to these on neighbors' gramophones, often while he was away from home, hunting rabbits.

The influence of Tex Morton and other early western stars on Buddy Williams's dress and style is evident in this photograph of Williams taken in the 1940s.

An early musical influence was Jimmie Rodgers. "He was my inspiration," Williams stated. "I knew I could never be Jimmie Rodgers, so I said 'Well you can't be Jimmie Rodgers, but you can be Buddy Williams.' And that's why I stuck to the Australian scene." Apart from Rodgers, Williams modeled his singing on that of Wilf Carter, the Canadian country singer whose discs sold well in Australia; Goebel Reeves; and, later, Tex Morton and Hank Williams. Morton's influence was especially potent. "I was the same as anybody else that followed Tex—I idolised his work from the beginning," Williams remembered in his later years.[35] "We both used to follow Jimmie Rodgers and Goebel Reeves, and I think that's where we both got our grounding."

Williams ran away from his foster parents when he was fifteen and worked as a potato digger and later as a rock crusher at a quarry near Grafton, supplementing his income by busking in the streets of Grafton. Later, he sang unaccompanied over Grafton radio station 2GF and appeared at the Jacaranda Festival in 1936, where he was popular with the crowds. From Grafton, he moved to Newcastle and then to Sydney.

Although he had commenced his career as an entertainer by busking in the streets, Williams had a burning ambition to make records. In 1939, he recorded a process (private) record, which included two songs, "Where the Jacarandas Bloom" and "They Call Me the Clarence River Yodeller," for radio station 2GZ in Orange. But the distinction of making commercial records for Columbia enticed him to Sydney. In September 1939, Williams caught a Homebush-bound train from the country and nervously auditioned for Arch Kerr.

Williams was Kerr's first major discovery. When he heard the young singer, Kerr probably couldn't believe his ears: Williams sang in a Jimmie Rodgers style, yodeled, played guitar, and had some self-penned songs to boot. Here at last was someone to keep the troublesome Morton in check. In a 1981 television interview, Kerr explained, diplomatically, why he signed Williams: "I discovered that he had something that I wanted. At this time, of course, we only had Tex Morton, and the field was bigger than Tex could cover, because he couldn't produce enough songs. We wanted a bit of variety, and of course, in a case like that you always have a backstop. You just don't rely on one artist to cater for the demand. You want a backstop, and that's what I was looking for at the time. Buddy fitted the bill excellently."[36]

Bernie Burnett recalled that Kerr was pleased to record Buddy Williams because he "was desperately wanting an Australian artist, and also to have some opposition to Tex Morton, as Tex was so good he outsold everyone in anything he recorded; also Tex was beginning to get a little too demanding."[37]

Another factor that might have influenced Kerr's decision to offer Williams a recording contract was new broadcasting regulations that specified that at least 5 percent of all songs played on radio had to be Australian compositions. Because Williams was a capable songwriter, Australian radio stations could use recordings by him to fulfil their required quotas of Australian material. To argue that Kerr signed Williams solely for this reason or as Columbia's "weapon" against Morton, however, overlooks Williams' considerable talent as a performer in his own right. Nevertheless, it is likely that these factors played some part in Kerr's decision to add a second yodeling cowboy to Columbia's roster.

Buddy Williams made his first records for Columbia on 7 September 1939, two days after his twenty-first birthday. Singing solo with his own guitar accompaniment, "The Yodelling Jackaroo," as he was called on Columbia's Regal Zonophone label, cut "That Dappled Grey Bronco of Mine,"

"They Call Me the Rambling Yodeller," "Lonesome for You Mother Dear," "Give a Little Credit to Your Dad," "The Orphan's Lament," and "My Moonlight Lullaby." The first two tracks were immensely popular in Australia, and established Williams as an important country singer. Williams's discs were similar in style to much of Morton's music, and would most likely have been bought by those people who had collected Morton's records.

Morton's immediate reaction to both Blinkhorn and Williams seems to have been a mixture of worry and bitterness. Kerr recalled that he, Morton, and Bill Scott had an agitated discussion at Homebush shortly after Columbia had signed Blinkhorn, whose contract, it seems, was enough to make Morton temporarily abandon his touring of city cinemas, where he sang during intermissions. Williams's singing undoubtedly rattled him. For the next three decades, he harbored a dislike for his rival, and even mocked him in a song he recorded late in his career and at a live performance in 1982.[38] Shortly after Williams signed with Columbia, Morton allegedly sent him the following tersely worded telegram: "Just to let you know I'm here with my solicitor. You've had a fair go and have been warned, so now just try to walk, talk, sing, dress or even look like me, once, and I'll go to the limit of the law." Although I have never seen the telegram, I have it on good authority that it was sent.[39] Bernie Burnett, who was married to Buddy Williams at the time, stated that "Tex was at one stage threatening to sue Buddy."

Morton quit recording for the Columbia Graphophone Company in 1943. Kerr was unconcerned about his absence from the recording scene, and told Ron Wills, "Tex knows where we are. Let him come and ask."[40] But country music enthusiasts regretted the dearth of new Tex Morton records in the ensuing years. "I have always regarded those years of silence as one of the great tragedies of country music," wrote author Eric Watson. "What gems would have been produced . . . we will never know."[41]

From 1943 to 1949, Morton continued to perform throughout the country with Sister Dorrie and The Roughriders, but the wartime rationing of gasoline brought about a marked reduction in the size of his show. Throughout this period, he continued to make radio broadcasts. In 1944, he helped start The Australian Hill Billy Club with Tex Banes (who taught aspiring country musicians the rudiments of country guitar playing) and Hawaiian guitarist Buddy Wikara. A sideline was selling "Tex Morton Guitars" by mail order. In 1946 his wife, Marjorie, took him to court seeking maintenance for their twin sons. Marjorie stated that he was earning five thousand pounds (about ten thousand Australian dollars) per year, but Morton argued that this was a three-fold exaggeration. After the war, he opened a dude ranch near Sydney, but it closed in 1949. At the time, Morton's assets included at least five cars, an airplane, caravans, trucks, and trailers.

In 1949 Ralph Peer visited Australia to open a branch of his Southern Music Publishing Company. Mrs. Peer wrote the following in her diary: "We had a most interesting visit today in our cramped quarters, with Tex Morton, the Australian cowboy singing star, who can best be described as the Gene Autry of Australasia. He does not call himself a Cowboy, but 'Australia's Singing Stockman.' He has a most engaging personality, and we got along very well. His friend and 'pardner,' Johnny Waikura [Wikara], came in later to play the guitar, and we had an old-fashioned hill-billy singfest. We certainly missed our old friends Bob Gilmore and Nat Vincent, because I am sure they would have appreciated this show as much as we did."[42]

On 15 December 1950 Morton signed three songs, "A Rolling Stone," "Soldier's Sweetheart," and "Stockman's Prayer," to Peer's publishing company in Sydney. Probably at Peer's instigation, Morton recorded some two dozen songs for the Tasman label in Sydney and New Zealand. In 1950, or thereabout, he flew to the United States to attempt to break into the entertainment scene there. In Hollywood, he met Gene Autry and reportedly struck up a friendship with him. Moving north to Canada—to avoid United States immigration restrictions—he later toured Canada with the Canadian country singer "Dixie" Bill Hilton.

In the early 1950s Morton was based in Montreal, but made forays into the United States. He toured with Pee Wee King in Pennsylvania and Illinois. King recalled that he performed his sharpshooting act and sang, and described him as "a personal friend" and a "great performer."[43] On 1 February 1953 Morton signed an exclusive contract with Okeh. His manager at the time was Oscar Davis. On 13 July 1953 he recorded seven sides in Nashville: "I've Known the Truth," "The Neighbor's Wife," "I've Got You Right Out of My Mind," "Circus Boy," "Kiwi Song," "Railroad Boomer," and "I Was Born in Old Wyoming." It is not known whether the recordings were intended for release in the United States or in Australia only. Four of these titles were released in Australia in 1954 on the Phillips label, but given the sounds of country music in the United States at that time, it is unlikely that songs such as "Railroad Boomer" and "I Was Born in Old Wyoming" would have made much of an impact on American record buyers.

Morton fronted a large traveling show that toured the United States and Canada during the 1950s, sometimes billing himself as "The Great Morton" or as "Dr. Morton." He featured hypnotism, memory recall, sharpshooting, and singing. He returned to Australia in 1959 with a *Grand Ole Opry*–type show, headlined by Roy Acuff. According to Pete Kirby, the venture was organized by Oscar Davis and Frankie Moore.[44] The tour was not popular with Australian audiences, however, and had to be called off after poorly attended performances in Sydney and Melbourne. Instead, Acuff and his Smoky Mountain Boys recorded 39 shows for Australian television. Morton appeared on some of these.

The country music scene had changed dramatically during Morton's decade-long absence from Australia. Buddy Williams had continued to record, despite being almost fatally wounded while on active service in a front-line battalion in Borneo, where the Army had put his marksmanship to good use. Although he had occasionally flirted with covers of American songs, Williams had recorded a solid repertoire of self-penned Australian songs during his career. Importantly, a new generation of Australian country singers, many of whom had been inspired and influenced by Morton and Williams, had emerged. One of these was Slim Dusty (David Gordon Kirkpatrick), whose first commercial recording, "When the Rain Tumbles Down in July," was described by Eric Watson as "no local imitation of an American cowboy song, but a sensitive poet observing and interpreting the life around him."[45]

The recordings of Tex Morton, Buddy Williams, and Slim Dusty helped to create what has become known as the "Australian bush ballad," described by some as a fusion of turn-of-the-century Australian poetry traditions with country music. The singer who has taken the bush ballad to its acme is Slim Dusty, who has freely acknowledged the immense influence of Tex Morton and Buddy Williams on his music. Country music is popular in many parts of the world, but very few countries have modified and adapted it to reflect their own regional forms.

Tex Morton and Buddy Williams temporarily patched up their differences in 1972 and even toured the eastern states of Australia together. During this time, the two recorded "I Like Country Music" with Sister Dorrie. Morton recorded sporadically and acted in movies before his death as a result of pneumonia and pleurisy in 1983. Five years later, Buddy Williams died of cancer. In 1976, Morton was the initial inductee into the Australian Country Music Roll of Renown (Australia's equivalent of the Country Music Foundation's Hall of Fame).[46] This award clearly acknowledged his seminal role in the development of a country music industry in Australia that was not always a clone of its United States counterpart, but one that gradually incorporated Australian influences, leading to the development of the Australian bush ballad.

The history of country music in Australia is inextricably linked with the story of Tex Morton. It was Morton who played a vital role in first transplanting the music of American hillbilly and western singers to Australian shores; it was Morton who first adapted this music to an Australian setting; and it was Morton who paved the way for other Australian country artists to follow in his footsteps. Indisputably, Tex Morton was the founding figure of Australian country music.

Notes

1. In Australia, "yodeller" and "yodelling" are commonly spelt with two ls.
2. E. Watson, *Country Music in Australia* (Kensington: Cornstalk Publishing, 1975), p.20. This quotation is unsourced in Watson's book, and the date given by Watson (1948) does not accord with Mrs. Peer's diary.
3. Harry McClintock, the artist usually associated with this song, visited Australia in 1901 and was arrested for riding a freight train. H. Young, *Haywire Mac and the Big Rock Candy Mountain* (Stillhouse Hollow Publishers, 1981), pp. 20–21).
4. National Country Music Jamboree interview.
5. Letter from Robert Gear, 8 January 1996.
6. Watson, p. 35.
7. G. Gibson, "The Tex Morton Story, Part 2," *Country and Western Spotlight* 66 (1970), p. 41.
8. G. Gibson, "The Tex Morton Story, Part 1," *Country and Western Spotlight* 65 (1969), p. 9.
9. *Country and Western Spotlight*, No. 65, p. 8.
10. J. Lapsley, *Slim Dusty: Walk A Country Mile* (Rigby, 1984), p. 47.
11. Letter from Gordon Spittle, 9 November 1993.
12. Spittle letter.
13. The date usually given is 1932, as Morton related to Watson (p. 13) but other accounts given by Morton suggest that the date might have been 1934. It is even possible that Morton traveled to Sydney in 1932, then returned to New Zealand, before traveling to Sydney again in 1934.
14. Interview with Smoky Dawson, April 1990.
15. Morton (in *Country and Western Spotlight*, No. 65, p. 11) stated that he recalled auditioning for Tyler on 1935 and was told "to come back."
16. Dawson interview.

17. Watson, p. 16.
18. Letter from Ron Wills, 1989.
19. Dawson interview.
20. Letter from Peter Colman, 5 September 1990.
21. Letter from Dick Carr, 22 August 1988.
22. Interview with Slim Dusty, 1990.
23. Carr letter.
24. Interview with Vince Walker, January 1996.
25. Colman letter.
26. Walker interview.
27. Dawson interview.
28. *Country Closeup* television show, 1981.
29. Interview with Slim Dusty, 4 June 1991.
30. Letter from Bernie Burnett, 12 March 1994.
31. *Country Closeup.*
32. *Country Closeup.*
33. According to John Edwards, this song was based on "The Orphan Girl."
34. Letter from Cleve McCarthy, 19 September 1990.
35. *Capital News,* vol. 12, no. 1, 1987, p. 7.
36. *Country Closeup.*
37. Burnett letter.
38. In "Tex Morton's Protest Song," Morton sang of a singer who was left with no ideas when Morton went to Canada, and in a live performance in Tamworth in 1982, Morton made a veiled criticism of Williams's yodeling.
39. In a letter dated 22 November 1990, John Minson stated that Williams had shown him the telegram. Bernie Burnett stated that "Tex was at one stage threatening to sue Buddy" (letter from Bernie Burnett).
40. Wills letter.
41. Watson, p. 20.
42. Mrs. Peer's diary (extract sent by Ralph Peer II).
43. Letter from Pee Wee King, 2 November 1989.
44. Letter from Pete ("Brother Oswald") Kirby, 30 June 1996.
45. Watson, p. 95.
46. Williams was inducted the following year.

Country Music Publishing Catalog Acquisition

John Gonas, David Herrera, James I. Elliott, and Greg Faulk

Overview

When a music publisher decides to acquire a country song catalog,[1] an estimation must be made of the future royalty income stream of the catalog, and a value must be ascribed to it. Using representative catalogs of country music songwriters, we will examine a popular method relied upon by music publishers to derive what they feel is a fair market value for an established song catalog. The valuation procedure used by music publishers, a multiple of recent Net Publishers Share (that portion of royalties for a catalog due to the publisher), is akin to the price/earnings multiple valuation used in the stock market. The major difference is that, on average, stocks sell for higher multiples of most recent earnings (twenty-one times) than do country song catalogs (six times to nine times).

There are two major reasons for this variance. First, royalty payments for song catalogs are complex and unpredictable. Song catalogs derive royalty from multiple sources: mechanical, performance, synchronization, print, foreign usage, and digital. The estimation and tracking of future song usage from these varied sources is extremely difficult. Second, song popularity tends to decline over time, reducing commercial potential. An examination of recent royalty payments of representative country songwriters reveals declines of 12.3 percent to 32.1 percent compared to stock price increases of 13.8 percent over the same time period.

The Music Publishing Business

The writing of a song can be rewarding both artistically and financially. A song is considered intellectual property and as such is protected by copyright law and entitles the owner to royalty payments by users. How valuable is a song or catalog of songs? History has shown they are quite valuable for a writer of country music. Alan Jackson received $13 million for his song catalog.[2] Sony/ATV reportedly paid $18 million for the song catalogs of the group Alabama.[3] The music publisher Tom Collins Music, which owned the rights to Tom T. Hall's songs, was purchased by Acuff-Rose Music Publishing in a deal valued at $5 million to $10 million.[4] These transactions underscore a complex process on which this discussion focuses. Determining an appropriate market value for intellectual property is a difficult task, and the valuation of a music catalog is no exception.

When a songwriter creates a song, that original work is protected under federal copyright law once the work is fixed in a tangible form of expression (e.g., tape recording). As the owner of a copyright, the songwriter has the right to be compensated for the use of his or her musical composition. Potential sources of income for a song include not only performances, recordings, lyric sheet sales, and radio broadcasts, but also use in television, film, videos, commercials, restaurants, night clubs, businesses, elevators, phone lines, websites, and even astronaut flights.[5] The songwriter usually does not have the time, expertise, or contacts to properly exploit the profit potential of a song, and therefore assigns control of these rights to a publisher. This assignment is accomplished in a songwriter contract where the songwriter transfers ownership to the music publisher in exchange for advances, collection of publishing royalties, registration of copyrights, and exploitation of the song. The songwriter retains the right of attribution (recognition as the songwriter) and the right to receive a percentage (usually 50 percent) of the royalties the song earns. The publisher then becomes the salesman, manager, and guardian of the rights of the song.[6] Current United States copyright law gives songwriters and music publishers some measure of protection for their efforts. Under the terms of the 1976 Copyright Act as amended by Congress in 1998 through the Sonny Bono Copyright Term Extension Act, copyrights are protected for the life of the owner plus seventy years.[7]

The music publisher's primary functions within the music industry are to (1) acquire the copyrights of music catalogs; (2) exploit or "pitch" the licensing of their collection of copyrights to users (recording artists, record companies, filmmakers, television networks, advertising agencies, etc.); and ultimately (3) collect royalties from end users (radio stations, recording studios, hotels, restaurants, nightclubs, etc.) who pay licensing fees to play, perform, or distribute the music in a variety of different formats. Depending on how a song is used, publishers collect a percentage of royalties from the following: each reproduction of a song, whether album, tape, CD, etc. ("mechanical royalties"); live or recorded public performances of a song ("performance royalties"); the recording of a song as part of a soundtrack of a motion picture or television program ("synchronization royalties"); the use of a song in a commercial for consumer products or services ("commercial sync royalties"); each printed copy of a song's sheet music ("print royalties"); each use (mechanical, performance, etc.) of a song outside of the United States ("foreign royalties"); and the use of a song on the Internet ("digital royalties").[8]

Given that the publisher retains exclusive rights of the copyrights it owns, the music publisher has several options regarding collecting royalties generated by a song catalog. Various licenses that require a licensing fee are issued on a nonexclusive basis. Some publishers issue their own licenses and others choose to use an independent licensing agency. Publishers employ Performing Rights Organizations (PROs) to issue performance licenses and collect royalties on their behalf. The major PROs in the United States are the American Society of Composers and Publishers (ASCAP) and Broadcast Music, Incorporated (BMI) and SESAC. Many publishers also use the services of The Harry Fox Agency (HFA) to collect their mechanical royalties. HFA also collects synchronization royalties for some of the music publishers it represents. Print royalties are usually collected from the major print publishers who have licensed the print rights from the copyright owners. The major print music publishers in the United States are Hal Leonard Publications, Warner Brothers Publications, Cherry Lane Music, Music Sales Corporation, and Columbia Pictures Publications.

A music publisher incurs significant risks when it purchases a song or catalog of songs from a songwriter or another music publisher. The most significant risk assumed by a publisher is revenue related. Will a song or catalog that it purchases have staying power and generate longstanding income? The publisher assumes the risk inherent in predicting the public's musical tastes and acceptance of its song collections. A publisher also risks capital that is tied to writers' advances and the promotion of songs. A partial list of these capital expenses includes writers' salaries, product acquisition, copyright purchase, product development, production of demo tapes and masters, marketing, copyright registration and administration, legal fees, operating overhead, equipment, and support salaries.[9]

When estimating the value of an established writer's catalog, the publisher has to make judgments about the future popularity of the songs as well as outlets where the songs can be placed. The music publishing business can be incredibly profitable if a publisher can acquire a catalog of popular songs that will have future demand from users. The publisher also has to identify songs that have peaked in popularity and usage. A music publisher's success is dependent on good fortune, insight into future trends within the music business, and the ability to recognize the potential use of a catalog and to successfully promote it. The track record of the songwriter is a critical component of this valuation. The initial cost and anticipated royalty income of a catalog containing "ageless" Beatles hits is entirely different from that of a catalog containing songs from a new writer and unknown artist.[10]

In addition to the problems and uncertainty associated with identifying the magnitude and duration of future revenues and expenses of a catalog, the music publisher is faced with the task of putting these cash flows in terms of today's dollars to arrive at a value for a catalog. In practice, song catalogs are valued using historical Net Publishers Share (earnings) multiplied by a market multiple, a process that is equivalent to stocks being valued using price/earnings multiples. A historical example can provide insight into how the value of a catalog for a representative songwriter is derived and measured.

Song Catalog Valuation Using a Market Multiple

The market multiple approach to valuing stocks uses recent income data—for example, the average net income, or earnings per share (EPS) over the last three years—multiplied by a price/earnings (P/E) multiple that is derived from the price of comparable stocks. For instance, if a stock had an average EPS of three dollars and similar stocks traded at a P/E multiple of twenty, it would be valued at sixty dollars.[11] If the company performed better than similar firms, then the multiple may be adjusted upward, re-

Table 1
Catalog 1

Year	Publisher's Gross Royalties to Publisher	Share of Performance Royalties	Publisher's Gross Mech./Other Royalties	Share of Mech./Other Royalties	Publisher's Share of Royalties
1992	$153,373.79	$87,231.23	$66,142.56	$33,071.28	$120,302.51
1993	$56,194.44	$17,828.75	$38,365.69	$19,182.85	$37,011.59
1994	$71,691.85	$10,649.59	$61,042.26	$30,521.13	$41,170.72
1995	$54,622.30	$9,165.12	$45,457.18	$22,728.59	$31,893.71

sulting in a higher stock price. Song catalogs are valued in a similar fashion. Average historical earnings, the Net Publishers Share, are multiplied by a market multiple to derive a value. The following discussion elaborates on this process.

Net Publishers Share

The first step in deriving the value of a catalog is to calculate the average Net Publishers Share (NPS) for the past three, four, or five years. The performing rights organizations (ASCAP, BMI, SESAC) and the mechanical rights organization (Harry Fox) collect the royalty income; however, they have different methods of disbursing the funds. The performing rights organizations separate performer and publisher royalties and send disbursements to each. The mechanical rights organization sends catalog royalty checks to the music publisher, who in turn remits the writer's portion (usually 50 percent) to the writer.[12]

Tables 1 and 2 illustrate how the music publishing industry derives the NPS for a song catalog. The numbers in the tables are taken from royalty income of existing catalogs of representative country music songwriters from 1992 to 1995. For example, in 1992 the total royalties received by the publisher of Catalog 1 were $153,373.79. The publisher's share of the performing rights, $87,231.23, was received directly from the performing rights organizations. The publisher also received the total royalties from the mechanical and other rights, which totaled $66,142.56. Per the stipulations of its contract with the writer, the music publisher received 50 percent of these royalties, or $33,071.28. The NPS, total royalties earned by the pub-

Table 2
Catalog 2

Year	Gross Royalties to Publisher	Publisher's Share of Performance Royalties	Gross Mech./Other Royalties	Publisher's Share of Mech./Other Royalties	Publishers Share of Royalties
1992	$11,648.27	$3,846.99	$7,801.28	$3,900.64	$7,747.63
1993	$40,416.64	$5,765.15	$34,651.49	$17,325.67	$23,090.90
1994	$9,433.49	$3,532.86	$5,900.63	$2,950.32	$6,483.18
1995	$11,304.12	$3,996.52	$7,307.60	$3,653.80	$7,650.32

lisher, was $120,302.51. In practice, the NPS may be greater than the contracted portion of the royalties due to cash advances, demo costs, and other fees recouped from the writer's share.

Multiples

Aside from the historical average NPS, the "multiple" is the most important number used in calculating what a music publisher might be willing to pay for a catalog of copyrights. A catalog's multiple comes from dividing the recent selling prices of comparable catalogs by their respective NPSs. The magnitude of a multiple is adjusted to reflect the purchaser's estimation of the catalog's future potential. The value of a catalog is estimated by multiplying the average of past years' NPSs by the multiple. Multiples for established song catalogs range between five and fifteen, with the more recent average in country music ranging between six and nine.[13] The multiple paid for a song catalog is an undiscounted estimate of the number of years that will elapse before the purchaser will recoup his or her investment. Beyond this payback period, all NPS from the catalog is profit for the publisher.

To get a sense for how a potential buyer of the two catalogs shown in tables 1 and 2 might value both as a single collective asset, see table 3. This table offers a combined summary of the NPS of Catalogs 1 and 2 over the past five years as well as a calculation of the average annual NPS over the past three and four years. Using these three- and four-year averages, the valuations are calculated with four different multiples (six, seven, eight, and nine).

Table 3
Combined Summary (Catalogs 1 and 2)

Year	Gross Royalties to Publisher	Publisher's Share of Performance Royalties	Gross Mech./Other Royalties	Publisher's Share of Mech./Other Royalties	Publishers Share of Royalties
1992	$165,022.06	$91,078.22	$73,943.84	$36,971.92	$128,050.14
1993	$96,613.38	$23,595.90	$73,017.48	$36,508.74	$60,104.64
1994	$81,125.34	$14,182.45	$66,942.89	$33,471.45	$47,653.90
1995	$65,944.42	$13,161.64	$52,782.78	$26,391.39	$39,553.03

Average Annual NPS for Three Most Recent Periods (1993–1995): $49,103.86

Average NPS x Multiplier	Catalog's Value
Average NPS x 6 Multiplier:	$294,623.16
Average NPS x 7 Multiplier:	$343,727.02
Average NPS x 8 Multiplier:	$392,830.88
Average NPS x 9 Multiplier:	$441,934.74

Average Annual NPS for Four Most Recent Periods (1992–1995): $68,840.43

Average NPS x Multiplier	Catalog's Value
Average NPS x 6 Multiplier:	$413,042.58
Average NPS x 7 Multiplier:	$481,883.01
Average NPS x 8 Multiplier:	$550,723.44
Average NPS x 9 Multiplier:	$619,563.87

Judgment

An issue of paramount importance to both the songwriter and publisher is the magnitude of the multiple. What differentiates a multiplier of six versus a multiplier of nine? Judgmental factors are considered. The most important factor is the distribution of "hit" songs. Is the catalog weighted to one or two hits, or is there an even distribution of strength or breadth within the collection? Another factor is the ability of the hit songs in the catalog to withstand the test of time. Songs that have generated income for more than eight years are considered "classics" and can be expected to maintain a steady revenue stream in the future. In the country market classics include songs such as "Crazy," performed by Patsy Cline, and "King of the Road," performed by Roger Miller. In the pop world, songs such as

"Rock Around the Clock" by Bill Haley and the Comets would fall into this category. Classic songs are expected to generate royalty income through licensing and even re-recording by current artists, as well as license fees from use in movies, television, and radio. Also factored in to the multiple valuation is the duration of the copyrights. Because U.S. copyright law has been modified several times in the past few decades, different copyrights have different durations. The remaining copyright life of a "classic" song may be shorter than its "economic life." In those cases where a catalog is being purchased from another publisher, an issue that affects the multiple is reimbursement of songwriter advances (payments to songwriters in anticipation of expected royalty revenues). The purchasing publisher may or may not reimburse the prior publisher for outstanding advances before disbursing funds to the songwriter. Contractual provisions vary with respect to repayment of advances on one or more other songs of a writer's songs that are cross-collateralized by the royalties of one or more other songs of the writer in the catalog. Copyrights attached to a songwriter's advances from the previous publisher may or may not be transferrable. Also considered are income trends over the past several years. Are there monies in the "pipeline" (units sold for which payment has not been collected)? A final factor is the appraiser's opinion of the catalog's future worth. This is based on the subjective reputation and past performance of the writer.[14]

The purchaser of a catalog factors in the above information to adjust contemporary market multiples and derive a multiple upon which to calculate the offering price for a songwriter's catalog. The Net Publishers Share is then multiplied by the multiple and a price is derived. In the example cited above (table 3), the value for a catalog could vary from $294,623.16 to $619,563.87 depending on the market multiple and the number of years used to calculate average NPS.

It is interesting to note that, when compared to average market multiples (market price per share divided by earnings per share) on a publicly traded company's common stock, average country music song catalog multiples are smaller. Common stock investors typically pay a much higher price compared to earnings per share than music publishers pay per NPS. In 1998, the P/E multiple for an average stock was twenty-one,[15] whereas the average NPS multiple in the country music industry was between six and nine. There are two reasons for this discrepancy. One is the uncertainty involved in estimating the future royalty income of a song catalog. The other is a result of differences in the rates of growth of stock prices versus royalty income from song catalogs.

Future Royalty Income

The publisher's motivation for valuing and purchasing a song catalog is, ultimately, to find users and collect royalty income. Even though there are hundreds, if not thousands, of variables that affect this process, the publisher still has the daunting task of trying to project future cash flows. However, each genre of music is different and each catalog of songs unique in its appeal and future potential, or profitability. Therefore, given that there does not exist a formal, "industry-standard" approach to projecting future royalty income, it is important to outline and explain how these sources of royalty income are actually created.

Mechanical royalties are the easiest to calculate and attempt to estimate. Under the current federally mandated statutory rate, a publisher receives $0.0755 for every reproduction (CD, tape, album, DVD, etc.) of a song that is sold. If a publisher owns the copyright of two songs on a CD and the CD "goes gold" (sells 500,000 copies), its mechanical royalties would be calculated as follows: 500,000 x $0.0755 x 2 = $75,500. A publisher can supplement its per-song mechanical royalty inflows by releasing the rights to record a song in multiple genres (for example, granting rights for the same song to be recorded by a popular artist in the pop market and by another artist in the country market).

Performance royalties, on the other hand, are much more difficult to quantify. The major sources of performance royalties are television and radio broadcasts and live performances.[16] Other sources of performance-royalty income include the use of music by businesses and enterprises in the United States, often as background music for offices, phones, or elevators. Because there are billions of performances of songs licensed by the PROs each year, it is not possible to track every single performance. Two primary methods of tracking are used: complete census and sampling. The American PROs have different methods of monitoring public performances. They also have different ways of calculating royalties and distributing them to their members. With respect to television broadcasting, ASCAP performs census surveys for all network performances on ABC, CBS, NBC, FOX, Paramount, and the Warner Brothers networks as well as many cable networks including A&E, Cinemax, Comedy Central, Showtime, TNT, and USA. ASCAP also samples millions of hours of local television programming. BMI relies on information provided by TV Data Corporation, which supplies performance information on TV shows broadcast on network, local (including syndicated programming), and cable television. Under a blanket license agreement with the PROs, the networks are required to provide program logs and music cue sheets, which list all of the music used on their stations.

The method for monitoring radio performances is different at each PRO. ASCAP does a sample survey yearly of hundreds of thousands of hours of radio broadcasts. Their sample includes taped broadcasts, radio station play lists, and Broadcast Data Systems (BDS) digital tracking.[17] BMI relies on a sample of radio station play lists.

The PROs also collect royalties for live performances. Both ASCAP and BMI conduct a census of the two hundred top-grossing concert tours in the United States. Other live performances are covered under general licensing agreements with the PROs. There are tens of thousands of customers in this category, and the monies collected from them are distributed based on performance tracking in other areas, primarily radio and television.

For businesses and enterprises that use songs for listening, dancing, or background music, the PRO grants a blanket license to the organization to play its entire repertoire of music covering thousands of catalogs. The fees for this license are collected and ultimately distributed to the owners of the copyrights, less a percentage for the PRO's efforts. Due to the enormity of tracking songs utilized by every business or organization in the United States, both ASCAP and BMI rely on television and radio airplay as proxies for determining royalty distribution from this source.

Synchronization royalties are received from users who have authorization to integrate a recording of a musical work into an audiovisual work, such as a movie or television series. If a song is "synchronized" with images on a screen, the user must acquire a synchronization right. This fee is usually negotiated based on the length of song being used, where in a film it is used, and whether the song is prerecorded or performed live.

Commercial synchronization royalties are fees paid by advertising agencies and their clients for using a song in a commercial. These fees are negotiated based on whether the commercial is on television or radio; the ad campaign is international, national, or limited territory; whether or not the original lyrics are changed; and if the song can be used exclusively for the product or service being advertised.

Print royalties are derived from licensing arrangements between the publisher and the creator of sheet music, folios, arrangements for a particular musical instrument, and concert editions of printed music.

Foreign royalties represent all performance, mechanical, print, synchronization, and digital royalty income from outside the United States. Given geographical constraints, publishers are typically dependent on PROs in other countries to track and collect these fees. Overseas piracy also poses problems for collecting such royalties.

Digital royalties represent all types of musical usage on the Internet. The designer of an Internet page usually deals directly with the publisher to negotiate a fee based on how a song is used (print, audible recording, etc). Because the use of the Internet is a relatively new form of communication, these royalties are difficult to track by PROs and copyright owners.

Given the difficulties involved in estimating future catalog royalties, it is no surprise that music publishers rely on average historical NPS as a baseline for estimating future NPS. Another important factor in establishing a market multiple for a song catalog is the anticipated growth rate of NPS. Considering that the strength of song catalog's royalty income ultimately reflects the musical tastes of the public, it seems unrealistic to expect it to remain fixed in perpetuity. If anything, the data should reflect the potential for a catalog to fall from the public's favor and experience downward trends in royalty income. This is exemplified in the decline in royalty income of Catalogs 1 and 2 from 1992 to 1995.

Growth or Decay Rates

From 1992 to 1995, the cash flows (annual NPS) of Catalog 1 decreased by 32.1 percent and those of Catalog 2 decreased by 12.3 percent.[18] In contrast, over the same time period, horizon returns on large company stocks had a compound growth rate of 13.8 percent.[19] Thus, purchasers of song catalogs pay smaller multiples of recent earnings than do purchasers of stocks because the popularity and commercial usage of songs tend to diminish over time.

Conclusion

The valuation of a country music song catalog consists of estimating the catalog's future Net Publishers Share and multiplying this amount by an appropriate market multiple. This is similar to the stock-market process of pricing a stock based on recent price/earnings (P/E) multiples. However, in the time period under study, stocks traded at an earning multiple of twenty-one, whereas song catalogs traded at earning multiples of between six and nine. The lower market multiples of song catalogs can be traced to two factors. First, estimating future song royalty payments is extremely difficult due to the various sources from which they are derived: mechanical, performance, synchronization, commercials, print, foreign usage, and digital. In addition, due to the enormity of song usages, the tracking and collection of song revenues is an imprecise process. Second, song popularity wanes, reducing a catalog's commercial viability over time. For example, in this study, royalty payments of established country songwriters declined 12.3 percent and 32.1 percent between 1992 and 1995, while stock prices showed an increase of 13.8 percent over the same time period.

Notes

1. A catalog is a collection of musical compositions written by the same songwriter or group of songwriters. It may include songs that are co-published (co-owned) with other music publishers. In the case of co-published compositions, the music publisher selling the catalog will only be selling their share (percentage) of the songs.

2. Carrington Nelson, "Songs for Sale," *The Tennessean,* May 22, 1999, Music Section, 1.

3. Jay Orr, "Sony/ATV: Sweet Home for Alabama," *The Tennessean,* June 16, 1999, Music Industry Section, 1.

4. Michael Scully, "Tom T. Hall Catalog Brings Worth to Deal, Analysts Say," *The Tennessean,* September 25, 1999, Music Section, 1.

5. See Brabec, 28–52, for a more complete listing of song royalty income sources.

6. Interview, Trigon Corporation (Dean Migchelbrink), summer 1999.

7. See ASCAP, *Music and Money, Where the Money Comes From for Writers and Publishers,* 5.

8. Interview, Sony/ATV Music Publishing LLC (Phil May), summer 1999.

9. Interview, Trigon Corporation (Dean Migchelbrink), summer 1999.

10. Interview, Sony/ATV Music Publishing LLC (Phil May), summer 1999.

11. Ross, Westerfield, and Jordan, 66.

12. See the ASCAP, BMI, SESAC, and Harry Fox Internet websites for a more detailed explanation of how royalties are disbursed.

13. Interview, Zeal Financial (Tim Smith), fall 1998. See also Carrington Nelson, "Songs for Sale," *The Tennessean,* May 22, 1999, Music Section, 1.

14. Interview, Sony/ATV (Donna Hilley), fall 1998.

15. Ross, Westerfield, and Jordan, 66.

16. Information on royalty collection procedures is drawn from Brabec, *Money, Music and Success, The Insiders Guide to the Music Industry, The ASCAP Advantage* and the ASCAP, BMI, SESAC and Harry Fox Internet Web sites.

17. BDS tracks radio play by initially creating a digital fingerprint for each song entered into its system. An automated listening station monitors the airwaves in each market, matching songs played on the air with their digital fingerprints.

18. The compounded rates of growth were estimated using log-linear least squares regression. See Brigham, Gapenski, and Ehrhardt, p. 418, for a detailed explanation.

19. Ibbotson, 181.

Works Cited

American Society of Composers and Publishers (ASCAP) Internet Web site. http://www.ascap.com/

ASCAP, *Music and Money, Where the Money Comes From For Writers and Publishers.* Los Angeles: ASCAP.

ASCAP, *The ASCAP Advantage.* Los Angeles: ASCAP.

Brabec, Jeffrey and Todd Brabec. *Music Money And Success, The Insiders Guide to The Music Industry.* New York: Schirmer, 1994, 2000.

Brigham, Eugene F., Louis C. Gapenski, and Michael C. Ehrhardt. *Financial Management Theory and Practice,* 9th ed. Fort Worth: Dryden, 1999.

Broadcast Music, Incorporated (BMI) Internet Web site. http://www.bmi.com/

Harry Fox Agency Internet Web site. http://nmpa.org/hfa/

Ibbotson and Associates. *Stocks, Bonds, Bills and Inflation 1999 Yearbook.* Chicago: Ibbotson Associates Inc., 1999.

Ross, Stephen, with Randolph Westerfield and Bradford Jordan. *Fundamentals of Corporate Finance,* 5th ed. Boston: Irwin McGraw Hill, 2000.

SESAC Internet Web site. http://www.sesac.com/

Postcards and the Promotion of Early Country Music Artists

Danny W. Allen

During the early part of the twentieth century, picture postcard collecting, sending, and exchanging became a mania in the United States. This phenomenon is largely forgotten today. Postcard clubs and collectors appeared across the nation within the first two decades of the century. Hundreds of millions of postcards were mailed. Lists of names were exchanged with people mailing postcards to collectors they would never meet.

The images on the postcards represented everything and anything. Usually a community, often through its merchants, would publish postcards carrying images of civic pride. Water works, main streets, fire stations, churches, and schools promoted the hometown. Businesses advertised with them, artistic cards were to be had, and musicians used postcards as well.

Through a collection of postcards, a large, clear picture of society emerges like the pieces of a jigsaw puzzle. This fingerprint of history tells us of culture, language, fashion, tools, furniture, musical instruments, and practically every other aspect of daily life. If you can think of it, it's likely on a postcard somewhere.

I am not trained as a historian. By education I am a paleontologist, but by avocation an inveterate collector of items of historical relevance—including postcards. But the two interests, earth sciences and history, are not at odds. The paleontology undergraduate is soon and often reminded of the inherent conceit and bias of the fossil record. For example, fossils of soft-bodied organisms are, in a relative sense, nearly nonexistent. The postcard record has a bias as well. It tells the history of only those who produced postcards. It is very easy, in both cases, to misinterpret the historical record. Still, when the pieces are put together, a larger picture emerges.

While there is considerable published material on the history of photographers and photography, there is very little scholarly work in the field of postcards. It is my hope that others will find some interest in pursuing a more scholarly approach to the history of postcards. The academic and professional historians with whom I have shared my collections usually admit that the idea of studying postcards has never occurred to them.

It is important to begin with a look at photography in general in order to better understand the use of photography in the postcards themselves. When the photographic body of the nineteenth century is compared to the postcard images of the first half of the twentieth century, one sees a distinct change from the posed shot to the candid. This change is due, in part, to the popularization of postcards.

The images of the nineteenth century were usually posed and rarely candid. This was due to several factors, including the weight and awkwardness of the equipment; the slow speed of some early film, which required long exposures; and the uncommonness of the event. The overwhelming genre was the portrait. Men, women, children, and babies posed, usually without props, but quite often with a studio backdrop of a mountain or some sylvan scene. Yet from the very beginning people posed with the objects they prized. Often these were musical instruments. Figure 1 is such an example.

At the beginning of the twentieth century, the development of lighter and cheaper cameras along with the worldwide popularization of postcards gave rise to the candid shot. It became relatively easy to photograph not just special events but also day-to-day life, make a postcard, and put it in the mail. People still posed in studios, often in order to acquire a postcard-backed photo to be mailed to friends and relatives. Few people realize today just how popular postcards became in the United States—particularly after 1907, when postal regulations allowed the inclusion of a written message along with the address.

Postcards probably first appeared in Europe around 1870. Different accounts place the first-known postcards in Austria, Eastern Europe, or any number of other places from 1860 to 1870. Much depends on the definition of "postcard." Oversized business cards and merchant trade cards were addressed, stamped, and postally used as well. The first postcard-

Fig. 1. Cabinet photograph, photographer N.J. Heywood, San Francisco (circa 1890). *From the collection of D.W. Allen.*

type issues by the United States government were offered to the public in 1873. Today, these are referred to as "postal cards" rather than postcards. The cards were imprinted with the stamp and required only a message and address. As part of this postal act, private postcards were prohibited, although some people occasionally still sent them successfully.

On May 19, 1898, Congress authorized private postcards. These were issued with what collectors call an "undivided back" (figure 2). No message was to appear on the address side.

Cards were printed—either in color or black and white—or produced photographically, developed by hand in a darkroom. Photographic paper with a postcard back was sold to both professional and amateur photographers. Collectors refer to these photographic paper postcards as "real photos."

In 1907 Congress authorized "divided back" postcards (figure 3), permitting a message along with the address. From about this time until the beginning of World War I, postcard collecting and trading became a social mania. Trading clubs were formed and lists of collectors were exchanged.

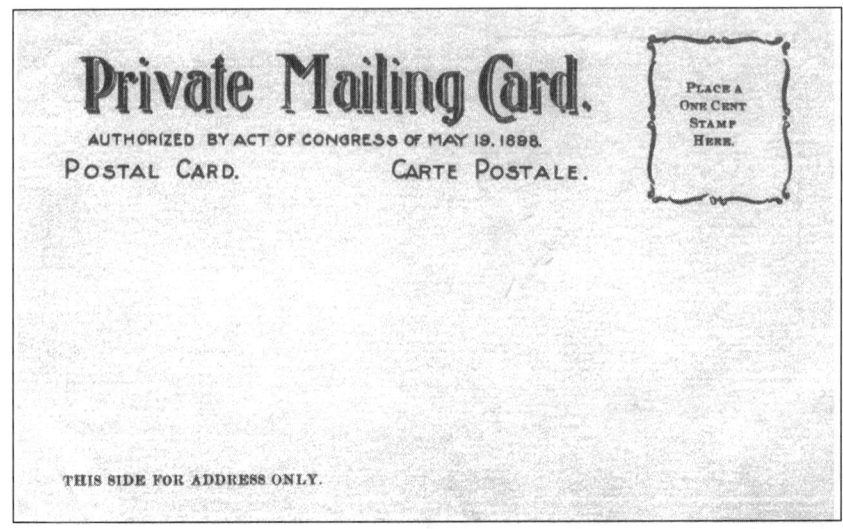

Fig. 2. An undivided back.

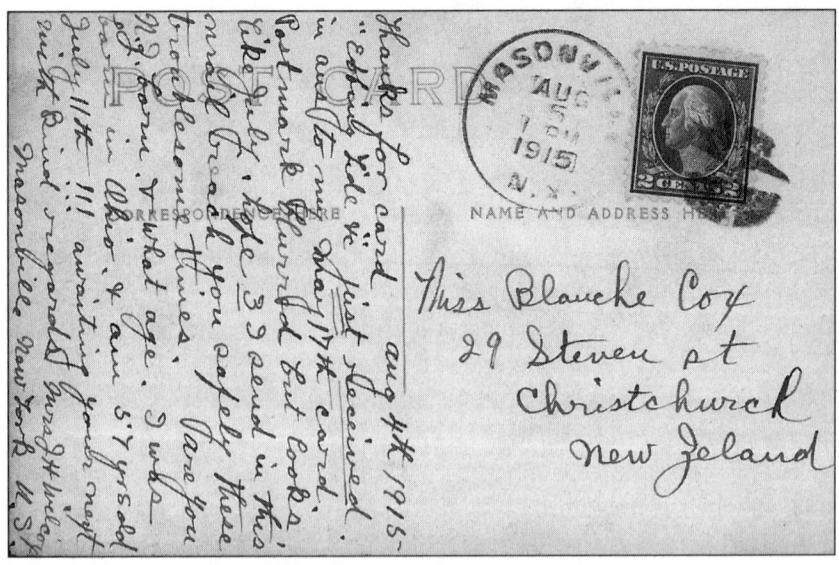

Fig. 3. A divided back. *From the collection of D.W. Allen.*

Postcards began to change hands and enter collections through the mail. For many people, particularly in rural- and small-town settings, life was incessant work with little contact outside the immediate community. Postcards provided color and a world view as they were exchanged and traded by the millions, if not billions.

At this time, smaller, lighter cameras became available and relatively inexpensive, making it possible for many Americans to purchase their first camera. The Eastman-Kodak Company sold a camera loaded with film, which could be mailed to the company for processing. Along with the processed postcard-back photos, the camera itself—loaded with a new roll of film—was returned to the owner. Others did their own processing, including the woman who mailed the postcard in figure 4.

Fig. 4. A real-photo postcard. This card, postmarked August 15, 1915, was mailed from Madisonville, New York, and reads: "Myself, & home, & husband on load of oats. I have Kodak & do all the work myself will send other of self later." *From the collection of D.W. Allen.*

Fig. 5. (left) An example of a cyanotype real photo postcard. On the back of this card is written: "Dewy Pierce 11 Adams Street, Salamanca, N.Y. Oct 10 1908." *From the collection of D.W. Allen.*

Fig. 6. (Below) Undivided-back, real photo postcard on U.S.–made photo paper. Unpostmarked. *From the collection of D.W. Allen.*

At last, a photograph could be taken without the planning and the trip to a photographer's studio. Relatives in another state or another country could see pictures of the new baby, the brother, or the cousin that left home. Communities and people across the country sent postcards all over the world. The images they sent were invariably objects of civic and personal pride such as the homestead, the town water treatment plant, and musical instruments. Figure 5 is a cyanotype, a process that yielded a blue and white photograph. Figure 6, a black and white "real photo" postcard, shows two men proudly displaying their instruments.

Figures 7 and 8 show other examples of early postcard images of musicians.

Fig. 7. These two women have donned some of their finest clothes for this portrait. Their handwritten note on the back asks the receiver to "come to our concert."

Fig. 8. A young boy holds his banjo in what might be a family portrait. Behind him is an older-generation fiddler. *From the collection of D.W. Allen.*

Professional musicians (figure 9) were quick to use the new medium, as were instrument makers and retailers (figure 10).

Of the many cards I have gathered through twenty years of collecting, this is the only one I have seen with saw players. But their claim to being the undisputed originators of handsaw music is one that should perhaps be scrutinized. Hyperbole and embellishment were as common on postcards as anywhere else.

The advertising card for a violin manufacturing company depicted in Figure 10 was probably sent out in the 1920s. On the postcard back were offered two violin models, the 210–A and the 210–B. The 210–A could be purchased for $18.83 with a $3.83 down payment and five monthly payments of $3.00. The 210–B was, apparently, a better model costing $4.95 down and five monthly payments of $5.00.

The real explosion in postcards with country musicians came with radio in the 1920s. Many stations would send postcards to listeners who had written to the station. Along with performers, many announcers appeared on radio stations' promotional postcards. A new color postcard format, the "linen," appeared around 1930. Figure 11, a linen card, is one of the many cards produced for WSM in Nashville.

Postcards and Promotion 125

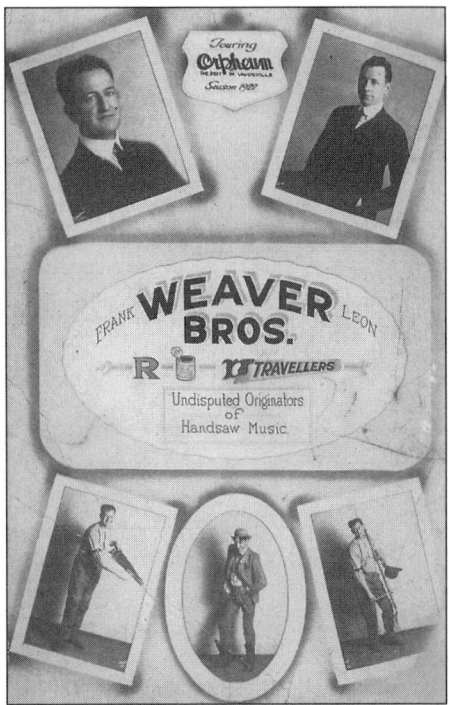

Fig. 9. This "real photo" advertising card pictures the Weaver Brothers, Frank and Leon, for the 1922 Orpheum Vaudeville season. The brothers make the claim of being "Undisputed Originators of Handsaw Music" and include a rebus that reads "Arkansas Travellers." *From the collection of D.W. Allen.*

Fig. 10. This violin was offered as "Post-Card Special No. 210" by the Quaker Valley Manufacturing Company of Aurora, Illinois. *From the collection of D.W. Allen.*

Fig. 11. The "Solemn Ole Judge" of Nashville radio station WSM poses with a hostess in this postcard issued in conjunction with the Texas Centennial Exposition. *From the collection of D.W. Allen.*

Linen cards and other types of lithographic, or printed, cards were much cheaper to produce than real photo in large quantities. However, most stations continued to produce and distribute real photo cards. This is fortunate for current collectors. Real photo cards are prized by collectors, in part, for their high resolution. Figures 12 and 13 show the detail that real photo postcards can provide when done by a competent photographer.

I have accumulated over one thousand cards of what could be considered images of country performers, and just as there is a bias in the fossil record, the postcards with radio performers from the early 1920s to 1950 do not always turn up in the numbers nor places one might expect. When looked at as a whole, certain patterns become apparent, but some intriguing questions arise. Areas of the country where one would expect to find many examples of radio performers have what would seem to be either an excess or lack of cards. Some states, such as North Dakota, which has a relatively small number of postcards of non-music-related views compared to other states, have considerably more radio performers in the postcard record than many other states. Postcards of early hillbilly and country music

Fig. 12. "Red River Dave" appeared in a series of advertising postcards for Gretsch Guitars. This especially sharp image yields great detail when magnified (figure 13). *From the collection of D.W. Allen.*

Fig. 13. Detail from figure 12.

radio performers from stations in the South, where one would expect to find them, are not nearly as common as those of the North. Many cards were sent out by New England stations. One can surmise that musicians went where there were populations that could support and sustain them; this often meant going North. Another anomaly in the collection is the absence of the famous. In my collection there are no prewar postcards of Bill Monroe, the Carter Family, Gid Tanner, nor Roy Acuff.

In amassing these images, it became apparent that a taxonomy, or some sense of order, was needed to keep track of the collection. Organizing the cards by performer or state is difficult since some country musicians appear in the collection with different groups and in different locales. So, I fell upon the idea of ordering the performers in the collection by gender and number. For example, the male musicians are arranged as single acts, duets, trios, etc., up to octets. The female performers are arranged in the same manner. Mixed gender groups are set out as one woman–one man, two women–one man, etc. Other groupings are announcers, jamborees, advertising, and "acknowledgment of signal received," perhaps one of the most interesting. Acknowledgment-of-signal-received postcards were sent commonly between ham radio operators documenting reception of radio frequencies. A few commercial stations sent them, also. Figure 14 is a card I found in New Zealand, sent there from Billings, Montana, on Jan 20, 1935, acknowledging a received signal of that station in September 1934 more than eight thousand miles away.

The influence of early country music and musicians of the southern United States on the rest of America is beyond question. That a U.S. radio station playing country/western artists could be heard in New Zealand in 1935 illustrates how international the music was and is. I have found New Zealanders to be so avidly interested in what they call "traditional country" that I wonder if the KGHL reception was an isolated event or a common one. Clearly, there are questions of interest to the scholar of country music that postcards can address.

In considering any study of postcards relating to early country music, it becomes clear that establishing boundaries and a framework is important. There are many sidebars and offshoots that can lead the researcher in any direction. When one begins to look at the full scope of musicians, instrument makers, radio personalities, and the business of music portrayed on postcards, the need for further study is readily apparent.

Postcards and Promotion 129

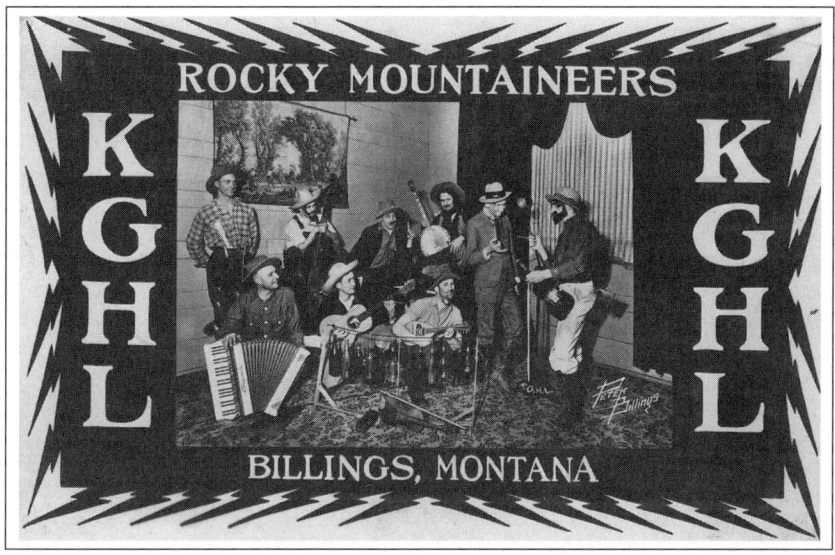

Fig. 14. Receipt-of-signal-received card mailed to New Zealand in January 1935.

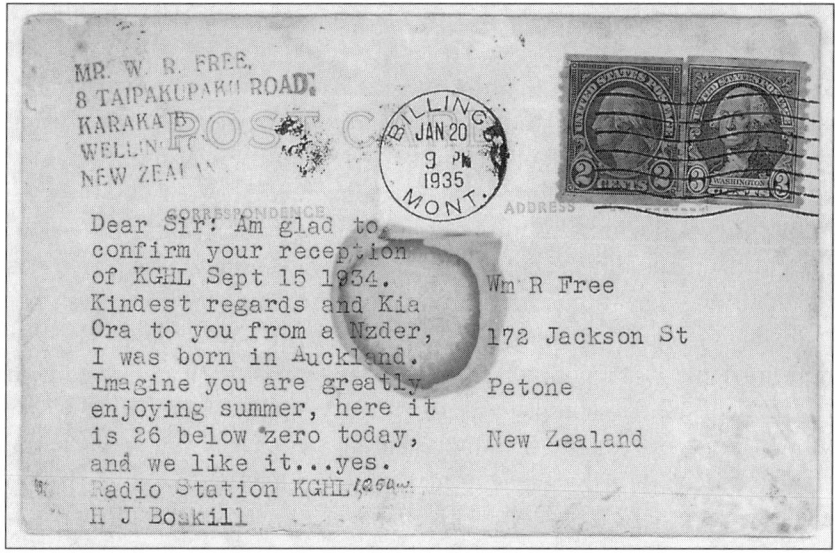

Fig. 15. Reverse of figure 14, showing postmark and message indicating that sender was a native New Zealander.

The Drive-by Truckers and the Redneck Underground
A Subcultural Analysis

S. Renee Dechert and George H. Lewis

> I got a pick-up that's up on blocks
> And I'm up to my ass in debt and hock.
> "Bulldozers and Dirt"

With "Bulldozers and Dirt," the Drive-by Truckers kick off their second album, *Pizza Deliverance*. "Bulldozers" is a dramatic monologue featuring every stereotype in the book, sung by the quintessential redneck as he addresses his girlfriend's thirteen-year-old daughter. The song describes the redneck's breaking into his future-girlfriend's trailer to steal her television; the girlfriend's holding a shotgun on him while waiting for the police and then putting up her trailer for his bail before promising to "learn [him] not to roam"; and details about the redneck's pickup on blocks, debt, and alcoholism—items that comprise his life and have always been associated with redneck culture.[1] To complete the picture, the singer offers the girl a beer in a clear act of seduction. Complimenting these low-brow lyrics is the song's music: a formal waltz with mandolin, upright bass, and the Truckers' perfect—indeed, gospel-like—harmony. This seeming contradiction embodies the artistic and rhetorical strategies of the Truckers. What becomes clear is that the band isn't exploiting the stereotype; instead, they're calling attention to it and to the socioeconomic issues it often obscures. So while, traditionally, the pickup truck on blocks may be a humorous staple of the

As this Jim Stacy sketch of the Drive-by Truckers' logo illustrates, creating unease is at the heart of the band's music.

redneck stereotype, the issues to which it points—poverty and the literal inability to leave, to change one's situation—are not particularly funny.

Cultural artifacts and stereotypes can be and are used to produce readings that stand in direct contrast to the interests of the dominant culture within which they were created and are currently situated. In most instances, popular culture acts as a mitigating force in society more than as a radical or revolutionary one. From this perspective, then, the sort of reworking of texts and stereotypes the Truckers engage in with songs such as "Bulldozers and Dirt" can be seen as an example of Michael de Certeau's "Brownian motion," or the resistance tactics used by the socially powerless against the dominant system and its created cultural meanings. Such tactics are not designed for power grabs; that is, there is no intention of taking over the dominant system. Instead, they are strategies for taking advantage of opportunities to resist the dominant political, economic, and ideological forces that work to neutralize individuals and groups, keeping them marginalized.

In this essay, we take the above perspective—and within it, the concept of subculture—to help explain the musical and cultural phenomenon of the Redneck Underground and the tactics of one of its seminal bands, the Drive-by Truckers. The Truckers resist the dominant culture's attempts to neutralize and marginalize rednecks by subverting the very stereotypes that have been most effective in keeping members of this subculture "in their place."

Subcultures

> I can kick ass and talk backward
> "Demonic Possession"

Dick Hebdige's study of British punks, *Subculture: The Making of Style,* remains one of the primary treatments of subculture. For Hebdige, "each subcultural 'instance' represents a 'solution' . . . to particular problems and contradictions," disrupting and violating the rules of hegemonized culture. As such, they become a source of anxiety for the dominant culture (81). He writes: "[S]ubcultures express forbidden contents (consciousness of class, consciousness of difference) in forbidden forms (transgressions of sartorial and behavioral codes, law breaking, etc.). They are profane articulations, and they are often and significantly defined as 'unnatural'" (Hebdige 91–92).

When these ideological ruptures occur, the hegemony is driven to what Hebdige terms "recuperation," a process through which "the fractured order is repaired and the subculture incorporated as a diverting spectacle within the dominant mythology from which it in part emanates" (94). Recuperation generally takes two forms. The first is the "commodity form," which is defined as "the conversion of subcultural signs (dress, music, etc.) into mass-produced objects" (94). That is, the Other is changed to "meaningless exotica." The second is the "ideology form," or the "'labelling' [sic] and re-definition of deviant behaviour by dominant groups" (94). Recuperation of the second form involves the creation of stereotypes that serve both to marginalize and neutralize those in the ideologically or politically threatening subculture or social grouping. These stereotypes can serve to trivialize or domesticate, or they can transform those to whom they are successfully applied, marginalizing them as either buffoons or threats to the social order. John Fiske has written of the process thusly: "[U]nruliness is characterized by the middle classes as immoral, disorderly, and economically improvident. These social threats were localized within the individual; the proletarian body became the individual body. So the pleasure and excesses of the body—drunkenness, sexuality, idleness, rowdiness—were seen as threats to the social order. Such a threat becomes particularly terrifying when allied with class interests . . . when pleasures are those of subordinated groups (whether the subordination is by class, gender, race or whatever) the threat is particularly stark" (75).

Tactics to resist such cultural control arise very quickly in subcultures and take, among other forms, the semiotic shape of reworking dominant texts and stereotypes, shifting their meanings and, to the extent this is possible, subverting them. Claude Levi-Strauss uses the term *bricolage* to refer to the way in which subcultures recombine the cultural artifacts of a dominant order to create a coherent new (or counter-) reality or message (Henaff 26). Manipulating the symbols and texts of the dominant culture, especially those of the subcultural stereotypes themselves, becomes a way of not only making these relevant to the members of the subculture, but also of resisting—even inauthenticating—the meanings assigned these symbols and texts by the dominant culture.

De Certeau suggests that this sort of resistance (even rebellion) is practiced most often by subcultures that are resisting assimilation into the dominant culture by creating a space in which they find ways of using the constraining orders of the place: "By an act of being in between, they draw unexpected results from their situation" (30). These "unexpected results" can be found reflected in the surfaces of subculture—in the created styles of *bricolage,* parody, and double meaning.[2] As Hebdige notes, "On the one hand, they warn the 'straight' world in advance of a sinister presence—the presence of difference—and draw down upon themselves vague suspicions, uneasy laughter, 'white and dumb rages.' On the other hand, for those who erect them into icons, who use them as words or as curses, these objects become signs of forbidden identity, sources of value" (2–3).

The ways in which redneck subculture has drawn this "uneasy laughter" while developing its own icons of value merit further examination.

Redneck Subculture

> If you see me on the street
> And I whup you on the head
> You probably got it comin'
>   "Sandwiches for the Road"

Redneck subculture has evolved for almost two centuries, and defining the term "redneck" is an uneven business. First, it is important to distinguish the difference between "redneck" and "white trash." Matt Wray and Annalee Newitz explain, "White trash . . . refers to actually existing white people living in (often rural) poverty, while at the same time it designates a set of stereotypes and myths related to the social behaviors, intelligence, prejudices, and gender roles of poor whites. That is, white trash is an identity generated in the dialectic of base and superstructure" (7). Certainly rednecks share some of these traits, but there are important distinctions: Perhaps most central, redneck is bound to geography in a way that white trash is not, for rednecks are traditionally tied to the South.[3] (However, this has shifted with the recent commodification of redneck iconography, which will be discussed later.)

Always a label of derision, the term "redneck," too, has clear alignment with questions of class given that early rednecks were field laborers whose class was inscribed on their bodies because of their sunburned, or "red," necks.[4] *The Oxford English Dictionary*'s primary definition is consistent with today's understanding of redneck: "A member of the white rural labouring class of the southern States; one whose attitudes are considered characteristic of this class; freq., a reactionary. Originally, and still often, derogatory, but now also used with more sympathy for the aspirations of the rural American."

Some of the most recognized markers of redneck "style" (to use Hebdige's term) are:

- Trailer houses surrounded by junk, especially broken-down cars;
- Men who are sloppy and overweight from too much beer and greasy food;
- Women with big hair, tight clothes, too much makeup, and too many children;
- Sexual (often incestuous), profane, and vulgar behavior;

- Poverty and ignorance; and
- Racism.

Consider, for example, James Dickey's *Deliverance*, a primary source of contemporary redneck stereotypes. Narrator Ed's initial assessment of Oree, Georgia, the small southern town where the men leave their cars, provides a case in point: "[E]verything in Oree was sleepy and hookwormy and ugly, and most of all, inconsequential. Nobody worth a damn could ever come from such a place" (Dickey 55). His discussion of rural life furthers this observation: "There is always something wrong with people in the country, I thought. In the comparatively few times I had ever been in the rural South I had been struck by the number of missing fingers. . . . There had also been several people with some form of crippling or twisting illness, and some blind or one-eyed. No adequate medical treatment, maybe. But there was something else. You'd think that farming was a healthy life, with fresh air and fresh food and plenty of exercise, but I never saw a farmer who didn't have something wrong with him, and most of the time obviously wrong" (55–56). The locals are little more than dangerous, deviant savages, and these figures, as seen in popular culture, are always Other. This has the effect of obscuring questions of class and economics that are at the heart of redneck subculture.

Redneck Recuperation

If the word "septic tank" appears anywhere on your résumé, you might be a redneck.

Sophisticated people have retirement plans. Rednecks, we play the lottery.

Jeff Foxworthy

With this in mind, let us turn to the dominant culture's "recuperation" of rednecks. First, the term "redneck" has been rendered almost meaningless. For example, Jeff Foxworthy of *You Might Be a Redneck If* . . . fame says, "My definition of redneck—it's just a glorious absence of sophistication. It really doesn't know any geographic bounds; it doesn't know any financial bounds" ("Redneck Humor"). In fact, Tom Anderson, executive producer of Foxworthy's short-lived tv sitcom, observes, "Redneck has become so generic. If you're a college kid drinking beer, suddenly you're a redneck. If

Cledus T. Judd's outrageous take on the redneck stereotype is apparent in this Judd album cover.

you fish, you're a redneck—and there are a lot of doctors who fish" (quoted in Hall).[5]

Second, through commodification, "redneck" has been recuperated, effectively rendered less threatening. For instance, the notion of "redneck" has been successfully disseminated across media, from the television program *Hee Haw* to southern redneck T-shirts to the E-mail-driven "redneck quizzes" that abound on the Internet. Consider, too, the antics of redneck comedians such as Jeff Foxworthy and Cledus T. Judd. Foxworthy has a safe, guy-next-door appearance and demeanor, and there is absolutely nothing threatening about him.[6] The approach Cledus T. Judd takes is quite different. Judd's look—outrageous, with his beer belly, tasteless clothes, and goofy antics—renders the redneck no more than a video buffoon as he lusts after Shania Twain or provides a visual component for Alan Jackson's cover of "Pop a Top." Gone is the threatening misfit—surly, alcoholic, violence prone—that threatens the safety (both physical and economic) of the middle class.

The Drive-by Truckers & the Redneck Underground

David Lee Murphy's brand of redneck chic is evident in this publicity photo.

Recuperation also occurs through country music. A case in point is Nashville's commercially viable (and carefully groomed), self-proclaimed redneck David Lee Murphy. Murphy explains, "I'm a redneck and proud of it. I like four-wheel-drive vehicles, and the food I eat is predominantly fried or boiled. Rural people, small-town people who work nine-to-five and are thoughtful of others, are my kind of people. It used to be they called us hillbillies or hicks, and now they call us rednecks, but we turned it around into a term of pride" (Himes 44). It's fitting that Murphy's description of redneck takes on the romance of a marketed stereotype rather than any kind of honest rebellion. His look and music are a kind of "redneck chic," comprised of boots and old jeans (with a flawless fit), too-long (but carefully groomed) hair, ragged (yet tasteful) shirts, a perfect smile, and videos that capture all this redneck rebellion and domesticate it.

The consequences of this recuperation are substantial. As Patrick Carr has noted in his discussion of subcultural stereotypes and their manipulation by the country music industry, "Not long ago, to 'be country' meant that you had been cast by a geo-socio-economic accident of birth with an almost automatically adversarial relationship with the dominant urban/suburban culture" (484). Today, with performers like Murphy, Judd, and Foxworthy, the country music industry has commercialized those earlier adversarial southern redneck voices, economically insinuating them into a capitalist order to which they have been traditionally opposed. To use Hebdige's terms, the redneck subculture has been "incorporated as a diverting spectacle within the dominant mythology" (94).

In the end, redneck subculture is neutralized by being made commercially viable and unthreatening.

The Redneck Underground

> Some people keep sayin' I can't last long,
> But I got my bands, I got my songs.
> "The Living Bubba"

The Redneck Underground music scene is not so safe, however. In the mid 1980s, the "Redneck Underground" emerged in the Atlanta/Athens, Georgia, bar scenes, a musical movement that denied the stifling economics and political correctness of Nashville and returned to southern themes and music. This network of bands and clubs, such as the Star Community Bar, Dottie's, and the Austin Avenue Buffet, has "no orthodoxy, other than a binding sense of Southern identity that embraces tradition with reverence and gooses it with tomfoolery" (Dollar P22).[7] Sara Kelly, manager of the Drive-by Truckers, describes the early Underground in 1991:

> On any given night [at the Star Bar] you could go see bands like the Continentals, the Jody Grind, Smoke, the Diggers, Blacktop Rockets, Useless Playboys, Redneck Grreece, Slim Chance and the Convicts, and too many others to even try and mention. The folks that bonded together through this neighborhood are what eventually came to be known as the "Redneck Underground." The thing about a scene is, you don't sit down and go, "Well, let's form a little collective of our posse and give it a name"—it just happens. Someone outside the circle gives it a name. . . . We all looked after each other, and ruled Little 5 Points with a [Pabst Blue Ribbon-] laden fist (by virtue of the fact that one of us worked at just about every store/bar/restaurant in the 'hood). They were great fucking days, no one could touch us. Everyone ate free, drank free and pretty much drugged free, too. It was goddamn beautiful.

Cornerstones of the early Redneck Underground were Deacon Lunchbox, Gregory Dean Smalley, and Slim Chance and the Convicts.

Lunchbox, who died in 1992, coined the term "Redneck Underground" and remains a patron saint of the movement. Steve Dollar describes him as "the NASCAR-loving, bra-wearing, Pabst Blue Ribbon–bellied Atlanta construction worker whose satiric performances were a lightning rod that galvanized the scene" (P22). Similarly, Convict Jon Byrd explains, "Something was genuinely lost when we lost him. . . . He was this vortex of gender and regional pride, the redneck sensibility and poetry, rock 'n' roll and country music" (Dollar P22). Lunchbox set the standard for the Redneck Underground and shows just how outside Nashville the Underground is. (After all, it's difficult to imagine Garth Brooks or George Strait trying Deacon Lunchbox's unorthodox approach.)

Gregory Dean Smalley's role in founding the Redneck Underground (RU) is especially important. As David Goodman has noted, Smalley "became the leading RU spokesman, ever ready to state in his blunt, down-home way just what is wrong with Nashville and so right about the RU" (290). Making his reputation was Smalley's practice of changing the lyrics of popular songs to lines that were hilarious—and often obscene. He was a member of over two dozen bands, perhaps most notably the Diggers, a group that prided itself on being "The Sorriest Band in Town." (That may have been the band's hope, but the consensus is that the Diggers were a fine group.) James Kelly, also known as "Slim Chance," notes that Smalley was "an excellent guitarist, with an uncanny ability to play along with anyone, even if he had never heard their music before" ("On My Way Home"), a point especially relevant given the collaborative nature of the early Redneck Underground. In addition, Smalley founded "Bubbapalooza," a parody of Lollapalooza with the focus on southern roots rock, which has become a semi-annual tradition and led to two compilation discs. Although he died of AIDS in 1996, Smalley drank, smoke, and played up until his death, at times even having to be carried to the stage. As Brandon Haynie remembers, "[W]e all saw him die before our eyes."

Slim Chance and the Convicts carry on the Redneck Underground torch. (Incidentally, Slim/James Kelly is currently finishing his doctoral dissertation in psychology at Georgia State. It's worth mentioning, too, that guitarist Jon Byrd is writing his dissertation—on Elvis—in American Studies at Emory.) Says singer/guitarist Slim, "The Redneck Underground is like the punk movement to us. . . . It's a subculture that's taking something in a different direction" (Dollar P22). Slim's mention of the punk movement is significant given punk's roots in anarchy, fighting against the constraints of the music business and, by extension, the dominant culture. In fact, Byrd sees this as a source of much of the Convicts' appeal: "It's like what the Sex Pistols did, breaking down barriers between the audience and the band, exploding the 'rock idol' (myth). This is what country music has always done" (Robert Kelly 8).

Today, the Redneck Underground maintains its diverse roots, including bands such as the Blacktop Rockets, Southern Culture on the Skids, Laura Tyler, Redneck Greece Delux, Truckadelic, and the Drive-by Truckers. Musically, the Underground defies the smooth production, syrupy lyrics, and easy commercial appeal of Nashville's Hot Country—artists like David Lee Murphy. Consider Slim Chance's assessment of the Underground's music: "What you do hear in a lot of RU bands' songs are themes of lower-class, southern lifestyles (farms, sharecroppers, trailer parks), blue-collar jobs (truck drivers, construction, auto repair), extreme acts of irrational behavior (killing, fighting, stealing heavy machinery), and regional leisure activities (stockcar racing, fishing, eating barbeque). You also hear about AIDS, mental illness, homelessness, domestic violence, loneliness, personal, family, and regional pride, poverty, and politics. These issues are usually addressed in one of two ways, either tongue-in-cheek, or with an honest and often heart-wrenching story" (Kelly "Re: The Redneck Underground").[8] That is, the Underground embraces a populist reality that has been lost in much of today's "hats and hair" Hot Country. Oddly enough, however, the Redneck Underground is even, to an extent, outside the world of alt.country, a genre that prides itself on its inclusion of diverse artists and defiance of Nashville. For example, *No Depression,* generally considered *the* publication of alt.country, consistently gives Underground bands and their music short shrift.[9]

The Redneck Underground and its seminal spokespersons act as "semiotic guerillas," opposing the dominant culture while—ironically and parodically—cloaking their messages in acceptable redneck symbols of dominant cultural interpretation. Patterson Hood, lead singer of the Drive-by Truckers, explains, "I personally like the whole Redneck Underground thing. It's kinda funny. It's definitely the more belligerent of the alt.country scene. And I like belligerent" (O'Neill).

Such is the role of subculture.

Drive-by Truckers

I'm tired of living in Buttholeville
   "Buttholeville"

In 1985 Patterson Hood, son of David Hood, a key session player in the original Muscle Shoals scene, met Mike Cooley at the University of North Alabama, and the two formed Adam's Housecat (AHC), a rootsy punk band. As Hood remembers, "I was writing record reviews for the university newspaper . . . [w]hen I got ahold of a copy of *Tim* by The Replacements. I loved it so much I decided to drop out of school. It sounded like shit . . . but I figured if they could do it, I could do it" (Slatton). In 1988, AHC won *Musician*'s "Best Unsigned Band" award and recorded an album that was never released. The band lasted until 1991.

In 1996 Hood got the idea for the Truckers, a group formed ultimately

The Drive-by Truckers send a holiday greeting (left to right: Rob Malone, Mike Cooley, Brad Morgan, and Patterson Hood).

by Hood (vocals, guitar), Mike Cooley (vocals, guitar), Rob Malone (bass), and Brad Morgan (drums). (Other musicians, such as Barry Sell on mandolin and John Neff on pedal steel provide additional studio support.) Hood does most of the writing and singing; his gravely voice is redneck through and through, and his work is suffused with humor—hinting that the best way to handle the mess that is the world is to laugh about it but never lose sight of the tragedy. In 1998, the Truckers released *Gangstabilly,* a disc chock-full of the Truckers' patented look at social issues. For example, "Late for Church," "Why Henry Drinks," and "Buttholeville" examine the frustration of blue-collar life.[10]

Gangstabilly opens with "Wife Beater," a track Hood cites in the liner notes as "pay[ing] homage to those great old Tammy Wynette singles from the late sixties." The song, with its dirge-like melody and rhythm, gets to the violence immediately as the singer recounts the victim's story, remembering the first show of violence: "He knocked out two of your front teeth." The singer then takes on the victim's litany of standard excuses ("He's changed"; "It's for the kids"), and while it's clear that the singer loves her, the song gives little hope for them or that, indeed, she'll survive her husband, known only as the "wife beater."

The song "18 Wheels of Love" is the true story of Hood's mother's second marriage to Chester, a truck driver. (Hood says he wrote the song as a wedding present for the happy couple because he couldn't afford a gift, "and every goddamn word is true.") The song opens with "Mama ran off with a trucker / Peterbilt, Peterbilt" and rolls on from there. Initially, this would appear to be the ultimate in redneck kitsch: After all, this song is about a trucker who falls in love and marries Mama at Dollywood—the ceremony, incidentally, is performed by a Porter Wagoner look-alike. However, closer inspection reveals that this is the story of two people living in an uncertain world (with unstable jobs) who manage to find each other, to give each other a sense of security and a home. She can stop working and make a home for her husband; he can switch to a local route that will keep him close to her. Or, as Hood puts it, "They can see the world from way up in the cab." This theme is underscored by the song's timbre, which grows increasingly harmonious as "18 Wheels of Love" progresses, reinforcing the love of Mama and Chester. Here the quintessential redneck tall tale—the kind of thing Foxworthy would have a field day with—is *real,* and the results are joyous.

"The Living Bubba" is a moving tribute to Greg Dean Smalley. The

The Drive-by Truckers & the Redneck Underground 143

attitude throughout the song is defiant—resigned but determined—opening with its angry, grungy guitar as Hood assumes the persona of Smalley, showing his courage and refusal to stop living, even in the face of AIDS:

> I'm sick at my stomach from the AZT
> Broke at my bank cuz that shit ain't free
> But I'm here to stay (at least another week or two)
> I can't die now cuz I got another show to do.

Hood adds, practically, "I ain't got no political agenda / Ain't got no message for the youth of America / 'cept 'Wear a rubber and be careful who you screw.'"[11] The issues Hood discusses here are real, the physical impact and financial burdens that comprise the reality of those with AIDS as well as the importance of safe sex. (Nashville has yet to produce anything that confronts AIDS this honestly.) The fact that Smalley is the *living* Bubba underscores how fully Smalley lived as well as his dedication to life and music, and, indeed, how his legacy continues. In effect, "The Living Bubba" is a portrait of Greg Dean Smalley, shaking his fist in the face of Fate.

The Drive-by Truckers' album's unusual title, *Gangstabilly*, gets to the core of the group. As Hood explains, "You know gangsta rap? Well, we're sort of gangsta country" (Thompson). That is, the Truckers have taken another subculture, the very in-your-face gangsta rap, and appropriated it to reflect their music, a point further reflected in the band's name. "Drive-by" is a term associated with rap music, a dangerous word; "truckers" gets back to the heart of country music and its tradition of rambling and truck driving. Moreover, it's an unconventional blending, for racism has long been a central element of the redneck stereotype.

While *Gangstabilly* met with generally positive reviews, its cover may have received even more attention. Jim Stacy's caricature highlights a number of redneck stereotypes: A lean younger man, complete with greasy hair, tattoos, cigarettes, and a beer, perches on the hood of his jalopy while groping the thigh of his redneck girlfriend with big hair, lots of makeup, and tight clothes. Hood observes, "[M]aybe because of the funny artwork, people respond to it and then in time see that there's something else there. If people miss some kind of profound message, that's fine. I'd rather just have fun with it" (Slatton).

Pizza Deliverance followed in 1999, adorned by songs like "Bulldozers and Dirt," "Too Much Sex (Too Little Jesus)," "Zoloft," and "The President's

The Drive-by Truckers' *Gangstabilly* album cover attracted attention thanks to Jim Stacy's caricature of redneck stereotypes.

Penis Is Missing"—and given the controversy of Stacy's first cover, the Truckers went with him again for their second disc. Here, however, the drawing is of an older working man, helping move the local Church of Christ to a new location. The visual juxtaposition is clear while the title makes fun of one of the most famous sources of redneck stereotypes, Dickey's *Deliverance*.

In August 2000, the Truckers released *Alabama Ass Whuppin'*, a live disc that captures the rocking vigor of the band's live performances.[12] The album includes some new material as well as a few Hood stories that ought not be missed, most notably "The Avon Lady." Currently, the Truckers are working on a full-length "redneck rock opera," *Soutnern Rock Opera*, dealing with the mythology of the quintessential redneck band, Lynyrd Skynyrd.

As songs like "Bulldozers and Dirt" illustrate, the Truckers have a great

The Drive-by Truckers & the Redneck Underground

Jim Stacy's cover artwork for the Drive-by Truckers' *Pizza Deliverance* album provides a visual play on Dickey's *Deliverance* and the disparate notions of pizza and religion.

sense of humor, but underneath it they are dead serious when taking on the redneck stereotype as well as the issues the stereotype too often makes light of. Perhaps Gregory Nicoll puts it best: "Hood sings about lowlifes and trailer trash not for cheap laughs, but for pathos and heartbreak." Their music is truly parodic.

Drive-by Truckers' *Pizza Deliverance*

Bulldozers and dirt, bulldozers and dirt
Most of all, I love bulldozers and dirt.
"Bulldozers and Dirt"

Patterson Hood has said, "There's a lot of dark stuff in the world, but the best defense to live through it is honestly but with a sense of humor" (Thompson), a point seen in the dry humor pervading most of the Truckers' songs. The rocking "Nine Bullets" tells of a broken-hearted man determined to use the nine bullets in his roommate's gun to solve his problems by shooting a slew of folks: his ex, his family, himself, and his roommate—it *is* his gun, after all. With "Too Much Sex (Too Little Jesus)," Hood assumes the voice of a radio evangelist, a raucous mandolin and upright bass bringing the fire and brimstone to his words. The preacher preys on insecure teens, telling them to "stop that dope smoking, stop that fornication / Take the Lord into your heart, and stop that masturbation." Instead, he says they need to send him money—a point he makes before a commercial break and promise of more drama from "another troubled teen." And a Hood-on-helium vocal brings home the point in the manic "Zoloft": The whole family—even the pit bull—is taking the anti-depressant, and now everyone's problems are miraculously gone. As the singer sums it up, "I'm so damned happy."

Some of *Pizza Deliverance* is more overtly political, calling attention to the reality of lower-class powerlessness. Cooley's angry "One of These Days" features the words of a son who finds himself caught in the same cycle that trapped his father: Neither can escape. Similarly, in "Uncle Frank," Cooley personifies the displacement of a culture as he describes one man affected by the TVA's damming of the Tennessee River. Frank cannot find a place in this promised Eden; instead, he hangs himself, unable even to leave a note because of illiteracy.

There is the Southern Gothic throughout. In the dark "Box of Spiders," Hood describes "Gran Gran," a death-obsessed woman who scared her grandson with tales of a box of spiders. But perhaps more unsettling is "Margo and Harold," the tale of a couple with unusual sexual and substance proclivities. The song is the monologue of a speaker explaining to his lover how terrified he is of the couple. However, that he's given in before is revealed as he confesses, "That night with Margo was a long time ago," thus calling into question whether the speaker fears Harold and Margo or himself. The slow, ominous bassline accompanied by a wicked mandolin is almost hypnotizing, echoing the singer's conflicting fear and fascination.

Songs like "The Company I Keep," "Tales Facing Up," and "The Night G.G. Allin Came to Town" take on a side of life that may make some listeners uncomfortable. Then there's the *Keystone Cops*-esque "The President's Penis Is Missing," with everyone obsessively looking for "Buffalo Bill." After listing other presidents and their indiscretions, Hood gets to the point: "Meanwhile the whole world suffers from hunger and meanness / But we're more concerned with the president's penis." Perhaps that's the point: We *should* be uncomfortable because, underneath the redneck trappings that some may find funny or offensive, the issues to which the Truckers call attention are important but too often ignored—and the music is never less than first-rate.

Final Thoughts: "18 Wheels of Love"

"Peterbilt, Peterbilt"
"18 Wheels of Love"

In the end, the Drive-by Truckers and the Redneck Underground represent a subculture that defies Hebdige's modes of recuperation—one that continues to threaten the dominant culture even in the face of that culture's usage of the redneck stereotype to trivialize and symbolically emasculate. As de Certeau would likely point out, the Drive-by Truckers subvert from within an order of power. They do this not by overthrowing or necessarily transforming it, but by appropriating its resources for their own purposes, using Levi-Strauss's process of *bricolage* in constructing their own space within its boundaries, while exploiting loopholes in its symbolic structure of dominance to acquire power for themselves. In effect, the Drive-by Truckers' parody takes the pickup on blocks, a symbol of powerlessness, and transforms it, giving it the semiotic strength of Chester's semi in "18 Wheels of Love," running on all cylinders as it gleefully inflates, then flattens the establishment's redneck stereotypes.

Notes

We would like to thank Sara Kelly, the Drive-by Truckers' manager, Jenn Bryant, their webmistress, and Slim Chance/James Kelly for their help with this essay. The Pabst Blue Ribbon's on us! Thanks also to the Drive-by Truckers for allowing the reproduction of these graphics.

All quotations used as epigraphs have been taken from Drive-by Truckers songs unless otherwise indicated.

    1. Certainly, we recognize that "redneck" can be perceived as a negative stereotype with political implications; indeed, that is one of our reasons for using the term. We address this in greater detail later in our essay.

2. We use Linda Hutcheon's definition of "parody": "[R]epetition with critical distance that allows ironic signalling of difference at the very heart of similarity" (26).

3. In *The Redneck Manifesto,* Jim Goad writes, "A redneck, as I define it, is someone both conscious of and comfortable with his designated role of cultural junk. . . . A redneck knows he's a villain, and he likes it" (84). While Goad makes a number of significant observations about class and describes rednecks at length, he never distinguishes between "white trash," "rednecks," "hillbillies," and other labels for social classes.

4. Originally, the term was one of derision first used in 1830 to denote the Presbyterians of Fayetteville, North Carolina. Oddly enough, it only came to have wide usage during the Great Depression.

5. As Pamela Wilson observes, "In today's cosmopolitan, rapidly globalizing society, the construction of cultural identities is increasingly becoming a symbolic process rather than the result of geographic positioning. Although the role of the media in this symbolic construction needs further exploration . . . the country music industry contributes to it by constructing notions of 'Southernness' . . . to which consumers can subscribe" (107). This same symbolic process has occurred with respect to "redneck," which in the dominant culture's semiotic vocabulary is fast becoming a media massaged generic construct, rather than a label for a distinct, geographically based subculture. In a similar vein, John Hartigan Jr. sees "redneck" as having been "valorized" as opposed to "white trash"; he links this valorization to the rise in social mobility experienced by country music performers and fans.

6. This is seen in the success of his act. Foxworthy is one of the best-selling comedians of all time. His first four CDs have sold over 11 million copies; sales of his videos, books, and calendars bring Foxworthy's worth is over $50 million ("Redneck Humor").

7. The notion of a supportive network is especially important, for a central tenant of the Underground is collaboration, a kind of musical extension of the southern "family."

8. Kelly has been outspoken in his criticism of Jeff Foxworthy's redneck "humor" and exploitation of the South: "I find [Foxworthy] to be comprehensively offensive, classist, and degrading. A much better example of 'good' country comedy would be the late Jerry Clower. Clower told true stories in an authentic, cornpone manner, and the essence of his style was his non-judgmental sincerity. Foxworthy has turned the degradation of the South into a cottage industry, and people fail to see just how offensive and stereotypical he can be" ("Re: The Redneck Underground").

9. This is probably the result of a lack of understanding of the Underground's very smart—indeed, at times uncomfortably honest—parody.

10. Of course, it's important to remember the Truckers' contribution to

Ghostmeat's 1996 *Flagpole Christmas* compilation CD, "Hope Santa's out of Rehab for X-mas."

11. Jen Bryant posted this on the Truckers' listserv: "Patterson [Hood] told me about a night Greg was playing, a night that he was so sick he had to have a stool to sit on. Between songs, Greg had a coughing fit so bad that they couldn't continue the music for a few minutes. At the end of the fit, he looked out at the audience and said, 'Sorry. I forgot to wear a rubber.'"

12. It's appropriate given the Truckers' politics that when the band released *Alabama Ass Whuppin'*, rather than have a traditional big-wig fete, the official release party was part of a pediatric AIDS benefit.

Works Cited

Bryant, Jenn. "The Living Bubba." 15 July 2000. On-line posting. Drive-by Truckers' listserv. dbts@egroups.com.

Carr, Patrick. "The Changing Image of Country Music." *Country: The Music and the Musicians*. Ed Paul Kingsbury. New York: Country Music Foundation, 1988. 482–517.

de Certeau, Michael. *The Practice of Everyday Life*. Trans. Steven Rendall. Berkeley: U of California P, 1984.

Dickey, James. *Deliverance*. New York: Delta-Dell, 1970.

Dollar, Steve. "Redneck Underground: Real-Life Country Spoken Here." Atlanta *Journal and Constitution*, 11 Feb. 1994: P22.

Drive-by Truckers. *Alabama Ass Whuppin'*. secondheaven.com. SHC-0008.

———. *Gangstabilly*. Ghostmeat Records. SDR-002.

———. *Pizza Deliverance*. Ghostmeat Records. SDR-003/GM-27.

Fiske, John. *Understanding Popular Culture*. London: Unwin Hyman, 1989.

Goad, Jim. *The Redneck Manifesto: How Hillbillies, Hicks, and White Trash Became America's Scapegoats*. New York: Touchstone-Simon & Schuster, 1997.

Goodman, David. *Modern Twang: An Alternative Country Music Guide and Directory*. Nashville: Deacon, 1999.

Hall, C. Ray. "The Whole Redneck Thing." *Courier-Journal*, 3 Oct. 1999: 01H.

Hartigan, John, Jr. "Unpopular Culture: The Case of 'White Trash.'" *Cultural Studies* 11 (1997): 316–43.

Haynie, Brandon. "The Living Bubba." 15 July 2000. On-line posting. Drive-by Truckers listserv. dbts@egroups.com.

Hebdige, Dick. *Subculture: The Meaning of Style*. New York: Methuen, 1979.

Henaff, Marcel. *Claude Levi-Strauss and the Making of Structural Anthropology*. Trans. by Mary Baker. Minneapolis: U of Minnesota P, 1998.

Himes, Geoffrey. "David Lee Murphy: Genuine Redneck Stuff." *Country Music* Jan./Feb. 1997: 44.

Hutcheon, Linda. *A Poetics of Postmodernism: History, Theory, Fiction.* New York: Routledge, 1988.
Kelly, James. "On My Way Home." *Creative Loafing,* 6 Apr. 1996.
———. "Re: The Redneck Underground." E-mail to authors. 15 June 2000.
Kelly, Robert. "Redneck Chic." *Highpoint,* Dec. 4–17, 1992: 1+.
Kelly, Sara. "The Living Bubba." 15 July 2000. On-line posting. Drive-by Truckers listserv. dbts@egroups.com.
Nicoll, Gregory. "Steve McQueen for a Day: Down the Road with the Drive-by Truckers." *Creative Loafing* 13 May 1999.
O'Neill, John. "Rebel Yell: Drive-by Truckers Skid on Southern Culture." *Worcester Phoenix,* 12–19 Mar. 1999. http://www.worcesterphoenix.com/archive/music/99/03/12/on_the_rocks.html
"Redneck." *The Oxford English Dictionary.* 2nd ed. 1989.
"Redneck Humor." CNN *Newsstand.* CNN, 14 July 2000.
Slatton, Jason. "Unchecked Redneck." *Flagpole,* 20 May 1998.
Thompson, Matt. "Gangsta Country at the Dish." *Gainesville Sun.* http://www.drivebytruckers.com/dbtreviews.html
Wilson, Pamela. "Mountains of Contradictions: Gender, Class and Region in the Star Image of Dolly Parton." *Reading Country Music: Steel Guitars, Opry Stars, and Honky-Tonk Bars.* Ed. Cecelia Tichi. Durham: Duke UP, 1998. 98–120.
Wray, Matt, and Annalee Newitz. Introduction. *White Trash: Race and Class in America.* Ed. Matt Wray and Annalee Newitz. New York: Routledge, 1997. 1–14.

WPAQ Radio

THE VOICE OF THE BLUE RIDGE MOUNTAINS

David B. Pruett

Located in Mount Airy, North Carolina, WPAQ Radio (740 AM) aired its first broadcast in February 1948. It has since served its community by broadcasting the music of the region, specializing in old-time and bluegrass music. WPAQ Radio is locally known as the "voice of the Blue Ridge Mountains." This expression has appeared, for example, in the titles of a video documentary produced in 1997 by the Surry Arts Council and a compact disc released in 1999 on the Rounder label.[1] The phrase suggests that WPAQ is recognized locally as a symbol and mouthpiece of the regional culture. But despite its local fame, the station has not been recognized in scholarly literature on rural music. This article aims to reveal the historical importance of WPAQ and the process by which this local radio station has contributed to the perpetuation of one of America's distinct regional cultures. It will do so by examining local events that the station sponsors, the station's archives, and well-known musicians who have performed at WPAQ.

By the late 1940s when WPAQ was founded, America had witnessed almost three decades of radio history, and country barn dances had become a staple fare on stations such as WLS (Chicago, Illinois), WSM (Nashville, Tennessee), and WBT (Charlotte, North Carolina). Radio's growth from the early 1920s had seen increasing commercialization through the selling of air time for advertisements.

Country music radio stations and musicians were affected both posi-

WPAQ Radio, located in Mount Airy, North Carolina, is dedicated to preserving old-time and bluegrass music heritage and providing a venue for Appalachian regional culture, earning it a reputation as the "voice of the Blue Ridge Mountains." (Photo by the author, February 2000)

tively and negatively by the presence of commercial advertising. It is difficult to imagine the national popularization of country music during the first half of the twentieth century without commercial sponsorship. For example, the *National Barn Dance* of WLS would not have reached audiences across America without the sponsorship of Sears, Roebuck, and Company. Moreover, National Life and Accident Insurance sponsored WSM, which produced the *Grand Ole Opry*. Radio helped to change the "hillbilly" music of the 1920s into mainstream country music, a lucrative industry since the 1940s controlled in large part by record companies and commercial advertisers. Later artists added instruments such as drums and the steel guitar, and the music evolved into a style dominated by stars.

However, not all stations welcomed the change in the music that was then identified with rural America. Since WPAQ's first broadcast in 1948, Ralph Epperson, the station's sole proprietor, has been using a mass medium to fight mass media in efforts to protect the regional heritage. Yet WPAQ's efforts have so far been documented only in various newspaper and magazine articles, a compact disc released in November 1999, and a fifteen-minute documentary film. In addition, it is not widely known that WPAQ made recordings of leading musicians such as Bill and Charlie Monroe, Lester Flatt and Earl Scruggs, and J.E. and Wade Mainer. Furthermore, I must emphasize that many of the over seven thousand recordings in WPAQ's archives have been heard by the general public only once—the day they were broadcast.

WPAQ Radio is located in Mount Airy, North Carolina, home to Andy Griffith and the model for Mayberry on the hit television series *The Andy Griffith Show.* Since its first broadcast in 1948, WPAQ Radio has remained dedicated to the goal of serving the community by broadcasting music of the region, primarily bluegrass and old-time music.

In his initial application to the Federal Communications Commission (FCC) in 1946, Epperson included a statement that has become a trademark of WPAQ. He guaranteed that each week, time would be set aside on the air to serve as "an outlet of expression for local talent."[2] With this in mind, in 1948 WPAQ began broadcasting the *Merry-Go-Round,* a weekly live broadcast that allowed local and regional musicians to perform on the air.

The barn dance format of the *Merry-Go-Round* was modeled after its much larger counterparts, namely WLS's *National Barn Dance* and WSM's *Grand Ole Opry.* The show has promoted and perhaps even started the careers of numerous musicians. Those who performed at one time or another on the *Merry-Go-Round* include: J.E. and Wade Mainer, Lester Flatt and Earl Scruggs, Mother Maybelle and the Carter Sisters, Donna Fargo, Andy Griffith, Tommy Jarrell, Charlie Monroe, Arthur Smith, Ralph Stanley, and Mac Wiseman. WPAQ has aired the show since early 1948, making it the third-longest-running live radio broadcast in America. Only the *Grand Ole Opry,* which went on the air in 1926, and Wheeling, West Virginia station WWVA's *Jamboree,* which started in 1933, are older.[3]

WPAQ's archives contain a wealth of music and information documenting the history of WPAQ as well as the history of country, bluegrass, and old-time music. Until now, very few individuals have had access to the archives, and their contents have been virtually unknown to the academic community. Consisting of four separate smaller archives (henceforth referred to as archives A, B, C, and D), WPAQ's collection of recordings dates back to its first broadcast in February 1948. Moreover, the archival holdings contain rare commercial recordings from the 1910s to today, which document not only the history of radio, but also the gradual evolution of country music style.

Performers, including "Pretty Blue-eyed" Odessa Johnson, "Uncle" Joe Johnson, and Mac Wiseman in the front row, line up on stage during a broadcast of WPAQ's *Merry-Go-Round* radio program in winter 1953. (Photo courtesy of Ralph Epperson)

Archive A is located in a room measuring five feet by nine feet and contains approximately 2,500 recordings. Sections of the shelf are partitioned by labels which identify style, namely bluegrass, old-time, and gospel. The albums are alphabetized and color-coded. They are used in much of the station's daily programming.

Archive B contains fourteen crates holding a total of 400 LP and 78-rpm discs. Stacks of cassette tapes, compact discs, and miscellaneous LPs comprise approximately 100 recordings, many of them now rare. This collection has not yet been cataloged, and the recordings are in no discernible order.

Archive C, a room approximately thirty feet by fifty feet, remains dimly lit, and a thin layer of dust blankets the various crates of cassette and reel-to-reel tapes, 78-rpm discs, and vintage radio equipment. One shelf contains approximately 1,000 78-rpm and 45-rpm phonograph discs from the station's first three decades of operation. The discs are numbered and cataloged on index cards. In addition, archive C contains over 1,000 other recordings which are not cataloged and are stored in unlabeled boxes.

Archive D is the largest of the four archives. Containing over 3,000 recordings, the collection is unique in that more than half of these recordings were made live at the station while broadcasting each performance. The archive is housed in a climate-controlled environment that protects against possible atmospheric hazards such as moisture, aridity, and sudden changes in temperature. Epperson has transferred many recordings from 78-rpm discs onto cassette tape. Each *Merry-Go-Round* performance since 1976 and most recordings of WPAQ's other live broadcasts reside in archive D.

WPAQ's archives contain recordings by a number of important musicians, and I will now turn to the station's involvement in some of these artists' careers. From the late 1940s to the early 1960s, J.E. Mainer and his Mountaineers, which included J.E. and his brother Wade, made several appearances at WPAQ. Epperson remembers how J.E. would perform at WPAQ for an hour on the *Merry-Go-Round* around noon and play in evening concerts at the National Guard Armory in nearby Hillsville. WPAQ was attractive to bands such as Mainer's Mountaineers, because other radio stations in the area in the late 1940s, such as WIS in Columbia, South Carolina, and WBT in Charlotte, North Carolina, would usually allot musicians only fifteen minutes of airtime. WPAQ, however, would always provide bands with an hour or more of airtime which allowed each band to perform more tunes, highlight soloists, and promote show dates.

Bill Monroe, widely recognized as the "Father of Bluegrass Music," and his brother Charlie visited Mount Airy and WPAQ on several occasions, including the opening of Brad's Card and Toy Shop in the summer of 1958. Monroe was present to sign autographs and to draw a crowd. WPAQ announcer Ronnie Pruett, who interviewed Monroe live on that occasion, recalls, "He [Monroe] was wearing thick glasses and was bareheaded with a receding hairline. I expected him to be wearing a big Stetson hat (like his entertainer brother Charlie Monroe whom I had met a year or so ago at the WPAQ studios). He [Bill] did not perform that day. The first series of questions I asked were answered by him with a simple 'yup' or 'nope.' Only after asking him about his music did he offer lengthy answers."[4]

The interview was recorded live, but the exact location of the recording remains as yet unknown. Epperson suspects that the tape is in the archive but is uncataloged. According to Ronnie Pruett, it is possible that the tape was reused due to the considerable expense of recording at the time.

After the Monroe Brothers disbanded in 1938, Charlie and Birch Monroe started a new group that included guitarist Lester Flatt. Billed as The

Kentucky Pardners, the band remained mostly in the Carolinas. The 1955 version of the group came to WPAQ and remained there for several months. The band was sponsored for the most part by Blackwelder Furniture Company and Bunker Hill Beef. While in Mount Airy, the Kentucky Pardners performed daily at WPAQ and Charlie advertised his group's upcoming show dates and song books over the air. Many recordings of Charlie Monroe's broadcasts still exist in WPAQ's archival holdings but remain as yet uncataloged. Local musician Johnny Vipperman recalls the car that Charlie used while in Mount Airy: a brand new, pink, stretch Cadillac that had been leased from the B & L Motor Company in North Wilkesboro.[5] Vipperman had toured the southeast for three weeks in the fall of 1951 as a guitarist with Monroe's Blue Grass Boys.

In 1948 Lester Flatt and Earl Scruggs left Bill Monroe's Blue Grass Boys and formed own their band, The Foggy Mountain Boys. This band performed throughout Appalachia in 1948, including three weeks in Hickory, North Carolina, before continuing onward to Bristol, Virginia. They performed at store openings, drive-in movies, country schools, and county fairs. They were sponsored by the Martha White Flour Company on a WSM early morning show beginning in 1953, but, at Bill Monroe's request, were not allowed to join the *Grand Ole Opry*. Eventually WSM gave in to the pressures of Martha White Flour and allowed Flatt and Scruggs to join the *Opry* roster in 1955.

It is locally believed that the group performed at WPAQ several times throughout their career, though I have found no archival recordings to support this. Lucy Bowman, station employee and sister to Ralph Epperson, recalls the band performing at the station in the early 1950s. The duo returned in the summer of 1958 and performed at the Mount Airy Drive-In Theater, according to Ronnie Pruett, who was present at the performance. In an interview with musician and NPR newscaster Paul Brown in the early 1990s, Scruggs recalled performing at WPAQ in 1950. He distinctly remembered the physical appearance of WPAQ disc jockey Uncle Joe Johnson and commented on the talent of Uncle Joe's band. Because Flatt and Scruggs were little known at the time, no special effort was made to record their performances in Mount Airy in 1950.

Mac Wiseman, born in 1925 in Crimora, Virginia, emerged as one of the great musicians of bluegrass and country music. In a career spanning over fifty years, he has left an impression on the history of bluegrass music as well as WPAQ. His life has been well documented in bluegrass literature,[6] though not his experiences in Mount Airy.

Wiseman first came to WPAQ in the summer of 1951. He remembers his involvement with the station as being "a most enjoyable association and one of the most pleasant in my career. I had just had a record come out and needed a way to promote it, and Ralph gave me the opportunity. It was a turning point in my career. . . . There was a family atmosphere around the station. Everything was done by handshake and word of honor. Ralph Epperson's been very successful with the music, but he's never been selfish about it. He's wanted the musician to gain from it, too, and he was always fair."[7]

During his time at WPAQ, Wiseman performed regularly on the *Merry-Go-Round* as well as daily broadcasts. While performing at the station, Wiseman was attracted to the talents of local banjo player Wade Macey, and hired Macey to tour with his group during the summer of 1953. The group was based in Richmond at WRVA's *Old Dominion Barn Dance*.

Renowned old-time fiddler Tommy Jarrell (1901–1985) also performed many times at WPAQ. He was born in Surry County, North Carolina, where WPAQ is based. Over the years, Jarrell was well known and respected at the *Merry-Go-Round* along with other musicians from the Round Peak community in Surry County, such as Kyle Creed, Paul Sutphin, Earnest East, and Fred Cockerham. Jarrell's last performance at WPAQ was on 1 September 1984, four months before his death, when he was featured on the *Merry-Go-Round* with Vernon Clifton, Frank Body, and Paul Brown. "Soldier's Joy" was among the tunes that Jarrell performed that day.[8]

Through its broadcasts and archives, WPAQ has greatly contributed to the preservation and dissemination of old-time and bluegrass music, and the station's impact on the Appalachian community has been significant. WPAQ's recordings fill gaps in the history of bluegrass and old-time music such as the whereabouts of particular musicians at particular times and exchange of influences with local artists. By disseminating this music, WPAQ has accomplished its original goal of preserving and promoting the regional culture, thus contributing significantly to American music history.

WPAQ's significance has been recognized by numerous organizations. In 1978 Epperson was presented with a Certificate of Appreciation from the American Folklife Center and National Park Service for his contributions to preserving music of the Blue Ridge Parkway. In 1991 he received an award for excellence in broadcasting from the International Bluegrass Music Association. That same year, WPAQ received the Hudson-Brown Folklore Award from the North Carolina Folklore Society. In 1994 the Society for the Preservation of Bluegrass Music recognized WPAQ as Bluegrass Station of the Year. Ralph Epperson received the J.E. Mainer Award in 1996 for his ongoing efforts to preserve the music of the region. WPAQ disc jockey Sherry Boyd has been named Top Bluegrass DJ in America four times by the Society for the Preservation of Bluegrass Music in America (SPGMA). In view of this recognition within the old-time and bluegrass world, it is surely time for the academic community to recognize WPAQ's significance.

WPAQ is more than a local radio station in the mountains of North Carolina. Its fifty-two years of operation have been spent representing the traditional cultural values of the region's inhabitants. It is clear that this radio station has lived up to its local reputation. Epperson and WPAQ have, indeed, become the "voice of the Blue Ridge Mountains."

Notes

1. *Voice of the Blue Ridge: 50 Years at Radio Station WPAQ*, directed by Frank Levering, Brack Lewellyn, and Hal Vaughn (Mount Airy, N.C.: Surry Arts Council, 1997), videocassette.

2. Ralph Epperson, FCC application, 1947, Washington National Archives, RG: 173, Stack 550/11/11/4, Docket #7658.

3. Sandra McKee, "Mayberry Lives on to a Bluegrass Beat," in *The Baltimore Sun*, 15 February 2000.

4. Ronnie Pruett, interview by author, E-mail, Charlotte, N.C., 1 December 1999.

5. Johnny Vipperman, interview by author, video recording, Low Gap, N.C., 1 April 2000.

6. Green 1972, Rhodes 1981, Henderson 1975, and Rosenberg 1993.

7. Jack Bernhardt, "WPAQ Radio," *Bluegrass Unlimited* 22, no. 2 (Aug. 1987): 20.

8. Tommy Jarrell, "Soldier's Joy," tape recording, Mount Airy, N.C., 1 September 1984, WPAQ Archive D.

Bibliography

Andrews, Amy. "Mount Airy." In *Winston Salem Journal*. Winston Salem, N.C. 1996.

Accessed 24 February 2000 at http://www.journalnow.com/hometown/mtairy/index.html.

Bennett, Cindy. "Country Music Pioneer, Mainer, Renews Ties to McDowell County." In *The McDowell Times,* Thursday, 29 November 1990.

Bernhardt, Jack. "WPAQ Radio." In *Bluegrass Unlimited* 22, no. 2 (Aug. 1987): 20–5.

Berrier, Ralph. "The Voice of the Blue Ridge Mountains." In *The Roanoke (Va.) Times,* 18 November 1999.

Brinson, Linda. "At WPAQ, the Mountain Music's Still Alive." In *Winston Salem (N.C.) Journal,* Sunday, 13 July 1983.

Cantwell, Robert. *Bluegrass Breakdown: The Making of the Old Southern Sound.* New York: Da Capo Press, 1992.

Chorba, Frank J. "The Golden Age of Radio." In *History of the Mass Media in the United States: An Encyclopedia.* Margaret A. Blanchard, ed. Chicago and London: Fitzroy Dearborn Publishers, 1998.

Collins, Paul. "WPAQ Keeps Up Old-time On the Airwaves." In *Winston Salem (N.C.) Journal,* Sunday, 22 May 1994: E1.

Davis, Amy. "Mount Airy Fiddlers Convention—25 Years!" In *The Old Time Herald.* 5, no. 4 (summer 1996): 20–44.

Green, Douglas. "Mac Wiseman: Remembering." In *Muleskinner News,* 4 July 1972: 2–8.

Kunkel, Karl. "With a Banjo on His Knee." In *Our State North Carolina,* June 2000: 50–53.

Langrall, Peggy. "Appalachian Folk Music: From Foothills to Footlights." In *Music Educator's Journal* 72, no. 7 (Mar 1986): 37–39.

Lomax, Alan. "Folk Song Style." In *American Anthropologist* 61, no. 6 (December 1959).

Lowery, H.H. "Radio Station at Mount Airy Seen in operation This Summer." In *Winston Salem (N.C.) Journal,* 3 June 1947.

Malone, Bill C. "Country Music." In *The New Grove Dictionary of Music and Musicians,* vol. 4. Stanley Sadie, ed. London and New York: Macmillan Publishers, 1980.

———. *Country Music, USA: A Fifty-Year History.* Austin, Texas: Univ. of Texas Press, 1968.

McKee, Sandra. "Mayberry Lives on to a Bluegrass Beat." In *The Baltimore Sun,* Tuesday, 15 February 2000.

Powell, Eleanor. "National Radio Group Honors Ralph Epperson." In *Mount Airy (N.C.) News,* 8 March 1998: 1–2.

Quinn, Christopher. "'Merry-Go-Round' Radio Show Filmed for Documentary on Bluegrass Music." In *Winston Salem (N.C.) Journal,* Sunday, 16 July 1988.

Robinson, Bradford. "Bluegrass Music." In *The New Grove Dictionary of Music and*

Musicians, vol. 2. Stanley Sadie, ed. London and New York: Macmillan Publishers, 1980.

Rosenberg, Neil V. "Bill Monroe." In *The New Grove Dictionary of Music and Musicians,* vol. 2. Stanley Sadie, ed. London and New York: Macmillan Publishers, 1980.

———. *Bluegrass: A History.* Urbana and Chicago: Univ. of Illinois Press, 1985.

Ross, Joe. "The Radio: Bringing Bluegrass to the Country." In *Bluegrass Unlimited* 23, no. 6 (Dec. 1988): 72–79.

Tribe, Ivan M., and John W. Morris "J.E. and Wade Mainer." In *Bluegrass Unlimited* 10, no. 5 (November 1975): 12–21.

Wolf, Charles K. *A Good Natured Riot: The Birth of the Grand Ole Opry.* Nashville: Country Music Foundation Press, 1999.

Discography

"Soldier's Joy." Performed by Tommy Jarrell at WPAQ's *Merry-Go-Round* on 1 September 1984. Musicians: Tommy Jarrell, fiddle; Frank Bode, guitar; Paul Brown, banjo; and Verlen Clifton, mandolin. Announcers are Clyde Johnson and Verlen Clifton. Recording housed in WPAQ archive D.

WPAQ: Voice of the Blue Ridge Mountains. 1999. Rounder Records ROUN 0404. Produced by Paul Brown. Liner notes by Paul Brown. Compact Disc.

Videography

Voice of the Blue Ridge: 50 Years at Radio Station WPAQ. Directed by Frank Levering, Brack Lewellyn, and Hal Vaughn. Mount Airy, N.C.: Surry Arts Council, 1997. 30 minutes. Videocassette.

Politics and Country Music, 1963-1974

Don Cusic

What has come to be known as "the sixties" may be defined as the period from 1963 to 1974, or from the assassination of President John Kennedy to the resignation of President Richard Nixon. During this period the two big political issues were civil rights and Vietnam; the biggest cultural and social issues centered on the "generation gap" between the Baby Boomers and their parents. Raised on Big Band music, the parents believed in patriotism, authority, a social hierarchy, and self-restraint. Their children, raised on the Beatles, believed in permissiveness, freedom, self-expression, and questioning authority.

The politics of this era represented a clash of cultures; the Kennedy administration was basically conservative until overwhelmed by civil rights. At this point, being "liberal" meant a pro-civil rights stance. After Kennedy's assassination, Lyndon Johnson presented "The Great Society" and an escalation of the Vietnam War. While John Kennedy inspired youth to be active and involved and Lyndon Johnson sought to bring the poor and disenfranchised into the political mainstream, Richard Nixon sat clearly on the side of the World War II–era generation, against the Baby Boomer's liberalism while at the same time overwhelmed by it. Nixon responded by dividing the country to unite his supporters; the result was a social revolution amongst the young who challenged the middle class's ideas, values, and leadership. But the middle class had a backlash of its own.

George Wallace was one of the most influential political leaders of this era. He became governor of Alabama on January 14, 1963, and said in his first speech, "Segregation now . . . segregation tomorrow . . . segregation forever." Wallace would be the most prominent anti–civil rights leader of his time, governing a state whose population was 30 percent black. Later in 1963, he made good on his promise to "stand in the schoolhouse door" when a Negro student tried to enroll in the University of Alabama. Federal officials intervened and the student was enrolled. Wallace would go on to run for the presidency in 1964 and 1968 on his racist rhetoric.

But Wallace touched a sympathetic chord in middle-class Americans all across the country with his tirades against hippies and communists and for the rights of private property, community control, and neighborhood schools. By the 1968 election, tens of millions of Americans despised antiwar demonstrators, civil rights, sexual freedom, and the decline of "fundamental values." America, they felt, had lost the cultural compass that guided it toward God, family, and country. For these Americans, what was most important was the sanctity of the traditional family, the importance of hard work and self-restraint, an autonomous local community, and the centralism of Christian religious beliefs. Uniting all of this was a muscular anticommunism; it was widely believed that the antiwar protests and civil rights activists were inspired and directed by Communists.

The movement Wallace led stirred racial fears, patriotism expressed as anticommunism, a cultural nostalgia, and right-wing economics. Throughout the rural South, there was an emphasis on "good country people" who were hardworking, law-abiding, churchgoing, soft-spoken, and poor. The South had long prided itself on "the southern way of life," which demanded subordination of all issues to that of white supremacy.

Although "white supremacy" was a term used by many to characterize the base of George Wallace's support, he would argue that it was "middle-class" supremacy that he was after, a rebellion against the elites who run the media, business, and government. In this light, George Wallace should be viewed as one of the founders of the conservative movement that nominated Barry Goldwater for the presidency in 1964 and elected Richard Nixon in 1968 and 1972 and Ronald Reagan in 1980 and 1984.

George Wallace was a Democrat and most southern voters were Democrats. Yet this had more to do with history than political belief: Abraham Lincoln, a Republican, had waged war on the South and ended slavery. But Democratic political leaders from the South were not cut from the same mold as Franklin Roosevelt, John Kennedy, or other liberal northern Democrats. The southern Democrats carried the name and created the organization that ran politics in the South, but they were not "liberal" by any stretch of the imagination.

However, by 1968 the national Democratic Party was considered by many southern whites as too pro-black; too tolerant of civil rights proponents (whose activism led to street riots and burning cities), antiwar marchers and campus demonstrators, and criminals (who threatened the idea of law and order in peaceful communities); and too strong an advocate of social programs giving handouts to the lower classes, which were paid for by the hard-working middle class.

Wallace played on the fears of whites, weaving a tapestry of respect for the law and Christianity against Communism, degeneracy, pornography, unbathed beatniks, socialists, atheists, sign-carrying degenerates, homosexuals, drugs, pornography, permissiveness, riots, and the backlash of kids against parents in the "generation gap," which led to an erosion of cultural values. White, working-class Americans felt powerless and afraid of all the changes that threatened their stable world. There was a sense of anguish and betrayal that America had gone from being a God-fearing nation that upheld family values to one that had gone down the slippery slope to degeneracy, lawlessness, and disrespect for the traditions and traditional values that had made America great. The voice of the hard-working white man had been drowned out by unwashed protestors and an overbearing government that sent bureaucrats into cities and towns to usurp the authority of local community leaders. Wallace's rhetoric convinced the white working class that they—not blacks or the young men being sent off to war in Vietnam—were the "victims" because everything they held dear was being swept away.

Because of its strong southern roots, country music played a part in all of this. Southern politics and country music were closely tied, since many country artists came from the South and most audience members were either southern or had family roots in the South. Moreover, country music played a role in the politics of the period because it is, essentially, the music of the white working class.

Southern politicians had often used country music in their campaigns; many began each political rally with a country music band—usually local talent—who played some big country hits, a patriotic song or two, and a gospel hymn. It was a way for these politicians to reach "the common man" and infuse a "common touch" into a campaign. It was also a good way to gather a crowd and keep them entertained as a warm-up for a political speech. George Wallace used country music during his political campaigns in Alabama beginning in the 1950s, when Minnie Pearl performed for him.

During the 1968 presidential campaign, a number of country music stars—including Hank Snow, Hank Williams Jr., and Stuart Hamblen as well as southern gospel groups such as the Oak Ridge Boys, Hovie Lister and the Statesmen, and Wally Fowler—openly supported George Wallace. By this time, Wallace had firmly positioned himself as the spokesman for the white South, and country music was considered the music of the white South. Thus, country music was linked with George Wallace and the emerging conservatism that was coming out of the 1960s.

In the 1968 election, Republican Richard Nixon was elected President with 43.3 percent of the vote. Democratic nominee Hubert Humphrey received 42.7 percent of the votes as runner-up in a close election. George Wallace received 14 percent of the vote. However, together, conservative candidates Nixon and Wallace received a majority of the votes: 57.4 percent—a harbinger of the coming trend in American politics.

Country Music, 1963–1974

In looking at country music between 1963 and 1974, this paper discusses songs on the *Billboard* country singles charts. These songs achieved significant airplay and thus reached a large listening public. Album cuts and songs that were sold under the counter (such as the racist country releases sold in the South) are not considered. By examining the songs that were commercially successful, an accurate reading about the public's tastes may be gained. All of the songs discussed in this paper achieved enough radio airplay to be on the *Billboard* country singles chart, and emphasis has been given to songs that reached the top fifteen positions.

Because country music is part of the commercial music industry and love is perennially the most popular topic with the radio-listening and record-buying public that supports that industry, it is not surprising that most of the songs on the country charts during the 1963–1974 period were about love—getting it, losing it, or keeping it. There are too many "love" songs to list in this article, but the clear message is that members of the country music audience preferred songs about their personal lives, not about social conditions or political trends. Approximately 80 percent of the songs charted during the 1963–1974 period were about love or, more accurately, relationships.

Most of the country songs that dealt with political, social, or cultural issues had either an underlying or overt patriotic theme; in general, country music is not protest music. There were a good number of songs in which country artists exerted pride in themselves as country people and in country music. These include "Bright Lights and Country Music" by Bill Anderson (1965); "I Take a Lot of Pride in What I Am" by Merle Haggard (1968); "Are You from Dixie (Cause I'm from Dixie Too)" by Jerry Reed (1969); "I'm Just Me" by Charley Pride (which reached number one in 1971); "You're Lookin' at Country" by Loretta Lynn (1971); "Listen to a Country Song" by Lynn Anderson (1972); "Southern Loving" by Jim Ed Brown (1973); "Rednecks, White Socks and Blue Ribbon Beer" by Johnny Russell (1973); "Hank and Lefty Raised My Country Soul" by Stoney Edwards (1973); "Country Sunshine" by Dottie West (1973); "Country Bumpkin" by Cal Smith (which reached number one in 1974); and "Country Is" by Tom T. Hall (which also reached number one in 1974).

Most political/social/cultural commentary in country music during the sixties came from the perspective of a working man trying to make ends meet, shown best by a series of records by Jim Nesbitt: "Livin' Offa Credit" (1963) and "Looking for More in '64," "Still Alive in '65," and "Heck of a Fix in '66," released in their respective years.

Other songs with political/social/cultural overtones were "The One on the Right Is on the Left" by Johnny Cash; "History Repeats Itself," Buddy Starcher's 1966 song about the similarities between Presidents John Kennedy and Abraham Lincoln; "Gallant Men" by Senator Everett McKinley Dirksen; "Skip a Rope" by Henson Cargill (1967); and "You Better Sit Down Kids" by Roy Drusky (a 1968 remake of a pop hit by Cher). In 1969, songs such as "This Generation Shall Not Pass" by Henson Cargill; "In the Ghetto" and "Clean up Your Own Back Yard" by Elvis Presley; "These Are Not My People" by Freddie Weller; and Tommy Cash's "Six White Horses"—about John and Robert Kennedy and Martin Luther King—fit this category.

Continuing in this vein, in 1970 Johnny Cash released "What Is Truth" while Tommy Cash had "The Tears on Lincoln's Face." In 1971 Johnny Cash sang "Man in Black" and Eddy Arnold released "A Part of America Died," a song about policemen being killed. The next year, 1972, saw the release of "The Monkey That Became President" by Tom T. Hall; "Made in

Japan" (number one) by Buck Owens; and "The Lawrence Welk–Hee Haw–Counter-Revolution Polka" by Roy Clark. In 1973, socially-conscious songs such as "Americans" by Byron MacGregor and "The Americans (A Canadian's Opinion)" by Tex Ritter hit the charts. "Ragged Old Flag" by Johnny Cash and "U. S. of A." by Donna Fargo were hits in 1974.

Some of the hardest-hitting social commentary came from women in country music. Loretta Lynn became a spokeswoman for women's rights with songs like "Don't Come Home A'Drinkin' (With Lovin' on Your Mind)," "Rated X," and "Fist City." Bobbie Gentry performed "Ode to Billie Joe" in 1967; Jeannie C. Riley released "Harper Valley P.T.A." (number one) and "The Girl Most Likely" in 1968; and Bobbie Gentry sang "Fancy" in 1969. These songs challenged the social status quo, and while most country fans (and female country singers) did not call themselves "feminists," they certainly stood up for themselves. These "feminist" country songs focused on the hypocrisy of judging women one way and men another—especially regarding sex and independence, where the woman let her man (and others) know she was no shrinking violet. Tanya Tucker, who began having country hits when she was thirteen years old, released "Delta Dawn" in 1972; "What's Your Mama's Name" and "Blood Red and Going Down," both number-one hits in 1973; and "The Man That Turned My Mama On" in 1974.

A hawkish attitude toward Vietnam pervaded country music songs during the first half of the 1960s, as evident in Johnny Wrights' number-one song, "Hello Vietnam," which reached the peak position on October 23, 1965, and stayed there for three weeks. In November, Dave Dudley's "What We're Fighting For" reached number four. The next year, Ernest Tubb reached number forty-eight with "It's for God, and Country, and You Mom (That's Why I'm Fighting in Viet Nam)." In January 1966, "Soldier's Prayer in Viet Nam" by Benny Martin with Don Reno reached number forty-six; the next month, Loretta Lynn's "Dear Uncle Sam" reached number four. Perhaps the biggest Vietnam "hit" was "The Ballad of the Green Berets" by S.Sgt. Barry Sadler, which reached number two on the country charts and number one on the pop charts in the spring of 1966. Also that spring, "Private Wilson White" by Marty Robbins reached number twenty-one, "Viet Nam Blues" by Dave Dudley reached number twelve, and "The Minute Men (Are Turning in Their Graves)" by Stonewall Jackson reached number twenty-four. "Distant Drums" by Jim Reeves, which does not mention Vietnam specifically but deals with leaving a loved one to go to war, reached number one on May 21 and stayed four weeks at the top of the charts. In 1967 Johnny Darrell's version of "Ruby, Don't Take Your Love to Town," about a Vietnam veteran whose wife is running around, reached number nine and "The Private" by Del Reeves reached number thirty-three. In 1968 "Little Boy Soldier" by Wanda Jackson reached number forty-six; "Ballad of Two Brothers" by Autry Inman reached number fourteen (and number forty-eight on the pop charts); and "My Son" by Jan Howard, whose son was killed in Vietnam, reached number fifteen. But there was a slight turning against the war in John Wesley Ryles's song "Kay"—about a taxi driver who lost his love to Nashville stardom—which contained the line "two young soldiers from Fort Campbell told me how they hate that war in Vietnam."

The most popular statement against the counterculture occurred with two Merle Haggard songs: "Okie From Muskogee," which reached number one on November 15, 1969, and remained there for four weeks and "The Fightin' Side of Me," which hit number one on March 14, 1970, and stayed at the top of the charts for three weeks. Both songs relayed a hawkish view of Vietnam. Bobby Bare's "God Bless America Again" reached number sixteen in 1969, and in 1970 Bill Anderson's "Where Have All the Heroes Gone" reached number six. Also in 1970, Jeannie C. Riley's "The Generation Gap" reached number sixty-two.

In 1971 Merle Haggard's "Soldier's Last Letter," a World War II song, reached number three, while "Battle Hymn of Lt. Calley" by C Company Featuring Terry Nelson—a song in support of the leader of the My Lai massacre—reached number forty-nine (and thirty-seven on the pop charts). Also in 1971 Johnny Cash's "Singing in Viet Nam Talking Blues" reached number eighteen.

But by 1972, the anti-Vietnam sentiment emerged slightly in country music with Skeeter Davis's "One Tin Soldier," which reached number fifty-four on the country charts after the original version by Original Caste was a hit on the pop charts. Another cover release, "Tie a Yellow Ribbon" by Johnny Carver reached number five (Tony Orlando and Dawn had the pop hit).

While country music never quite embraced "flower power," there were some songs that promoted a general cosmic goodness. Examples are "It Takes People Like You (To Make People Like Me)" by Buck Owens (1967); "I Wanna Live" by Glen Campbell (1968); "I Believe in Love" by Bonnie Guitar (1968); "Less of Me" by Bobbie Gentry and Glen Campbell (1968); "Try a Little Kindness" by Glen Campbell (1969); "Everything Is Beautiful" by Ray Stevens (which reached number one on the pop charts but only number thirty-nine on the country charts in 1970); "Let's Get Together," a remake of the Youngbloods' pop hit by George Hamilton IV and Skeeter Davis (1970); "Bridge over Troubled Water," a remake of the Simon and Garfunkel hit by Buck Owens (1971); "I Wanna Be Free" by Loretta Lynn (1971); and "I'm Just Me" by Charley Pride (1971). In 1973 "I Love" by Tom T. Hall hit number one. In 1974 songs such as "You Can't Be a Beacon (If Your Light Don't Shine)" by Donna Fargo (number one), "Love Is Like a Butterfly" Dolly Parton (number one), and "I Care" by Tom T. Hall hit the country charts.

Mainstream country music generally avoided the racial issue, although Kenny Rogers's "Ruben James," a song about a white child being raised by a black woman, reached number forty-six in 1969.

Songs addressing the working life in the early 1960s include "Get a Little Dirt on Your Hands" by Bill Anderson, which reached number fourteen in 1962; "Busted" by Johnny Cash, which rose to number thirteen; "Detroit City" by Bobby Bare (which made it to number six on the country charts and number sixteen on the pop charts); and "Last Day in the Mines" by Dave Dudley (1963). In 1967 Tex Ritter had "A Working Man's Prayer," a song that went to number fifty-nine. Merle Haggard, country music's chief social commentator, presented an anthem to the working class with "Working Man Blues," which reached number one in 1969.

Other songs that addressed the working life included "If I Were a Carpenter" by Johnny Cash and June Carter (1970); "I Never Picked Cotton" by Roy Clark" (1970); "Oney" by Johnny Cash (1972); and "Working Class Hero" by Tommy Roe; "If We Make It through December" by Merle Haggard; and "That Girl Who Waits on Tables" by Ronnie Milsap, all in 1973. The most significant of these is the number-one hit "If We Make It through December," which tells of a man facing Christmas with his family after being laid off during an economic downturn.

Truck driving songs, which became anthems to the blue collar working man, were popular in country music during the 1960s. In 1963 Dave Dudley released "Six Days on the Road," which reached number two on the country charts and number thirty-two on the pop charts, and Hank Snow saw his "Ninety Miles an Hour (Down a Dead End Street)" go to number two. In 1964 George Hamilton IV went to number eleven with "Truck Driving Man." In 1965 Del Reeves's "Girl on the Billboard" reached number one. That same year, Dick Curless released "A Tombstone Every Mile," which went to number five, and Dave Dudley came out with "Truck Drivin' Son-of-a-Gun," which peaked at number three.

The popularity of Red Sovine's "Giddyup Go," which reached number one in January 1966 and remained in that position for six weeks, led to two answer songs: Minnie Pearl's "Giddyup Go—Answer," which reached number ten, and Don Bowman's "Giddyup Do-Nut," which reached number forty-nine. Also in 1966, Red Simpson—who made a career out of singing trucking songs—released "Roll Truck Roll" (number thirty-eight), "The Highway Patrol" (number thirty-nine), and "Diesel Smoke, Dangerous Curves" (number forty-one). Kay Adams's trucking song "Little Pink Mack," which reached number thirty, was also released in 1966.

Several trucking songs reached into the top fifteen positions in 1967: "Phantom 309" by Red Sovine (number nine), "How Fast Them Trucks Can Go" by Claude Gray (number twelve), and "Anything Leaving Town Today" by Dave Dudley (number twelve). Trucking songs that landed in the top fifteen in 1968 include "There Ain't No Easy Run" by Dave Dudley (number ten) and "Looking at the World Through a Windshield" by Del Reeves (number five).

Dave Dudley reached number twelve in 1969 with "One More Mile" and number eight in 1971 with "Comin' Down." Also in 1971, Red Simpson's "I'm a Truck" hit number four. In 1973, Dave Dudley topped the charts again with "Keep On Truckin'" (number ten). Finally, C.W. McCall's "Wolf Creek Pass" peaked at number twelve in 1974.

In the 1963–1974 period, only two songs mentioned welfare. One, "Waitin' in Your Welfare Line" by Buck Owens (1966), is a semi-humorous attempt to compare his undying love to welfare stereotypes. The other, Guy Drake's number-six hit "Welfare Cadillac," promotes the idea that those on welfare are driving Cadillacs—a forerunner to Ronald Reagan's view of "welfare queens."

The issue of class is evident in country songs throughout 1963–1974, with the country singer generally being poor and up against the rich or privileged. In 1963 Lester Flatt and Earl Scruggs had a number-one hit with the theme song to the television series *The Beverly Hillbillies*, "The Ballad of Jed Clampett." The theme of a poor but proud country native who, while naive, possesses a native intelligence that allows him to take advantage of greed is also central in the song "Saginaw, Michigan" by Lefty Frizeill, which reached number one in 1964. In 1964 Johnny Cash had a hit in "The Ballad of Ira Hayes," which tells the tale of a Native American who helped hoist the flag at Iwo Jima but is an outcast back at home.

Two other songs of the period are also strong examples of class struggle: "Coal Miner's Daughter" by Loretta Lynn, which reached number one in 1970, and "Coat of Many Colors," released by Dolly Parton in 1971. In both these songs the singer is proud of her heritage, while at the same time acknowledging the pain of poverty.

The idea of "family values" is prevalent in country music throughout the 1960s and early 1970s. In 1962 Jimmy Dean had a hit with "To a Sleeping Beauty" about a father's love for his daughter. In 1964 Porter Wagoner offered "Howdy Neighbor Howdy," which welcomes visitors to a country home.

In 1965 Ned Miller offered fatherly advice in "Do What You Do Do Well"; Jimmy Dean sang a love song to his wife, "The First Thing Ev'ry Morning (And the Last Thing Ev'ry Night)," which reached number one; and Sonny James had "True Love's a Blessing." Meanwhile, Loretta Lynn gave a warning to her wayward husband in "The Home You're Tearin' Down."

In 1968 Glen Campbell had a number-three hit with "Dreams of the Everyday Housewife," Bobby Goldsboro sang "The Straight Life," and Eddy Arnold sang "They Don't Make Love Like They Used To."

In 1969 Johnny Cash had a number-one hit with "Daddy Sang Bass," about a family that sang together and stayed together, while Merle Haggard had a number-one hit with "Hungry Eyes," about love defined through their family's poverty.

In 1971 two songs about children, "Watching Scotty Grow" by Bobby Goldsboro and "Two Dollar Toy" by Stoney Edwards, were released. That year also saw the release of "Daddy Frank" (number one) by Merle Haggard; "Take Me Home, Country Roads" by John Denver; and "One's on the Way" by Loretta Lynn, which reached its number one position the following year. Three family- or home-oriented songs hit number one in 1972: "Bedtime Story" by Tammy Wynette; "Grandma Harp" by Merle Haggard; and "Happiest Girl in the Whole U.S.A." by Donna Fargo. In 1973 Loretta Lynn released "Love Is the Foundation" (number one) as well as "Rated X," a feminist plea to not judge by appearances. Strong family-values messages are also evident in other artists' releases of 1973, including "Kids Say the Darndest Things" (number one) by Tammy Wynette; "Kid Stuff" by Barbara Fairchild; "We're Gonna Hold On" (number one) by George Jones and Tammy Wynette; and "Daddy What If" by Bobby Bare with Bobby Jr. In

1974 songs such as "(We're Not) The Jet Set" by George Jones and Tammy Wynette; "They Don't Make 'em Like My Daddy" by Loretta Lynn; "Country Bumpkin" (number one) by Cal Smith; "No Charge" (number one) by Melba Montgomery; and "Back Home Again" by John Denver (number one) dealt with themes of home and family.

Although country music can be labeled "conservative" when measured against the "liberal" ideas of civil rights, anti–Vietnam War protests, feminism, individual freedom, personal independence, and criticism of society in general and the United States in particular, an examination of the songs of this 1963–1974 period show a mixed bag. In general, country music songs were more conservative through the 1960s but seemed to become more liberal as the 1970s began. Part of this increased liberalism was likely the result of growing dissatisfaction with the Vietnam War. The middle and working classes turned against the war not only for political reasons, but for personal reasons as well: Most of the young men who served were from poor, working-class families. And these families were often country music's audience.

After the first wave of anti-integration sentiment, led by George Wallace, had passed, it was hard to be against addressing the injustices brought to light by the civil rights movement. While most southerners who came of age during this era privately carried the racist baggage of their parents to some degree or another, those who continued to be staunchly racist could no longer voice those views to wide support in the public arena. Moreover, the creative community tends to be more tolerant than society at large, and the musicians, songwriters, and singers who make up the country music community were more open to a racially mixed society, especially since many of them had grown up enjoying integrated music like rock 'n' roll, being influenced by rhythm and blues, and cheering black sports stars.

There is no doubt that country music in general rejected the counterculture during the years between 1963 and 1974. Yet this fact was expressed most vociferously in country musicians' casual conversations, rather than in their songs. Hints of it can be seen in occasional public documents like Paul Hemphill's book *The Nashville Sound* and Robert Altman's 1975 film *Nashville*. By and large, most singers were more interested in releasing a hit record than in making a social statement. And when making a social statement threatened to get in the way of their career, they were likely to keep their views to themselves. This is the market at work.

On one hand, many individuals felt conservative and were more comfortable with George Wallace or Richard Nixon. Because country music has traditionally appealed to an older audience (over twenty-five years old) and the sixties counterculture was dominated by young people, there was a generational gap in the country music business. The country music community, by virtue of its overall age, was on the older, more conservative side of that generation gap.

On the other hand, the conservative movement led to the "outlaw" movement in country music, beginning around 1976, when Waylon Jennings and Willie Nelson led the way for hippies and rednecks, beer drinkers and pot smokers to live in peace together. This was country music's sexual revolution and many in this new country audience were comfortable with the counterculture.

Presidential politics used country music during the 1963–1974 era. Marty Robbins was active in Barry Goldwater's campaign; Lyndon Johnson had Gene Autry and Eddy Arnold perform at his ranch; Jimmy Carter instilled southern pride in the White House and invited Willie Nelson, Tom T. Hall, and others to perform there; and George Bush Sr. regularly invited country performers like the Oak Ridge Boys and Lee Greenwood on the campaign trail. Ronald Reagan invited Merle Haggard to the White House to perform, but his major connection to country music was an empathy with show business from his years in Hollywood. But Reagan is a key figure: his *attitude* toward a wide variety of issues and particularly his disdain of 1960s liberalism struck a responsive chord in the country music community.

As a genre, country music has certainly evolved since the fiddle tunes of the early 1920s. But it has been less evolutionary as a musical form than rock. Particularly since the end of World War II, country music has evolved more slowly than other kinds of popular music. It is easier to hear the link between Hank Williams and Alan Jackson than it is between Frank Sinatra and Limp Bizkit. If one defines "conservative" as resisting change and keeping things the way they are, then it seems country music will reflect conservative politics for the foreseeable future.

Sources

Carter, Dan T. *The Politics of Rage: George Wallace, The Origins of the New Conservatism, and the Transformation of American Politics.* New York: Simon & Schuster, 1995.

Whitburn, Joel. *Top Country Singles 1944–1988* Menomonee Falls, Wisc.: Record Research, Inc. 1989.

Songs on Vietnam

1965

"Hello Vietnam" by Johnny Wright (#1)
"What We're Fighting For" by Dave Dudley (#4)

1966

"It's for God, and Country, and You Mom (That's Why I'm Fighting in Viet Nam)" by Ernest Tubb (#48)
"Soldier's Prayer in Viet Nam" by Benny Martin with Don Reno (#46)
"Dear Uncle Sam" by Loretta Lynn (#4)
"The Ballad of the Green Berets" by S.Sgt. Barry Sadler (#2; #1 pop)
"Private Wilson White" by Marty Robbins (#21)
"Viet Nam Blues" by Dave Dudley (#12; #127 pop)
"Distant Drums" by Jim Reeves (#1; #45 pop)
"The Minute Men (Are Turning in Their Graves)" by Stonewall Jackson (#24)
"The 'A' Team" by S.Sgt. Barry Sadler (#46; #28 pop)

1967

"Ruby, Don't Take Your Love to Town" by Johnny Darrell (#9)
"The Private" by Del Reeves (#33)

1968

"Little Boy Soldier" by Wanda Jackson (#46)
"Ballad of Two Brothers" by Autry Inman (#14; #48 pop)
"My Son" by Jan Howard (#15)
"Kay" by John Wesley Ryles (#9; #83 pop)

1969

"Ruby, Don't Take Your Love to Town" by Kenny Rogers (#39; #6 pop)
"Okie from Muskogee" by Merle Haggard (#1; #41 pop)
"God Bless America Again" by Bobby Bare (#16)

1970

"The Fightin' Side of Me" by Merle Haggard (#1; #92 pop)
"Where Have All Our Heroes Gone" by Bill Anderson (#6; #93 pop)
"The Generation Gap" by Jeannie C. Riley (#62)

1971

"Soldier's Last Letter" by Merle Haggard (#3; #90 pop)
"Battle Hymn of Lt. Calley" by C Company Featuring Terry Nelson (#49; #37 pop)
"Singing in Viet Nam Talking Blues" by Johnny Cash (#18; #124 pop)

1972

"One Tin Soldier" by Skeeter Davis (#54)

1973

"Yellow Ribbon" by Johnny Carver (#5)

Songs on Watergate

1973

"Watergate Blues" by Tom T. Hall (#16; #101 pop)

Songs on Welfare

1966

"Waitin' in Your Welfare Line" by Buck Owens (#1)

1970

"Welfare Cadillac" by Guy Drake (#6; #63 pop)

Songs Dealing with Race

1969

"Ruben James" by Kenny Rogers (#46; #26 pop)

1972

"(Old Dogs, Children and) Watermelon Wine" by Tom T. Hall (#1)

Religion

1970
"If God Is Dead (Who's That Living in My Soul)" by Connie Smith and Nat Stuckey (#59)
"Jesus, Take a Hold" by Merle Haggard (#3; #107 pop)

1971
"I Saw the Light" Roy Acuff with the Nitty Gritty Dirt Band (#56)

1972
"Me and Jesus" by Tom T. Hall (#8; #98 pop)

1973
"Why Me" by Kris Krostofferson (#1)
"I Knew Jesus (Before He Was a Star)" by Glen Campbell (#48; #45 pop)

Country Pride

1965
"Bright Lights and Country Music" by Bill Anderson (#11)
"I'm Just a Country Boy" by Jim Ed Brown (#37)

1968
"I Take a Lot of Pride in What I Am" by Merle Haggard (#3)

1969
"Are You from Dixie (Cause I'm from Dixie Too)" by Jerry Reed (#11)

1970
"Coal Miner's Daughter" by Loretta Lynn (#1)

1971

"I'm Just Me" by Charley Pride (#1)
"You're Lookin' at Country" by Loretta Lynn (#5)
"Country Green" by Don Gibson (#5)

1972

"Listen to a Country Song" by Lynn Anderson (#4; #107 pop)

1973

"Southern Loving" by Jim Ed Brown (#6)
"Rednecks, White Socks and Blue Ribbon Beer" by Johnny Russell (#4)
"Hank and Lefty Raised My Country Soul" by Stoney Edwards (#39)
"Country Sunshine" by Dottie West (#2; #49 pop)

1974

"Back in the Country" by Roy Acuff (#51)
"Country Bumpkin" by Cal Smith (#1)
"I Believe the South Is Gonna Rise Again" by Bobby Goldsboro (#62)
"Country Is" by Tom T. Hall (#1)
"Mississippi Cotton Picking Delta Town" by Charley Pride (#3; #70 pop)

Family Values

1964

"Howdy Neighbor Howdy" by Porter Wagoner (#10)

1965

"Do What You Do Do Well" by Ned Miller (#7; #52 pop)
"The First Thing Ev'ry Morning (And the Last Thing Ev'ry Night)" by Jimmy Dean (#1)
"Six Times a Day (The Trains Came Down)" by Dick Curless (#12)
"The Home You're Tearin' Down" by Loretta Lynn (#10)

1966

"The Men in My Little Girl's Life" by Tex Ritter (#50)

1967

"My Elusive Dreams" by David Houston and Tammy Wynette (#1; #89 pop)
"My Elusive Dreams" by Johnny Darrell (#73)
"Mother, May I" by Lynn Anderson and Liz Anderson (#21)
"Dreams of the Everyday Housewife" by Glen Campbell (#3; #32 pop)
"The Straight Life" by Bobby Goldsboro (#37; #36 pop)
"They Don't Make Love Like They Used To" by Eddy Arnold (#10; #99 pop)

1968

"Honey" by Bobby Goldsboro (#1; #1 pop)

1969

"Stand by Your Man" Tammy Wynette (#1)
"Daddy Sang Bass" by Johnny Cash (#1)
"Hungry Eyes" by Merle Haggard (#1)
"Yesterday, When I Was Young" by Roy Clark (#9; #19 pop)
"Growin' Up" by Tex Ritter (#39)

1970

"She's a Little Bit Country" by George Hamilton IV (#3)
"Wonder Could I Live There Anymore" by Charley Pride (#1; #87 pop)
"Daddy Was an Old Time Preacher Man" by Dolly Parton and Porter Wagoner (#7)

1971

"Watching Scotty Grow" by Bobby Goldsboro (#7; #11 pop)
"Two Dollar Toy" by Stoney Edwards (#68)
"Take Me Home, Country Roads" by John Denver (#50; #2 pop)
"One's on the Way" by Loretta Lynn (#1)
"Daddy Frank" by Merle Haggard (#1)
"Coat of Many Colors" by Dolly Parton (#4)

1972

"Grandma Harp" by Merle Haggard (#1)
"Do You Remember These" by The Statler Brothers (#2; #105 pop)
"The Happiest Girl in the Whole U.S.A." by Donna Fargo (#1; #11 pop)
"These Are the Good Old Days" by Roy Rogers (#73)

"One's on the Way" by Loretta Lynn (#1)
"Bedtime Story" by Tammy Wynette (#1)
"Manhattan Kansas" by Glen Campbell (#6; #114 pop)
"Grandma Harp" by Merle Haggard (#1)
"Happiest Girl in the Whole U.S.A." by Donna Fargo (#1)
"Comin' after Jinny" by Tex Ritter (#67)
"(Old Dogs, Children and) Watermelon Wine" by Tom T. Hall (#1)

1973

"Rated X" by Loretta Lynn (#1)
"Kids Say the Darndest Things" by Tammy Wynette (#1)
"Love is the Foundation" by Loretta Lynn (#1)
"Kid Stuff" by Barbara Fairchild Columbia (#2; #95 pop)
"We're Gonna Hold On" by George Jones (#1)
"Daddy What If" by Bobby Bare with Bobby Jr. (#2; #41)

1974

"(We're Not) The Jet Set" by George Jones and Tammy Wynette (#15)
"They Don't Make 'em Like My Daddy" by Loretta Lynn (#4)
"Country Bumpkin" by Cal Smith (#1)
"No Charge" by Melba Montgomery (#1)
"Back Home Again" by John Denver (#1)
"Hoppy, Gene and Me" by Roy Rogers (#15; #65 pop)

Cosmic Goodness

1966

"I'm a People" by George Jones (#6)

1968

"I Wanna Live" by Glen Campbell (#1)

1969

"Games People Play" by Freddy Weller (#2)

1967

"It Takes People Like You (To Make People Like Me)" by Buck Owens (#2; #114 pop)

1968
"I Wanna Live" by Glen Campbell (#1; #36 pop)
"I Believe in Love" by Bonnie Guitar (#10)
"Less of Me" by Bobbie Gentry and Glen Campbell (#44)

1969
"My Life (Throw It Away If I Want To)" by Bill Anderson (#1)
"Try a Little Kindness" by Glen Campbell (#2; #23 pop)

1970
"Everything Is Beautiful" by Ray Stevens (#39; #1 pop)
"Let's Get Together" by George Hamilton IV and Skeeter Davis (#65)
"One Hundred Children" by Tom T. Hall (#14)

1971
"Bridge over Troubled Water" by Buck Owens (#9; #119 pop)
"I Wanna Be Free" by Loretta Lynn (#3)
"Life" by Elvis Presley (#34; #53 pop)
"I'm Just Me" by Charley Pride (#1; #94 pop)

1972
"If It Feels Good Do It" by Dave Dudley (#14)
"If You Can't Feel It (It Ain't There)" by Freddie Hart (#3)
"All His Children" by Charley Pride with Henry Mancini (#2; #92 pop)

1974
"I Love" by Tom T. Hall (#1)
"You Can't Be a Beacon (If Your Light Don't Shine)" by Donna Fargo (#1; #57 pop)
"Love Is Like a Butterfly" by Dolly Parton (#1)
"I Care" by Tom T. Hall (#1)

Songs Dealing with Political/Social/Cultural Issues
1962
"P.T. 109" by Jimmy Dean (#3)

1963

"Livin' Offa Credit" by Jim Nesbitt (#28)

1964

"Looking For More In '64" by Jim Nesbitt (#7)
"The Ballad of Ira Hayes" by Johnny Cash (#3)

1965

"Still Alive in '65" by Jim Nesbitt (#34)
"Mr. Garfield" by Johnny Cash (#15)
"Skid Row Joe" by Porter Wagoner (#3)

1966

"The One on the Right Is on the Left" by Johnny Cash (#2; #46 pop)
"History Repeats Itself" by Buddy Starcher (#2; #39 pop)
"Heck of a Fix in '66" by Jim Nesbitt (#38)

1967

"Gallant Men" by Senator Everett McKinley Dirksen (#58)
"Skip a Rope" by Henson Cargill (#1; #25 pop)

1968

"You Better Sit Down Kids" by Roy Drusky (#28)
"Harper Valley P.T.A." by Jeannie C. Riley (#1)
"The Girl Most Likely" by Jeannie C. Riley (#6; #55 pop)

1969

"This Generation Shall Not Pass" by Henson Cargill (#40)
"In the Ghetto" by Elvis Presley (#60; #3 pop)
"These Are Not My People" by Freddy Weller (#5; #113 pop)
"Clean Up Your Own Back Yard" by Elvis Presley (#74; #35 pop)
"Six White Horses" by Tommy Cash (#4; #79 pop)
"Fancy" by Bobbie Gentry (#26; #31 pop)

1970

"What Is Truth" by Johnny Cash (#3; #19 pop)
"The Tears on Lincoln's Face" by Tommy Cash (#36)

1971

"Man in Black" by Johnny Cash (#3; #58 pop)
"A Part of America Died" by Eddy Arnold (#49)
"Delta Dawn" by Tanya Tucker (#6; #72 pop)

1972

"The Monkey That Became President" by Tom T. Hall (#11)
"Manhattan Kansas" by Glen Campbell (#6; #114 pop)
"One's on the Way" by Loretta Lynn (#1)
"Made in Japan" by Buck Owens (#1)
"The Class of '57" by The Statler Brothers (#6)
"The Lawrence Welk–Hee Haw–Counter-Revolution Polka" by Roy Clark (#9)
"Rated X" by Loretta Lynn (#1)

1973

"Lord, Mr. Ford" Jerry Reed (#1)
"Uneasy Rider" by The Charlie Daniels Band (#67; #9 pop)
"Rated X" by Loretta Lynn (#1)
"Kids Say the Darndest Things" by Tammy Wynette (#1)

1974

"Americans" by Westbound (backed by "America the Beautiful" by Byron
    MacGregor) (#59; #4 pop)
"The Americans (A Canadian's Opinion)" by Tex Ritter (#35; #90 pop)
"Ragged Old Flag" by Johnny Cash (#31)
"U. S. of A." by Donna Fargo (#9; #86 pop)
"The Credit Card Song" by Dick Feller (#10; #105 pop)
"Hoppy, Gene and Me" by Roy Rogers (#15; #65 pop)
"The Man That Turned My Mama On" by Tanya Tucker (#4; #86 pop)

Songs Dealing with Class

1962

"The Ballad of Jed Clampett" by Lester Flatt & Earl Scruggs (#1; #44 pop)
"Ruby Ann" by Marty Robbins (#1; #18 pop)
"Second Hand Rose" by Roy Drusky (#3)

1964

"Saginaw, Michigan" by Lefty Frizzell (#1)
"The Ballad of Ira Hayes" by Johnny Cash (#3)

1965

"I'm Just a Country Boy" by Jim Ed Brown (#37)

1966

"The Streets of Baltimore" by Bobby Bare (#5; #124 pop)

1967

"Ode to Billie Joe" by Bobbie Gentry (#17; #1 pop)

1970

"Coal Miner's Daughter" by Loretta Lynn (#1)

1971

"Coat of Many Colors" by Dolly Parton (#4)
"Delta Dawn" by Tanya Tucker (#6; #72 pop)

Truck Driving Songs

1963

"Six Days on the Road" by Dave Dudley (#2; #32 pop)
"Ninety Miles an Hour (Down A Dead End Street)" by Hank Snow (#2; #124 pop)

1964

"Truck Driving Man" by George Hamilton IV (#11)

1965

"Girl on the Billboard" by Del Reeves (#1; #96 pop)
"A Tombstone Every Mile" by Dick Curless (#5)
"Truck Drivin' Son-of-a-Gun" by Dave Dudley (#3; #125 pop)

1966

"Giddyup Go" by Red Sovine (#1; #82 pop)
"Giddyup Go—Answer" by Minnie Pearl (#10)
"Roll Truck Roll" by Red Simpson (#38)
"The Highway Patrol" by Red Simpson (#39)
"Giddyup Do-Nut" by Don Bowman (#49)
"Little Pink Mack" by Kay Adams with The Cliffie Stone Group (#30)
"Diesel Smoke, Dangerous Curves" by Red Simpson (#41)

1967

"Diesel on My Tail" by Jim & Jesse (#18)
"Trucker's Prayer" by Dave Dudley (#23)
"Phantom 309" by Red Sovine (#9)
"How Fast Them Trucks Can Go" by Claude Gray (#12)
"Anything Leaving Town Today" by Dave Dudley (#12)

1968

"My Big Truck Drivin' Man" by Kitty Wells (#35)
"There Ain't No Easy Run" by Dave Dudley (#10)
"Truck Drivin' Cat with Nine Wives" by Jim Nesbitt (#63)
"Truck Drivin' Cat with Nine Wives" by Charlie Walker (#54)
"Truck Drivin' Woman" by Norma Jean (#53)
"Looking at the World through a Windshield" by Del Reeves (#5)
"Big Rig Rollin' Man" by Johnny Dollar (#48)

1969

"Big Wheels Sing for Me" by Johnny Dollar (#65)
"One More Mile" by Dave Dudley (#12)

1970

"Truck Driver's Lament" by Johnny Dollar (#71)
"Freightliner Fever" by Red Sovine (#54)

1971

"Comin' Down" by Dave Dudley (#8)
"I'm a Truck" Capitol (#4)

1972

"White Line Fever" by Buddy Alan (#68)
"Country Western Truck Drivin' Singer" by Red Simpson (#62)

1973

"Trucker's Paradise" by Del Reeves (#54)
"Keep on Truckin'" by Dave Dudley (#10)
"Awful Lot to Learn About Truck Drivin'" by Red Simpson (#63)
"Rollin' Rig" by Dave Dudley (#47)

1974

"Old Home Filler-Up an' Keep On-A-Truckin' Café" by C.W. McCall (#19; #54 pop)
"Wolf Creek Pass" by C.W. McCall (#12; #40 pop)

Songs on Work

1962

"Get a Little Dirt on Your Hands" by Bill Anderson (#14)

1963

"Busted" by Johnny Cash (#13)
"Detroit City" by Bobby Bare (#6)
"Last Day in the Mines" by Dave Dudley (#7)
"D.J. for a Day" by Jimmy C. Newman (#9)

1967

"A Working Man's Prayer" by Tex Ritter (#59)

1968

"Ballad of Forty Dollars" by Tom T. Hall (#4)
"Wichita Lineman" by Glen Campbell (#1)

1969

"Workin' Man Blues" by Merle Haggard (#1)

1970

"If I Were a Carpenter" by Johnny Cash and June Carter (#2)
"I Never Picked Cotton" by Roy Clark (#5; #122 pop)
"Money Can't Buy Love" by Roy Rogers (#35)

1972

"Daddy Frank" by Merle Haggard (#1)
"Oney" by Johnny Cash (#2; #101 pop)

1973

"Working Class Hero" by Tommy Roe (#73; #97 pop)
"If We Make It through December" by Merle Haggard (#1; #28 pop)
"That Girl Who Waits on Tables" by Ronnie Milsap (#11)

Honky-Tonk Angels and Rockabilly Queens

Oklahoma Divas in American Country Music

George Carney

Historians, folklorists, and cultural geographers have long recognized the role that Oklahoma has played in the evolution of American country music. Music scholars Richard Peterson and Russell Davis determined that the number of country musicians born in Oklahoma during the first and third decades of the twentieth century was above average, given the state's relatively small population. Only Texas in the Southwest produced a comparable number of country musicians, and its population base was greater than Oklahoma's.[1] Historian William W. Savage Jr. maintains that country music has been an important segment of the culture of Oklahoma for almost a century because it appealed to a predominantly rural audience in the state. Moreover, he attributes the phenomenon to the rural, white composition of the population that migrated to the state from the upper and lower South more than one hundred years ago. According to Savage, country music was a key item in the "cultural baggage" they transported from the South to Oklahoma during their move. Savage concludes that these are the people who have always played, sung, and listened to country music and remain as loyal fans.[2] Folklorist Guy Logsdon contends that the early families who migrated to Oklahoma were restless, creative types. He also theorizes that music was an avenue for leaving the small towns and rural areas and getting away from poverty—especially for those who lived on tenant farms and were sharecroppers. Talented young performers, Logsdon states, viewed country music as a potential occupation. And several Oklahomans—including Bob Wills, Gene Autry, and Hank Thompson—helped make country music a viable profession. Thus, a young person could stand back and say, "Hey, that's what I want to do," adds Logsdon.[3] Billy Parker, a KVOO disc jockey and successful country artist, believes that Oklahoma has always been a heart-of-the-matter state. He emphasizes the country tradition in Oklahoma: "We've been country people raised in a country atmosphere, especially the numerous country music radio programs. Oklahoma has that type of heritage. If you live in St. Louis, for example, you would not hear all that country music on radio."[4] Cultural geographer George O. Carney's study of country music radio stations in the 1970s indicates that Oklahoma ranked fourth in terms of the ratio of all-country radio to total AM stations.[5] Carney's 1979 analysis of birthplaces of country music notables ranks Oklahoma fourth behind Texas, Kentucky, and Tennessee in total output as well as fourth behind Kentucky, Tennessee, and Arkansas in per capita production.[6] Clearly, the evidence suggests that Oklahoma is a key state in the "Fertile Crescent of Country Music" as outlined by Peterson and Davis.

Importance of Oklahoma Country Music

Country music has proven to be one of Oklahoma's most important cultural resources. The state has produced performers, composers, institutions, and songs that have significantly shaped the entire realm of American country music. One need only mention performers like Garth Brooks, Vince Gill, and Joe Diffie, as well as composers Dallas Frazier, Floyd Tillman, and Stoney Edwards to demonstrate the profound role that Oklahoma has played in American country music. The state has spawned influential country music institutions—including ballrooms such as Cain's in Tulsa and Trianon in Oklahoma City and radio stations KVOO in Tulsa and WKY in Oklahoma City—and nurtured such groups as the Texas Playboys and Wiley and Gene. It has also produced some of the most respected country music promoters and producers, including Lucky Moeller, Tim Dubois, and Scott Hendricks. Noted country music instrumentalists, such as Eldon Shamblin and Bob Dunn, were also natives of Oklahoma. Finally, songs such as "Oklahoma Hills," "You're the Reason God Made Oklahoma," and "Take Me Back to Tulsa" evoke images of Oklahoma and remain a vital part of the American country music legacy.

Oklahoma Women in Country Music

One facet of Oklahoma's country music heritage often overlooked is the contribution of native-born Oklahoma women. Linda Williams Reese's recent history of Oklahoma women pays tribute to the political and social leaders associated with the development of the state; however, nothing is mentioned regarding the significance of Oklahoma females in any genre of American music, including country. Similar to the individuals covered in Reese's volume, country music's Oklahoma-born women came from humble economic circumstances and had little formal education. As Reese states, "Oklahoma women understood their importance as individuals and as members of the family unit." But of primary importance, according to Reese, was their "desire to secure a better economic condition, if not affluence."[7] These attributes described by Reese are applicable to the fourteen women investigated by this study. All were interested in searching for their identity as individuals and promoting the family unit, but utmost in their minds was the search for a better life. One of the opportunities through which Oklahoma women sought economic stability was music as a profession.

Individual accomplishments of Oklahoma women in country music have been addressed in a few biographical accounts and journal articles, however, little or no research has examined the social, historic, and geographic background of the Oklahoma women collectively. This analysis thus focuses on the fourteen women artists born in Oklahoma after 1907 as identified by one or more of the major biographical dictionaries or encyclopedias of American country music[8] (see table 1). Additional biographical data was collected from a variety of secondary sources (journals, books, theses and dissertations, and manuscripts) on Oklahoma-born women in American country music. Finally, a systematic comparison of the production of Oklahoma's country music women with other states was calculated. Final results of this analysis reveal that Oklahoma ranks in the top four states in total production of women country artists. Topping the list are Tennessee (19) and Kentucky (15), while Texas and Oklahoma are tied for third (14). More importantly, Oklahoma ranks second after Tennessee based on a per capita production formula.[9]

Although biographical data for the female musicians is incomplete and, in some cases, unavailable, an analysis of several variables provides a number of sociocultural characteristics concerning the fourteen women artists native to Oklahoma: (1) time and place origins (when and where each was born),

Table 1. Oklahoma-Born Women in American Country Music (alphabetized) N=14

Name	Birthplace	DOB	Specialty
Bee, Molly (Molly Beachboard)	Oklahoma City	1939	Singer/Yodeler
Collins, Lorrie	Tahlequah Vicinity	1942	Singer/Guitar
Davies, Gail	Broken Bow	1948	Singer/Composer/Guitar
Hardin, Gus	Tulsa	1945	Singer
Hobbs, Becky	Bartlesville	1950	Singer/Composer/Piano
Jackson, Wanda	Maud	1937	Guitar/Singer/Composer
Jean, Norma	Wellston	1938	Singer/Guitar
McBride, Laura Lee	Bridgeport	1920	Singer
McEntire, Reba	Chockie	1954	Singer/Composer/Fiddle/Guitar/Piano/Drums
Owens, Bonnie	Blanchard	1932	Singer/Composer/Guitar
Page, Patti (Clara Ann Fowler)	Claremore	1927	Singer
Place, Mary Kay	Tulsa	1947	Singer/Composer
Shepard, Jean	Paul's Valley	1933	Singer/Composer/Bass
Willis, Kelly	Lawton	1968	Singer/Composer

(2) family background (parents and siblings) and role of social institutions (school and church experiences), (3) amateur and professional opportunities within Oklahoma, (4) achievements and recognition outside Oklahoma, and (5) contributions to and innovations within American country music.

Time and Place Origins

The 1930s produced the most Oklahoma women in country music, with five being born during this decade (Bee, Jackson, Norma Jean, Owens, and Shepard), followed by the 1940s with four (Collins, Davies, Hardin, and Place). Three were born in the post-1950 era (Hobbs, McEntire, and Willis), while Page and McBride were born in the 1920s. By combining the periods from statehood to 1950, it is evident that more than 78 percent of Oklahoma's female country musicians were born prior to 1950 (see table 2).

Origin of Oklahoma Women in Country Music (N-14)
(By City Size and Period of Birth)

City Size (Population)	Periods of Birth					Total
	1907-1919	1920-1929	1930-1939	1940-1949	1950-Present	
>2,500	1	3	1	1		6
2,501-25,000		1	1	1		3
25,001-50,000					1	1
<50,000			1	2	1	4
Total	0	2	5	4	3	14

Table 2

Birthplace distribution patterns suggest that, in general, the eastern half of Oklahoma is the area of highest productivity. More specifically, two clusters emerge. First is the central section of the state with five (Bee, Norma Jean, Owens, Shepard, and Jackson), while the second concentration is the northeast, also with five (Collins, Hardin, Hobbs, Place, and Page). The remaining four (Davies, McEntire, McBride, and Willis) are randomly distributed in the southeastern and western sections of the state (see figure 1). It is hypothesized that two factors account for this distribution pattern. First, higher population densities in the northeastern and central portions of Oklahoma, both located in the "population corridor" of the state, undoubtedly have affected production. Second, the eastern half of Oklahoma has been strongly influenced by the cultural forces of the three states to the east—Missouri, Arkansas, and Louisiana—where country music traditions have historically flourished, especially in the Ozark-Ouachita region of Missouri and Arkansas. The women performers originated in communities ranging from Bartlesville (Hobbs) in the northeast to Broken Bow (Davies) in the southeast to Lawton (Willis) in the southwest. Only one (Bee) was born in Oklahoma City, the largest urban center in the state. Ten of the fourteen (Collins, Davies, Hobbs, Jackson, McBride, Norma Jean, McEntire, Owens, Page, and Shepard) were born in communities with a population

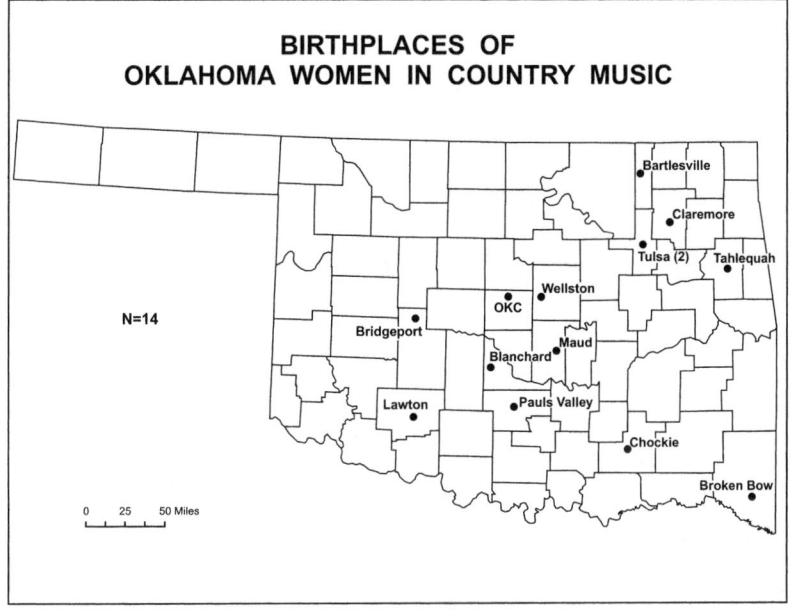

Figure 1

less than 50,000, a figure used by the United States Bureau of the Census to designate metropolitan areas (see table 2). Therefore, roughly 71 percent of the women artists were born outside the two metropolitan areas in Oklahoma (Tulsa and Oklahoma City). The towns of 2,500 or less (today considered rural by the Bureau of the Census) produced five of the fourteen, or more than 35 percent of the total. Included were Wanda Jackson (Maud), Norma Jean (Wellston), Laura Lee McBride (Bridgeport), Bonnie Owens (Blanchard), and Reba McEntire (Chockie).

Oklahoma women represent a broad spectrum of American country music ranging from Lorrie Collins of the Collins Kids' rockabilly sound to the honky-tonk subgenre of Jean Shepard. Their performance characteristics disclose that these Oklahoma women were a talented group that demonstrated a wide array of musical skills. All were primarily vocalists. Several were known for their yodeling abilities, particularly Molly Bee and Bonnie Owens. Eight of the fourteen (57 percent) were instrumentalists (Collins, Davies, Hobbs, Jackson, Norma Jean, McEntire, Owens, and Shepard), with three playing multiple instruments (Hobbs, Jackson, and McEntire). McEntire was competent on the most instruments (fiddle, guitar, piano, and drums). The most popular instrument was the guitar (6) followed by the piano (2). Nine of the fourteen (64 percent) were composers/songwriters (Collins, Davies, Hobbs, Jackson, McEntire, Owens, Place, Shepard, and Willis). In terms of songwriting capabilities, Hobbs is the most prolific, having composed songs for such country music luminaries as Alabama, John Anderson, Shelly West, George Jones, Loretta Lynn, and Moe Bandy. Finally, it should be noted that in 1986 Davies organized the first female songwriters roundtable for the PBS series *Austin City Limits* that included Emmylou Harris, Rosanne Cash, and Lacy J. Dalton.

Demographic Profile

In terms of racial and ethnic background, all fourteen are Caucasian, not uncommon in the history of country music. The data is sketchy, but sources indicate that all fourteen either received a high school diploma or completed some high school training, while only three (Hobbs, Place, and McEntire) attended college.

The most significant musical influence on these Oklahoma women country artists was that one or both parents or one of their siblings played an instrument or sang. Fathers played an important role in the musical development of Hobbs (fiddler), Jackson (guitar and piano), McBride (singer), and Davies (guitar), while mothers influenced Collins (singer), McEntire (singer), and Willis (singer). Sibling musicians also affected the group, including Collins (brother was guitarist), Page (sisters sang and formed the Fowler Sisters who performed for local events and in church), Davies (brother sang and formed a duet in high school as well as influenced her songwriting), McBride (sister was vocalist and formed a duet known as Joy and Jane who performed on a radio program starring their father, Tex Owens), and McEntire (brother and sister sang and formed The Singing McEntires in high school). Outside the home, little data was located on the influences of church or school music programs. Hardin, Jackson, McEntire, Shepard, and Page (member of the Fowler Sisters) sang in church either as a child or teenager. Finally, Owens, McEntire, and Place sang at school assemblies or talent shows while in elementary or high school.

Little is known of the politics of the fourteen women, although McEntire has sung the national anthem at Republican Party conventions in the past. Religious background data is likewise scarce, although Jackson became a born-again Christian during the latter stages of her career. This is evidenced by her recording of "Jesus Put a Yodel in My Soul," while Norma Jean, after confessing alcoholism, became a devout Christian.

Marital problems plagued many of the Oklahoma artists. With reliable data, seven (Davies, Hardin, McEntire, Norma Jean, Page, Shepard, and Willis) of the fourteen (50 percent) were divorced at least once. Hardin holds the record with six and was dubbed the "Elizabeth Taylor of Country Music." Based on available data, eight (Collins, Davies, Hardin, Jackson, Norma Jean, McEntire, Owens, and Shepard) of the fourteen had children (57 percent), either adopted or by birth, with Shepard having the most with three. Davies was one of the first single parents in country music. She gave birth to a son out of wedlock in 1982 (Gary Scruggs was the father and Earl Scruggs the grandfather.)

Amateur and Professional Opportunities in Oklahoma

Half of the fourteen began their amateur/professional careers in Oklahoma. Collins won a talent contest in Tulsa at age eight. It was hosted by Leon McAuliffe, western swing notable and member of Bob Wills's Texas Playboys. Hardin sang in talent contests while in junior high in Tulsa, performed in Tulsa nightclubs for fifteen years, and was promoted by a Tulsa-based entertainment group. Hobbs was a member of two all-female bands (Four Faces of Eve and Sir Prize Package) while completing high school and as a student at the University of Tulsa. Jackson first performed on KLPR radio in Oklahoma City at the age of fifteen. She also joined the Merle Lindsay and Hank Thompson bands while in high school in Oklahoma City. Norma Jean was also on KLPR, at the age of twelve, and she toured with western swing bands while in high school in Oklahoma City. McEntire began her singing career with the Singing McEntires (brother Pake and sister Suzie) while in high school. Clem McSpadden, rodeo announcer and Oklahoma politician, arranged for her to sing the national anthem at the National Finals Rodeo in 1974 in Oklahoma City. It was at this event that McEntire was discovered by Red Steagall, who assisted in obtaining her first recording contract. Page began her career as Clara Ann Fowler on KTUL in Tulsa on a show sponsored by the Page Milk Company (hence the name Patti Page). The remaining seven (Bee, Davies, McBride, Owens, Place, Shepard, and Willis) either left Oklahoma as children or after high school to launch careers elsewhere.

From Oklahoma to National and International Prominence

Because of its rural orientation, sparse population, lack of a major metropolitan center, and shortage of recording facilities, Oklahoma failed to retain most of its country music women. The allure of major recording studios, more and better-quality performing venues, and larger radio markets affected the decisions of Oklahoma women to migrate from the state in order to achieve fame and fortune. The West was the most attractive region, with seven of the fourteen (Bee, Collins, Davies, Hobbs, Owens, Place, and Shepard) migrating to California (4), Arizona (2), and Washington (1). Bee migrated with her family to Tucson, Arizona, where she appeared on the Rex Allen radio show at the age of ten. Collins and her family moved to the Los Angeles area where she appeared at the age of eleven on the *Town Hall* television show hosted by Tex Ritter. Davies moved at the age of five to Point Orchard, Washington (near Seattle), with her mother and two brothers following the divorce of her parents. Hobbs and her band moved to Los Angeles in 1971. Owens, like Bee, first migrated to Arizona, where she performed on radio in Mesa. After graduation from the University of Tulsa, Place moved to Hollywood to seek a career in some form of entertainment. Finally, Shepard moved in 1946 to Visalia, California, where she and friends formed the Melody Ranch Girls (an all-female western swing band).

Rivaling the *Grand Ole Opry* in Nashville in the 1950s was the Ozark Jubilee in Springfield, Missouri. Hosted by Red Foley, it became a primary destination point for Norma Jean and Wanda Jackson. Patti Page and Laura Lee McBride both headed for large midwestern cities. At the age of twenty, Page left Oklahoma for Chicago, where she eventually became a regular performer on Don McNeill's *Breakfast Club* on the ABC network. As a teenager, McBride and her family relocated to Kansas City, where she and her sister performed on their father Tex Owens's radio program on KMBC in Kansas City. Willis was the only Oklahoman who left the state for the East Coast. Reared in the Washington, D.C., area, she began performing professionally at the age of nineteen with her own group, Kelly and the Fireballs. Surprisingly, none of the Oklahoma women made Nashville their first professional home base. However, several eventually joined the *Grand Ole Opry* during their careers, including Jackson, Norma-Jean, Shepard, Collins, Hobbs, and McEntire. Only McEntire migrated to Nashville directly from her southeastern Oklahoma ranch, and that did not occur until 1987, three

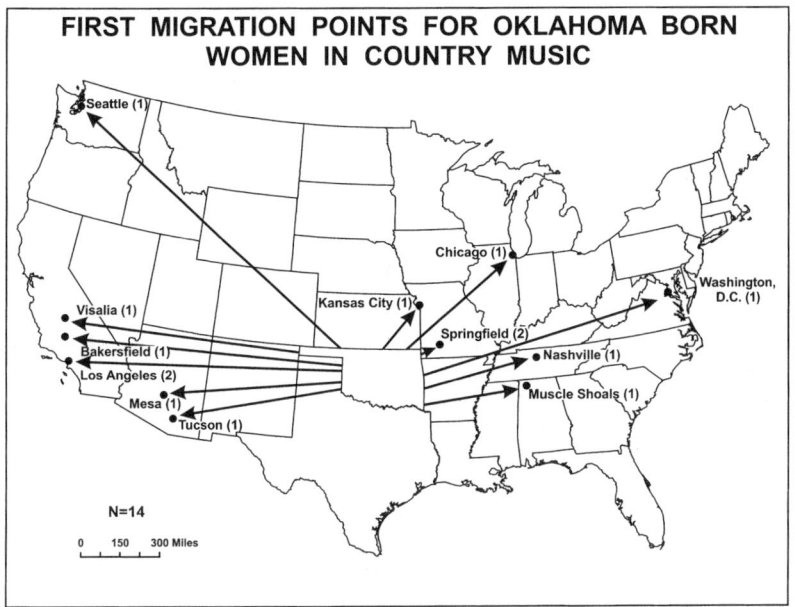

Figure 2

years after her first number-one hit and her divorce from Charlie Battles. Other than McEntire's move to Nashville, the South as a region attracted only one of the women performers—Hardin to Muscle Shoals, Alabama (see figure 2).

A number of the Oklahoma women have received recognition at the national level. During the 1960s, several Oklahoma-born women vied for the title of "Queen of Country Music," including Owens, Jackson, Norma Jean, Bee, and Shepard. The most lauded, McEntire has been named Top Female Vocalist or Entertainer of the Year with honors from the Country Music Association, Academy of Country Music, American Music Academy, The Nashville Network/Music City News, People's Choice, Billboard, and the Grammy Awards. In addition, Jackson and Shepard were recipients of Grammy Awards, while Owens and Shepard have gained top honors from the Academy of Country Music and Cash Box. Several achieved a national reputation via radio, television, film, and Broadway. Bee, Page, and McEntire have appeared in motion pictures, Page had her own television show, and McEntire has starred in two network television specials as well as playing the lead role of Annie Oakley in *Annie Get Your Gun* on Broadway.

Although most Oklahoma women artists remained as prominent figures in American country music, several gained distinction on the global country music scene by participating in overseas tours. Jackson has appeared in more foreign countries than any of the fourteen artists. She was one of the members of the first United Nations/Country Music Association–sponsored tours to Australia, New Zealand, and Japan. In addition to these countries, she has toured Canada, Europe (where she recorded an album in Sweden), the Philippines, Korea, and the Middle East. Other artists appearing overseas include Hobbs (England, Switzerland, and Africa), Bee (Europe and Japan), Owens (England), Shepard (England), Davies (England), and McEntire (Australia).

Innovations/Contributions by Oklahoma Women Artists in Country Music

The accomplishments of Oklahoma women in American country music are noteworthy. In addition to the numerous awards and honors given by various organizations and academies, the multitude of innovations and contributions made by these women is often overlooked. Jackson entered the country music charts in 1954 with "You Can't Have My Love," a duet with Billy Gray, one of Hank Thompson's sidemen. After joining the Ozark Jubilee in 1955, Jackson appeared on tour with Elvis Presley, who encouraged her to change styles. After recording "Hot Dog (That Made Him Mad)" in 1956 and "Let's Have a Party" in 1958, she became known as "The Queen of Rockabilly," and was often referred to as the female counterpart of Elvis Presley. By the early 1960s, she returned to the honky-tonk substyle with such recordings as "Right or Wrong" and "In the Middle of a Heartache," both released in 1961. During the 1970s, she became a born-again Christian and recorded six country gospel albums. In the 1980s and 1990s, she has fluctuated between the rockabilly, honky-tonk, and country gospel subgenres (depending upon who was booking her). Thus, Jackson was one of the first female artists to successfully embrace three different substyles of American country music.

In terms of crossover music, Page was the first woman artist to claim the Top Five in both country and pop, with "The Tennessee Waltz" reaching number one on the pop charts and number three on the country charts in 1951. Page was also the first woman to employ multi-track recording, a technological breakthrough in the music industry. Her use of this technique on "The Tennessee Waltz" predated that of Les Paul and Mary Ford.[10] Finally, Page was considered a role model by many later country stars, including Patsy Cline and K.T. Oslin.

The first woman in country music to record a concept album was Shepard. Her 1956 LP *Songs of a Love Affair* featured songs from a single woman's point of view on one side, while the other side portrayed the wife's perspective. Additionally, Shepard was the first female in country music to sell a million records and the first woman to hold membership in the *Grand Ole Opry* for more than forty-five years.

McBride became the first female vocalist in the subgenre of western swing when she joined Bob Wills in 1943. Labeled as the "Queen of Western Swing," she recorded with Wills in the 1940s and 1950s. As a member of Cliff Bruner's Texas Wanderers western swing ensemble in 1938, she provided the vocal for the first recording of "It Makes No Difference Now."

Norma Jean was the first woman to record a woman-oriented truck driving song in country music with her "Truck Drivin' Woman" in 1968. Furthermore, she recorded one of the best albums reflecting the plight of the poor. Recorded in 1972, *I Guess That Comes from Being Poor* included such songs as "Hundred Dollar Funeral," "There Won't Be Any Patches in Heaven," and "The Lord Must Have Loved Poor Folks [He Made So Many of Them]."

Davies also deserves special attention because of her role in the country music industry. She was the first woman in country music to produce and arrange her own recordings (Warner Brothers, 1980–1983) as well as being hired as the first female staff producer for Liberty Records (formerly Capitol Nashville) in 1990. "When I first came to Nashville, the industry was not open to a woman . . . having much to say about production," according to Davies, "but I feel strongly about my music, and I don't believe being firm about my convictions and standing up for them is in conflict with my femininity."[11] She sang several benefits for the Nashville women's shelter after recalling her upbringing in a childhood home where considerable domestic violence occurred because of her father's alcoholism. After becoming pregnant in 1982, Davies decided not to marry Gary Scruggs and had son Christopher on her own in late 1982. During the pregnancy, Davies was confronted with a great deal of criticism. "I discovered a whole side of society that bothered me very much . . . I started seeing how women are looked at, like my behavior was bad, yet nothing was said about the man. And so I started reading a lot of books on women and our self-image."[12] During this time, Davies released two feminist-oriented albums—*Givin' Herself Away* (1982) and *Where Is a Woman to Go?* (1984). Finally, Davies demonstrated further initiative by forming her own record label in 1994—Little Chickadee Records.

Conclusions

In his state-based study of country music in Tennessee, Charles K. Wolfe remarks that country music should be examined from a regional perspective. He also notes that one cannot fully understand country music without an evaluation of the social context that produced and maintained it. This context, according to Wolfe, "seems most easily and obviously defined in terms of geography."[13] The preceding examination of Oklahoma country music women fulfills both objectives set forth by Wolfe. As a regional analysis, this study affords one an opportunity to better comprehend the entire American country music story. It also provides a social context for these fourteen women relevant not only to their musical training, but also their geographic origins, family life, educational and religious backgrounds, and economic circumstances. Additionally, understanding country music traditions in Oklahoma offers a key to a more holistic view of country music in the United States.

The questions remains, however, why Oklahoma is such a fertile ground for the production of women country music artists when compared with other states? One must first consider the settlement patterns of Oklahoma because they reflect the cultural diversity of the state. Charles N. Gould, an early twentieth-century travel writer and geographer, emphasizes Oklahoma's multicultural traditions: "Oklahoma is a meeting place of many different peoples. Nowhere else is there such a mingling of types. Practically every state in the Union and every civilized nation on the globe is represented among the state's inhabitants."[14] Many different cultural groups brought music in their "cultural baggage" that resulted in the development of a myriad of vibrant musical subcultures: songs and dance music of the Native Americans from the southeastern United States and western plains, Anglo-Celtic ballads from the upland South, country blues from the Mississippi Delta, black and white spirituals from the lowland South, European immigrant music from Italy, Germany, and Czechoslovakia, polka music from the Upper Midwest, and Mexican *mariachi* from the Rio Grande Valley. This cultural confluence of different genres of American music allowed Oklahomans to experiment, innovate, and improvise—traits necessary in the formulation of the various subgenres of American country music. Within this Oklahoma cultural mosaic, music knew no color. Black, white, and red musicians borrowed freely from each other, exchanged repertoires and musical ideas, and adopted new techniques and styles. These cross-cultural experiences favored the development of country music in Oklahoma.

A second factor is Oklahoma's population and economic history. The state was small town- and rural-oriented, both in terms of composition and mentality. Moreover, the rural and small town residents of the state have experienced considerable poverty throughout the state's history. Both the rural nature of the state and the poverty challenges confronted by its residents favored the development of country music. Oklahomans identified with country music lyrics that spoke to their rural way of life and economic conditions. Many of the women in this study were exposed to country lyrics via the state's flourishing live country music radio shows being broadcast over KFRU in Bristow (later to become KVOO in Tulsa), and WKY, KFJF, and KLPR in Oklahoma City. Furthermore, Oklahoma's high percentage of tenant farmers and sharecroppers in the 1930s forced many to seek music as an avenue for leaving poverty. Several (Bee, Jackson, Norma Jean, Owens, and Shepard) were children of Great Depression parents who had survived the hard times and dust—parents who longed for their children to realize a better life. Therefore, they encouraged their daughters to practice their musical talents and promoted them at any venue available within Oklahoma. A number of Oklahoma-based musicians helped turn music into a profession, including Otto Gray and the Oklahoma Cowboys, Gene Autry, Bob Wills, and Hank Thompson. Many of those young women in rural areas and small towns sought a more secure economic lifestyle. And when they listened to the radio broadcasts of Otto Gray over KFRU and Gene Autry and Bob Wills on KVOO during the first half of the twentieth century, it helped inspire them to become professional country musicians.

A third factor focuses on the availability of performance venues. As these young Oklahoma women in country music honed their musical skills at county fairs, churches, school assemblies, nightclubs, honky-tonks, and rodeos throughout the state, many of them were eventually given the opportunity to perform on the live country music radio shows, such as KLPR in Oklahoma City (Jackson and Norma Jean) and KTUL in Tulsa (Page). As a result, these local experiences helped launch their professional careers in country music and simultaneously inspired younger women in Oklahoma to seek country music as a profession.

A fourth and final factor was the numerous local musicians who were influential in the early development of these Oklahoma women's careers in country music. Individuals such as Merle Lindsay, Leon McAuliffe, and Hank Thompson offered the fledgling artists opportunities such as singing in their bands, scheduling them on live radio shows, and assisting them in securing recording contracts.

Country music and the influence of women on the genre are some of the cultural traits that make Oklahoma a unique place. These cultural markers distinguish the state from other places and give special meaning to its residents—a feeling of pride in place, or, as geographers call it, place consciousness. Place itself embodies meaning dependent upon the personal history that one brings to it. It is through these people-place interactions that one develops a deep psychological attachment with a specific place, such as Oklahoma.

Oklahoma women in country music are a significant part of the rich and diversified musical heritage of the state, but, more importantly, this regional perspective provides us with a fuller and deeper appreciation of the American country music landscape. As the scholarship associated with American country music continues to increase, so does the need for more in-depth research into regional studies of country music. When completed, fuller documentation of country music at the state level will become a vital component of American country music historiography.

Notes

1. Richard A. Peterson and Russell Davis Jr., "The Fertile Crescent of Country Music," *The Journal of Country Music* 6 (spring 1975): 19–27.

2. William W. Savage Jr., *Singing Cowboys and All That Jazz: A Short History of Popular Music in Oklahoma* (Norman: Univ. of Oklahoma Press, 1983).

3. Guy Logsdon, "Hit the Road, Jack!" *Oklahoma Monthly* 26 (February 1976): 7–16.

4. Personal interview with Billy Parker, Tulsa, Oklahoma, October 1999.

5. George O. Carney, "From Down Home to Uptown: The Diffusion of Country Music Radio Stations in the United States," *The Journal of Geography* 75 (March 1977): 104–10.

6. George O. Carney, "T for Texas, T for Tennessee: The Origins of American Country Music Notables," *The Journal of Geography* 78 (November 1979): 218–25.

7. Linda Williams Reese, *Women of Oklahoma, 1890–1920* (Norman: Univ. of Oklahoma Press), 283.

8. See Colin Larkin, ed., *The Virgin Encyclopedia of Country Music* (London: Virgin Books, 1998); Paul Kingsbury et al., *Country: The Music and the Musicians* (New York: Abbeville Press, 1994); Country Music Magazine, eds., *The Comprehensive Country Music Encyclopedia* (New York: Random House, 1994); Fred Dellar et al., eds., *The Harmony Illustrated Encyclopedia of Country Music* (New York: Harmony Books, 1994); Patrick Carr, ed., *The Illustrated History of Country Music,* rev. ed. (New York: Times Books, 1995); Barry McCloud et al., *Definitive Country: The Ultimate Encyclopedia of Country Music and Its Performers* (New York: Perigee, 1995); Kurt Wolff, *Country Music: The Rough Guide* (London: Penguin Books, 2000); Paul Kingsbury, *The Encyclopedia of Country Music: The Ultimate Guide to the Music* (New York: Oxford Univ. Press, 1998); and David Goodman, *Modern Twang: An Alternative Country Music Guide and Directory* (Nashville: Dowling Press, 1999).

9. Data on country music women (N=108) were collected from the nine most recent biographical dictionaries (see note 8), and per capita results were calculated using a location quotient formula. (First, the number of country music women produced by a state is divided by total number of country music women produced in the United States. Second, the total population of a state is divided by the total population of the United States. Finally, the first division using production of women country artists is divided by the results of the second division using population data).

10. McCloud et al., *Definitive Country,* 614, and Larkin, *Virgin Encyclopedia,* 321.

11. Davies quoted in Mary A. Bufwack and Robert K. Oermann, *Finding Her Voice: The Saga of Women in Country Music* (New York: Crown Publishers, 1993), 438.

12. Ibid., 438–39.

13. Charles K. Wolfe, *Tennessee Strings: The Story of Country Music in Tennessee* (Knoxville: Univ. of Tennessee Press, 1977), vii.

14. Charles N. Gould, *Travels Through Oklahoma* (Oklahoma City: Harlow Publishing Company, 1928). See also Michael Frank Doran, "The Origins of Culture Areas in Oklahoma, 1893–1900," Unpublished Ph.D. dissertation, Department of Geography, University of Oregon, 1974, and Michael Roark, "Searching for the Hearth: Culture Areas of Oklahoma, *The Chronicles of Oklahoma* 70 (winter 1992–1993): 416–31.

THE BRISTOL SYNDROME
FIELD RECORDINGS OF EARLY COUNTRY MUSIC

Charles K. Wolfe

The year 2002 marks the seventy-fifth anniversary of the 1927 field recording session held in Bristol, Tennessee, by talent scout Ralph Peer from the Victor Talking Machine Company. This session, which has been called "the big bang of country music," resulted in the discovery of the genre's first great stars: Jimmie Rodgers and the Carter Family. It has been studied rather exhaustively for a number of years. Yet most students of the music know that the Bristol event was not an anomaly, and that it was only one of a number of such sessions held around the South and Southwest by major record companies in the 1920s. It was by no means the first such session, nor was it the only one to result in the discovery of significant artists. For a couple of generations now, popular histories and media documentaries have seized upon the romantic image of the cynical northern record company executive standing in a drafty hotel room with blankets hung around the walls recording amazing old-time fiddlers and singers fresh from the nearby mountains. The recent reissue of the Harry Smith Anthology, the influential 1952 collection of early field recordings, along with the attendant publicity effort by the Smithsonian, generated even more interest in the practice. Yet aside from accounts of the Bristol sessions, there has been far too little hard evidence presented about the exact nature and scope of these early field recordings. This paper is an attempt to present a general overview of this activity and how it related to the recording industry in general.

To begin with, there is the basic question of just what percentage of early country music recordings—what was then called "old-time music"—were in fact recorded outside the big studios in New York. The first generation of country music scholars, working at a time when the study of the music's discography was in its infancy, assumed that most of the recordings, like those of jazz or pop, had been made in New York or (in the case of Victor) Camden, New Jersey. The expeditions into the rural South by men like Ralph Peer and his counterparts Frank Walker (Columbia), Dick Voynow (Brunswick), H.C. Spier and Polk Brockman (Okeh), Harry Charles (Paramount), and later Art Satherly (ARC) were seen as exceptions to the rule, and the general consensus was that while the talent hunters were indeed busy, they sent more of their discoveries up to New York than recorded them on location.

Since then we have learned a great deal more about this body of recordings. By networking with record collectors, exchanging data with other researchers, and harrowing old company catalogs, we were able to create a series of "numericals" for each of the labels of the 1920s. This formed a sort of bibliography, a numerical listing of the released sides, and was essential in understanding the scope of such recordings. Later, with the help of discographer Tony Russell and his quarterly *Old Time Music,* I learned how to use "master numbers" (the original serial number given a disc before it released) to recreate the original field sessions. Whenever I did interviews with older musicians, I always asked how they felt about Peer, or Walker, or whoever their talent scout was, and how this person got in touch with them, and whether he influenced their choice of songs to record.

The handful of interviews that had been done with Peer, Walker, and others began to reveal a picture of the overall scope of field recordings. First, we learned that there were far more record releases in this body of material than we had suspected. When we began to get access to some of the actual sales figures, they also appeared to be much higher than we suspected, making the discs not only valid in a passive sense (as preservers of the music) but also in an active sense (as carriers and influences in their own right). But most interesting of all, we were able to verify that, indeed, most of these discs were recorded "in the field" at various cities and towns across the South.

As to specifics: in 1925, the first year of Columbia's "Old Familiar Tunes" catalog—the term they used to designate the specific series for old-time music—the company released some fifty-three records in the series. These sides included works by such genuine traditional performers as Gid Tan-

A 1926 Victor Record catalog.

ner, Charlie Poole, Ernest Thompson, and Riley Puckett, but only six of the records were recorded in the field—mainly in Atlanta. The rest of the time, the company either coaxed the artists to come into New York, or they used nontraditional New York–trained singers like Vernon Dalhart. But in later years, this percentage changed dramatically. To illustrate just how high this percentage was, I have charted below sample years from three of the major companies involved in issuing old-time music in the 1920s (see table 1).

Table 1. Number of Recordings by Year Recorded in the Field.

Year	No. of releases	No. of field recordings	No. of N.Y. recordings	Percent recorded in field
COLUMBIA				
1926	59	33	26	56%
1927	94	74	20	79%
1928	121	108	13	89%
1929	155	138	17	87%
OKEH				
1927	102	84	18	82%
1928	109	87	22	80%
VICTOR				
1929	170	121	49	71%
1930	164	131	33	80%

Several things are noteworthy here. One is the way the companies in general increased the number of releases as the decade wore on. The second is that, once the record series really got going, the percentage of the pieces recorded out of New York rose toward 80 or even 90 percent. Even in 1926, Columbia was still recording a high percentage in New York; many of these recordings reflect the early popularity of "city-billy" singers like Vernon Dalhart, whose popularity quickly waned as audiences were allowed to hear more authentic singers like Rodgers and the Carters. The 1929 Victor releases were all part of their 40,000 issues, the "Old Familiar Tunes and Novelties" series. During the year, the series released some 170 records, of which only 49 were from the company's permanent studios—a field percentage of 71 percent. Most of the New York–Camden sessions were now being done by studio regulars like Dalhart, Carson Robison, Frank Luther, and the NBC network stars The McCravy Brothers. Jimmie Rodgers recorded some 28 songs this year, and only 5 of them were done in New York. The others were done in Dallas (14), Atlanta (8), and New Orleans (1). Major artists who recorded often, such as Charlie Poole, the Carter Family, and Uncle Dave Macon, still routinely went up north to record. But by the late 1920s, field sessions had emerged as the best way to find and document grassroots talent.

While the kind of data needed for a complete analysis of the old-time record series (such as the exact release dates, as opposed to recording dates) is lacking, it seems likely that a similar pattern existed for other companies—with the exceptions of Gennett and Paramount, who made few field session trips.

There is some evidence that record executives in the 1920s looked upon old-time music and blues as similar to the ethnic recordings they had been making for specialized markets for a decade. To that end, they ghettoized many of their non-popular releases by placing them in special numerical series, each with a separate numerical prefix and even with a series name. Thus Columbia put its old-time records into a special 15000 series, with release numbers starting at 15001 and running on to 15782; they dubbed the series "Familiar Tunes—Old and New" and even issued catalogs and catalog supplements for the series. Such a series might be called a "dedicated" series, to contrast it with the more general numerical series that included everything from light classical to dance bands. Though the companies began releasing old-time records in 1923 and 1924—as a response to Fiddlin' John Carson's famous "first" country record ("The Little Old Log Cabin in the Lane")—it wasn't until 1925 that they got around to creating the special dedicated series.

How many different country records were released through such dedicated series in the 1920s? Documentation on some of the minor labels is still sparse. Furthermore, several of the companies had leasing arrangements with big mail-order retailers like Sears-Roebuck and Montgomery Ward, and chain dime stores like Woolworth. In these cases, a record that came out on, say, Victor, might also appear on the Montgomery Ward label. Company executives at the time referred to such records as being released on a "stencil" label, and those fortunate artists who had a royalty arrangement for their discs usually got paid at half the normal royalty rate for such stencil issues. In some cases, the stencil release out-sold the original release.

We do, however, have fairly complete numericals of the major companies producing old-time music in the 1920s. Seven companies dominated the field, each with its own numerical series and title. The following chart lists these seven companies, the title of their series, their numerical identity, the duration of the series, and the total number of records (not sides) released in the series. A "release" is defined as a two-sided record bearing the same catalog or release number on either side.

Table 2. Major companies producing old-time music in the 1920s

Columbia. "Familiar Tunes—Old and New" and "Old Familiar Tunes" (title varies). 15000 series; 1925–end of 1932; *782 released records.* Important artists in this series were Gid Tanner, the Skillet Lickers, Riley Puckett, Charlie Poole, and the Leake County Revelers.

Okeh (General Phonograph Company). "Old Time Tunes;" 45000 series; 1925–1934; *579 releases.* Key artists included Fiddlin' John Carson, Narmour and Smith, Earl Johnson, Henry Whitter, Frank Hutchison, and The Jenkins Family.

Brunswick. "Songs from Dixie;" 100 series; ca. 1927–1932; *501 releases.*

Vocalion. "Old Southern Tunes;" 5000 series, late 1926–May 1935; *504 releases.* Artists on both labels included Uncle Dave Macon, The Kessinger Brothers, and McFarland and Gardner (Mac and Bob).

Victor. "Native American Melodies" and later (1929) "Old Familiar Tunes and Novelties"; Victor started the 40,000 series ("Old Familiar Tunes") in January 1929. In January 1931 they started a new series, the 23,500 series. Prior to 1929, the company issued most of its pop and old-time (and blues) in their general 20,000—every one from Jelly Roll Morton to Jimmie Rodgers. The 40,000 series produced some *335 releases,* while the 23,500 series, in the depths of the Depression, released some *359 records.* Key artists: Jimmie Rodgers, Carter Family, Ernest V. Stoneman, Carson Robison, and The Allen Brothers.

Paramount. Unnamed 3,000 series; April 1927–July 1932; *323 releases.* This does not include sides from the general series, nor the extensive stencil issues on the Broadway label. Artists include Welling and McGhee, Fruit Jar Guzzlers, Kentucky Thorobreds, and Wilmer Watts.

Gennett. Unnamed series, 6000 and 300 numericals; 1925–1934; old-time records in these general series number approximately *323 releases.* Artists include Gene Autry, Bradley Kincaid, and Doc Roberts.

Note: The last two companies, Gennett and Paramount, were located in the Midwest, in the Chicago area; the others were based in New York.

The total for these old-time releases in dedicated series, ranging from 1925 to 1932, is *3,577 records*—an average of slightly over 500 a year. This meant that about every year, almost 1,000 songs were circulated throughout the South, having an incalculable effect on the repertoires of musicians in the area. During this same period, blues releases, which were also issued by the same companies in similar dedicated numerical series, totaled 3,318. Most individual companies had dedicated blues series that released about the same number of sides as the old-time series.

Of the various companies listed above, Paramount and Gennett did not record much old-time music in the field; Gennett had a lone session in Birmingham in 1927. Victor and Columbia did huge amounts of recording in Memphis and Atlanta, respectively. Vocalion, Brunswick, and Okeh fall somewhere in between. As a general rule, there were fewer field sessions in 1924 and 1925, when much of the recording was done in the old acoustic method requiring a cumbersome horn to play into. Once Western Electric developed the electrical recording process, and it became possible to fit all the needed recording gear into the back of a 1927 touring car, the number of field sessions mushroomed. Yet by 1932 the Depression and hard times in the record business had curtailed many of them.

Indeed, so much was being done by some companies, like Columbia, that the very term "field session" may need to be qualified. While the popular image of field engineers hanging blankets around the wall of an empty loft, or hunched over their portable cutters in a cheap hotel room, is certainly still accurate in many cases, in other cases things were not so dramatic. Columbia, who had begun having long sessions in Atlanta every spring and fall, eventually developed quite an infrastructure there. It included local talent scouts and recording managers like Atlanta natives Bill Brown and Dan Hornsby, who worked year-round setting up artists and rehearsing songs; it also included a crack cadre of local studio musicians, including Clayton McMichen, Lowe Stokes, and Riley Puckett, who were paid a monthly retainer just for being available to help out other newer artists who came in, and to make new records themselves. The Columbia studio, at 15 Pryor Street in Atlanta, may have started out as the second floor of a warehouse, but was soon used as a studio on a very regular basis. Thus though the Atlanta studio was still able to attract regional artists who were by no means professional, it did not fit the image of a make-shift, temporary field studio.

Though favorite locations, like Atlanta and Dallas, were visited on an almost annual basis, others were visited only once or twice. The extent of the sessions may be seen from table 3.

Examining this list, the first noticeable thing is really how wide an area the field sessions covered. Between 1923 and 1932, the commercial record companies staged a total of 107 field sessions—most averaging 40 or 50 sides. Most of the main regions from the South are represented. Mississippi, with its unique string band and fiddle styles, had only one session, but many of its musicians made the drive up to Memphis, where regular

Table 3. Recording sessions in the South

Columbia	Atlanta (1925–1932)	New Orleans (1925–1927)
	Memphis (1928)	Johnson City, Tenn. (1928–1929)
	Dallas (1927–1929)	
Okeh	Asheville (1925)	St. Louis (1925–1926)
	Atlanta (1923–1932)	Winston-Salem (1927)
	Richmond, Va. (1929)	Jackson, Miss.(1930)
	San Antonio (1930)	
Victor	Atlanta (1927–1932)	Houston (1925)
	New Orleans (1925)	Memphis (1927–1932)
	Nashville (1928)	Charlotte (1927, 1931)
	Louisville (1931)	Savannah (1927)
	Dallas (1929, 1932)	El Paso (1929)
	Bristol (1927–1928)	
Brunswick & Vocalion	Atlanta (1927–1932)	Ashland, Ky. (1928)
	Birmingham (1928)	Knoxville (1929–1930)
	Indianapolis (1928)	Memphis (1928–1930)
	New Orleans (1928–1929)	Dallas (1928–1930)
Gennett	Birmingham (1927)	

Note: While most of these sessions included blues as well as old-time music, and thus are to some extent interchangeable with the list of field sessions given in the fourth edition of *Blues and Gospel Records 1890–1943*, other sessions were virtually all old-time and do not appear in that book. Among these were ones from Ashland, Kentucky; Winston-Salem, North Carolina; and Asheville, North Carolina.

---

sessions were held. Alabama was also not a favorite spot (only two sessions), but dozens of its musicians made the easy trek to Atlanta. West Virginia hosted no sessions, but many musicians traveled to the ones at Ashland, Kentucky (just across the river), and to Bristol or Johnson City in Tennessee. There were areas, though, that were seriously under represented. One was Arkansas, which never hosted a session, and whose musicians had to travel to Memphis, New York, or even Chicago to record. Louisiana and Oklahoma hosted no sessions. Kentucky hosted only two sessions, and these recordings barely scratched the surface of the complex music scene found there. Many Kentucky musicians had to go north to the Gennett studio at Richmond, Indiana, to make records that are among the worst sounding in the business (from a technical aspect), and the most poorly distributed. It is no coincidence that today the rarest and most collectible of all early country records are by Kentucky bands: The Walter Family and the Shepherd Brothers.

While it is beyond the scope of this study to list details about every field session (or "session lists"), an examination of a couple of them gives some idea of how far they flung their net, and from what distances people came. The famous Bristol session of July and August 1927, where Jimmie Rodgers and the Carters first recorded, documented nineteen acts. Some, like the Tenneva Ramblers, worked right out of Bristol, while others like B.F. Shelton and Blind Alfred Reed traveled over 120 miles, one way. After researching the background and hometowns of the participants and computing the distances to Bristol on 1928 maps, we can create the following table:

Table 4. Distances musicians traveled to Bristol

Within 20 miles of recording site	5 acts
Within 50 miles of recording site	4 acts
Within 100 miles of recording site	5 acts
Over 100 miles to recording site	5 acts

A second sample session list comes from the Vocalion-Brunswick session of March 29–April 7, 1930, held in Knoxville, Tennessee. This session produced no startling new artists, but did include legendary *Grand Ole Opry* stars Uncle Dave Macon and Uncle Jimmy Thompson, as well as the black string band headed by Howard Armstrong. Again, some nineteen old-time acts were documented. And again, there were some performers who were actually based in Knoxville: the sentimental singers McFarland and Gardner, blues singer Leola Manning, and the string band called The Smoky Mountain Ramblers. Macon, however, traveled over 200 miles, and The Perry County Music Makers came some 260 miles, from Linden, near the banks of the Tennessee River. A summary of distances from the artists' homes to Knoxville is shown in table 5.

One thing is obvious from looking at the last three charts: whereas the Library of Congress folksong collectors, like John and Alan Lomax, Sidney Robertson, and Herbert Halpert, often did set up their recording machines in small, out-of-the-way hamlets and front rooms, the commercial companies often chose large or medium-sized cities. Indeed, Atlanta, Dallas, and Memphis—all favorite sites—were among the largest cities in the South.

The Bristol Syndrome

Table 5. Distances musicians traveled to Knoxville

Within 20 miles of recording site	6 acts
Within 50 miles of recording site	2 acts
Within 100 miles of recording site	5 acts
Over 100 miles to recording site	6 acts

Note: Background information is uncertain with two of the above acts (Louis Bird and The Kentucky Holiness Singers) and their home base is partly guesswork.

Of the lesser locations, the smallest was probably Ashland, Kentucky, with a population of around 15,000, according to the 1920 census. Bristol and Johnson City, in Tennessee, were small individually, but were part of a "Tri-Cities" complex that also included Kingsport and Bristol, Virginia, creating a population area of well over 25,000. Jackson, Mississippi, was slightly over 22,000, but was also the state capitol. In sum, none of the commercial

Recording equipment from the 1930 Knoxville session.

field recording sessions came from "small sleepy southern towns." It was the cities and small cities, after all, that had the radio stations and theaters to support the increasingly commercial old-time music of the day.

A second point that emerges is just how far typical performers would come to make records. During the two sessions in question (Bristol and Knoxville), almost 25 percent of the musicians came from over 100 miles away. Some came to Knoxville from a distance of as much as 260 miles. At a 1929 Dallas session, fiddler Eck Robertson traveled some 350 miles from his home in northwest Texas to Dallas. At least one group from a Columbia Atlanta session traveled from Louisiana, while another were hauled in a cattle truck from Muhlenberg County in western Kentucky to Atlanta—well over 200 miles. But the average distance the musicians traveled to these sessions was only 87.3 miles (Bristol) and 81.6 miles (Knoxville). This seems to suggest that the "regionality" of field sessions is valid, and that, in spite of the locations in urban areas, the music captured at them at least came from a homogenous area within a hundred-mile radius of the recording site.

Part of the myth of the field recording sessions involves how the talent was found. This started with the Peer-Bristol session of 1927, when Peer himself admitted that he planted stories in the local newspaper and held "open auditions" for the dozens of folk musicians who wandered in—including Jimmie Rodgers. Yet we now know that Peer had been through Bristol some six months earlier, talked to A.P. Carter, and set up at least some of his artists to record in advance. Others, such as the Stoneman Family from Galax, Virginia, he contacted by mail and invited to the session. In fact, he did not advertise in the local papers; what he did was to plant stories about how much money his record artists were making, and let the story do its magic. I have found only two cases where a talent scout actually took out advertisements for musicians in the local papers. One was in 1928, in Johnson City, Tennessee, where Columbia's Frank Walker actually placed a display ad in the local paper asking "Can you sing or play old-time music?" The other was when Brunswick's Jack Kapp took out the ad that "discovered" the Stripling Brothers in Birmingham in 1928.

As might be expected, a big-time record company coming to record in a small city was news, and many local papers did cover the event. We know of news stories in Bristol, Asheville, Winston-Salem, Dallas, Johnson City, Birmingham, and Knoxville. The latter was the most dramatic of all coverages: a full page on the session, under the banner headline "Preserving Our

> **Can You Sing or Play Old-Time Music?**
>
> Musicians of Unusual Ability --- Small Dance Combinations--- Singers --- Novelty Players, Etc.
>
> **Are Invited**
>
> To call on Mr. Walker or Mr. Brown of the Columbia Phonograph Company at 334 East Main Street, Johnson City, on Saturday, October 13th, 1928—9 A. M. to 5. P. M.
>
> **This is an actual try-out for the purpose of making Columbia Records.**
>
> You may write in advance to E. B. Walker, Care of John Sevier Hotel, Johnson City, or call without appointment at address and on date mentioned above.

Frank Walker of Columbia Records placed this ad seeking old-time music talent at a 1928 field recording session in Johnson City, Tennessee.

Hill-Billie Harmonies." There were very few stories in the Atlanta papers, and virtually none in Memphis or Nashville. Furthermore, many of the stories list the people who were already set up to record, or in fact had already recorded, suggesting again the sessions were organized before the recording crew hit town. Such stories could have hardly been used as advertising for the sessions.

While there were undoubtedly cases where talent just wandered in off the street at auditions—it happened in Bristol, Johnson City, and in Birmingham—there was normally a good deal of advance planning that went into many sessions. They were, after all, expensive undertakings for the companies, and were not to be entered into casually. Men like Peer, Walker, and Brockman had a ready-made grassroots network in the dozens of local phonograph dealers and distributors for their labels. Often, such people would know about a local favorite fiddler or singer and get word to the talent scouts. Dick Burnett, of Columbia's Burnett and Rutherford, got his Columbia audition when a local storekeeper in West Virginia heard the team play in a company town and contacted Columbia about them. Gus Nennsteil, a furniture store owner and Vocalion distributor in Knoxville, recommended artists like Uncle Dave Macon, George Reneau, and Charley Oaks to his head office. Cecil McLister, the Bristol store owner who was the Victor agent, told Peer about The Carter Family. By 1929 and 1930, regional radio stations were up and running, and serving as sources for talent. All of this eventually evolved into a second tier of talent scouts—local people who understood how the record business worked, and who would be good for it. It was they who actually prowled the back roads and country dances looking for artists. Columbia's Frank Walker had such second-tier scouts in Bill Brown, an Atlanta native, and Dan Hornsby, an Atlanta native and singer. Peer had a black bandleader named Charlie Williamson as his organizer for many of the Memphis blues sessions. Okeh's Polk Brockman utilized the services of H.C. Spier and Tommy Rockwell in Mississippi, and the Gennett company relied on the work of Dennis Taylor from Richmond, Kentucky. By the 1930s such Artist and Repertory men as Eli Oberstein, W.R. Calaway, and Art Satherly were continuing the tradition of field sessions.

Almost from the start of the era, record companies on occasion would dictate the repertoire their artists would record. "Cover" versions (imitations of an already established hit), which many associate with the pop music of the 1940s and 1950s, were also quite common in the 1920s. When Uncle Dave Macon had a hit on Vocalion with the car song "On the Dixie Bee Line," studio man Vernon Dalhart was rushed into the studio for a rival company in a surrealistic effort to copy Macon's song, even down to the spoken jokes and Macon laugh. Ernest Stoneman was asked by Victor to rerecord some of the earlier hits by Fiddlin' Powers, and was even sent a set of the records so he could learn the songs. The files of Kentucky fiddler Doc Roberts were filled with letters from the Gennett Company asking him to learn certain songs that "our clients" wanted. After the Mississippi band The Leake County Revelers had a best-seller with "Wednesday Night Waltz" on Columbia in 1927, rival company Brunswick asked The Kessinger Brothers to cover it at their first session, in 1928.

Once Ralph Peer figured out that he could make money copyrighting and publishing the songs he recorded, he began to demand more and more that his artists come up with "original material." In 1931, when the Delmore

Gennett Records relied on A & R man Dennis Taylor to find their talent.

Brothers were trying to get on records with Victor or Columbia, they once crossed paths with The Allen Brothers, who were recording regularly with Victor. Alton Delmore wrote in his autobiography that the Allens' advice was simple: get some new, original songs if you wanted to get on Victor records. This meant an aspiring artist had to either actually write new songs (which a surprising number did), discover an old ballad or folksong that had not been previously recorded (such as "Frankie Silver" or "Tom Dula"), or take an old song and rework it. All of these methods were used by the Carter Family, though they utilized the third option more often than the others. "Ralph Peer very seldom told them what to sing," recalls A.P. and Sara's daughter Jeanette. "And he usually accepted the songs they brought up with them." In general, other companies were less stringent about "originality." Columbia was releasing well-recorded traditional songs like "Devilish Mary" and "Over the Waves" as late as 1931.

All of which raises the question crucial to the romantic theory essential to seeing the early A & R men as folksong collectors: How representative of local musics were the commercial field recordings? There are two ways to get at this. One is to examine the statements and recollections of the A & R men themselves. The second is to contrast the repertoire formed by the commercial field recordings with the repertoires from various printed collections. We have interviews with Ralph Peer, Frank Walker, and Art Satherly, each of whom were major players, but each of whom tended to romanticize their accomplishments. Peer was doing this as early as 1928, when he returned to Bristol for follow-up sessions, and again in 1938 for a dramatized portrait in *Colliers*. Similarly, Frank Walker insisted that he sold thousands of copies of a record about the Scopes "Monkey" Trial in Dayton, Tennessee, while the trial was still in session—an impossible feat given the recording dates and logistics. When Mike Seeger asked Walker in 1962 what kind of songs he had been interested in recording, Walker answered: "Four kinds. There were only four kinds of country music. One is your gospel songs, your religious songs. The others were your jigs and reels. . . . Your third were your heart songs, sentimental songs that came from the heart, and the fourth, which has passed out to a degree today and was terrific in those days, were the event songs." Looking over the Columbia 15000 series and its sales figures, one can see why Walker made these four particular divisions. The great Columbia best-sellers, the ones that topped one hundred thousand in sales, were indeed from these ranks. Walker's biggest seller was "Pictures from Life's Other Side" by the gospel group Smith's Sacred Singers; close rivals were The Skillet Lickers' "A Corn Licker Still in Georgia" and, especially in 1925, event songs like "The Death of Floyd Collins." Another of the biggest sellers was a heart song, "My Carolina Home," done by Riley Puckett and Clayton McMichen as a harmony duet. The term "folk" or "traditional" was not mentioned in Walker's categories, though virtually all four categories contain traditional items. But Walker omitted several important categories that do show up throughout the 15000 series and through dedicated numericals of other companies: the comic or novelty song, as featured by Uncle Dave Macon or Charlie Poole; the so-called "white blues," stimulated to a large extent by the success of Rodgers; original instrumentals, or non-fiddle instrumentals; and new compositions.

Research by Norm Cohen has shown that there is a scant handful—less than 1 percent—of identifiable Child ballads (ballads that have an undeniable British pedigree) in the body of commercial recordings. There are considerably more recordings of Native American songs and ballads: From 1925 to 1931, the Columbia series contained on the average some 23 percent songs of this type. Cohen estimates that the number of ballads in the combined Okeh, Brunswick, and Columbia series is around 4 percent. However, recordings featuring the most common singing style of old ballads—the unaccompanied and ornamented solo voice—are extremely rare. I can think offhand of fewer than ten. And while there are occasional examples of the print folksong collectors getting to the same people the A & R men recorded—Sharp got to a relative of the Carter Family, and Richardson got to Gid Tanner—what is more remarkable is the lack of overlap between the two bodies of song. Was the art of *a capella* singing such an acquired taste that the Peers and Walkers of the world simply ignored it? Did it have something to do with a folk aesthetic which made a distinction between public and private performance, and decreed that ballads were "family" music? Or did it have to do with the fact that many who were brazen enough to record were the Young Turks of the time, the new generation who were using the relatively new instrument, the guitar, to accompany virtually all their singing?

There were other types of music the companies did not cover well. We know now that many communities had large ensembles with as many as ten members, some of them mixing stringed instruments with horns and even drums. Musicians all over north Georgia remember the Armuchee Band at Rome, which included a baritone sax, a clarinet, and fiddlers like Lowe Stokes. From western Kentucky came the E.E. Hack Band that included mandolins, guitars, banjoes, a tuba, fiddles, and a "jazzhorn" (a giant kazoo). Touring vaudeville bands like those of Otto Gray (Tulsa) and H.M. Barnes's Blue Ridge Ramblers (Tennessee and Virginia) often included seven or eight acts within the larger ensembles. In Knoxville, the Wise

Brothers Orchestra included nine players, including a piano and a drum, and a veritable nest of mandolin players. While a few of these larger ensembles did go into the studio, they seldom recorded as a group: most of the time, two or three of the members would be featured on a given record. The Wise Brothers' Vocalion sides only featured the guitar and fiddle of the two leaders.

A third missing genre is the church ensemble. Most of the labels released impressive numbers of performances by African American preachers and their congregations; some, like the Reverend F.W. McGhee, became media stars. Yet little like this exists in the history of Anglo preachers and congregations; the only example widely known is Victor's documentation of Holiness preacher Ernest Phipps and his congregation from Kentucky. The makeshift studios might have made it difficult to record large groups, but the fact that the companies did record glee clubs, civic choirs, Sacred Harp singers, and black preacher-congregation groups suggests that there were other reasons that this segment was largely ignored.

A fourth omission was the black string band. Once a common feature in the nineteenth-century rural landscape, there were many such ensembles still functioning in the 1920s. A handful did get recorded, but most did not. One reason was that the companies very soon ghettoized the music, assuming that any black musician played the blues. Dorris Macon, the son of Uncle Dave Macon, recalled an incident in a Knoxville session when a black string band, with whom Uncle Dave had been joking and playing during the wait, was turned down by the Vocalion company because they couldn't play the blues.

In general, even though the various series like "Old Familiar Tunes and Novelties" and "Old Southern Tunes" contained a great deal of material that was not folk music by any standard definition, they did capture an impressive amount of traditional music. In every year from 1925 to 1931, for instance, Columbia released more "traditional" records (vocals or fiddle tunes) than any other type—old pop, gospel, or originals. Usually the traditional releases constituted from 30 to 40 percent of the total.

The last major concern in this survey of field sessions involves the bread and butter issues of sales, payments, and royalties. Much of the data necessary for a cogent analysis here is simply missing. Record companies, which even today are wary of giving out sales figures, have not been especially interested in keeping such data from seventy years ago. Trade publications like *Billboard* did not start publishing their best-seller country charts until January 1944, and the occasional list of "top hits" from the 1920s and 1930s that appear in some publications have no real basis in fact. They are educated guesses, compiled from various clues (such as in a legal action) and the frequency with which record collectors discover certain titles. Other barometers of sales come from a handful of performers who kept their old royalty statements and shared them with researchers. My own files contain copies of royalty statements from figures like Eck Robertson, Fiddlin' Doc Roberts, The Georgia Yellow Hammers, Ernest Stoneman, Welling and McGhee, The Allen Brothers, Jimmie Rodgers, and The Girls of the Golden West. Two files of sales for individual numerical releases have been retrieved from company archives: a complete run of the entries in the Columbia 15000 series, and a complete run of the Victor 40,000 series (see below). In many cases, though, artists were paid a flat rate of, say, fifty dollars a side for their work, with no royalties at all. When Ralph Peer signed artists, he usually had them sign two contracts: one was a flat fee agreement for making the record, but a second was an agreement to publish the song with Peer's company, Southern Music. Most of the Victor artists who later got royalty statements got them from Southern, not Victor, and they were for what are today called "mechanicals"—publisher's fees earned by copyrighted songs. (Such statements did, of course, also reflect the sales of the artists' own records, and give data in that respect.)

The data from Victor and Columbia has not been well studied or analyzed as of yet. While these were the two major companies during the 1920s, there were five other companies for which we have virtually no data. Thus the following conclusions are highly tentative. On Columbia, the 725 records released in the 15000 series from 1925 through 1931 sold a total of 11,315,869 copies—each with two songs on it. This was an average sale of 15,600 per record, though the best-seller of the series topped out at just over 300,000 and the worst-seller (at the series's Depression-wracked end) managed barely 500. On Victor, the sales for the "Old Familiar Tunes and Novelties" 40,000 series, for the year of 1929 alone, totaled some 845,000 copies, or about 5,000 per disc. Their range extended from 236,000 (Rodgers's "Lonely and Blue"/"Sailor's Plea") to less than 3,000 (M.S. Dillegay's "Mother in Law"/"Mexican Jumping Bean").

If we estimate that the other companies sold, in toto for their dedicated series, some four million records each, then the overall number of country records that entered the households of the South and Midwest from 1925 to 1931 might well exceed some thirty-three million two-sided discs. Furthermore, many of these records were heard by more than one listener. Little wonder, then, that for generations, folksong collectors kept finding and publishing "traditional songs" that were drawn from records, of which they knew very little. Little wonder that as early as 1935 a folksong collector from Putnam County, Tennessee, was already turning up songs learned from Jimmie Rodgers and Carter Family records—very few of which she recognized. This massive infusion of songs, tunes, and performing styles into the vernacular culture of the South was far greater than has been previously thought. Indeed, its impact is almost incalculable, and may well have changed the entire nature of American music.

Notes on Sources

The numerical lists of various dedicated series have been drawn from the author's files and from several key scholars and collectors, including Steve Davis, Robert Nobley, Malcolm Blackard, Bob Pinson, Tony Russell, and Norm Cohen. Some of the numericals are available to the public. The Okeh 45000 series and the Columbia 15000 series, replete with useful indexes, appear in a long appendix to William Randle's dissertation, "History of Radio Broadcasting and Its Social and Economic Effect on the Entertainment Industry. . . ." Western Reserve University, 1966 (Dissertation Abstracts # 67–4619). The Brunswick 100 series was serialized in the *JEMF Quarterly* 31–34 (1973–1974).

Major archives such as the Country Music Foundation Library and the Southern Folklife Collections have copies of taped interviews with people like Ralph Peer, Frank Walker, and Art Satherly. A good portion of Mike Seeger's interview with Frank Walker can be found in Josh Dunson and Ethel Raim, eds., *Anthology of American Folk Music* (New York: Oak Publications, 1973). The best account of Peer's career, drawn from the unpublished interviews done by journalist Lillian Borgeson, is the "Mr. Victor and Mr. Peer" chapter of Nolan Porterfield's *Jimmie Rodgers: The Life and Times of America's Blue Yodeller* (Urbana: Univ. of Illinois Press, 1992). The names of the various dedicated series come from the author's own collection of 1920s catalog supplements, and from advertising on the original 78-sleeves.

A detailed analysis of the Columbia 15000 series and its sales patterns can be found in the author's "Columbia Records and Old-Time Music," *JEMF Quarterly* 51 (1978): 118–26. Details about the musicians who participated in the Bristol sessions are available on a CD set of the same name, produced by CMF and BMG, and in an article on the sessions by the author in Paul Kingsbury, ed., *A Country Reader* (Nashville: Vanderbilt Univ. Press/Country Music Foundation Press, 1997).

Most of the details about the "second tier" of talent scouts come from my own interviews; likewise, data on how companies sometimes interfered with repertoire comes from my own files and from my interviews with numerous musicians and/or their relatives. The early content analysis of the Okeh, Brunswick, and Columbia sessions comes from a long review in *The American Folk Music Occasional* (New York: Oakm, 1970): 78–80.

Sales figures in my files were compiled by my own searches through the Columbia (CBS/Sony) archives in New York, as well as earlier searches by David Freeman. The Victor sales figures were made available by Tony Russell, and by Richard Weize of Bear Family records.

CONTRIBUTORS

DANNY W. ALLEN divides his time between his native West Virginia and Mendocino County, California, where he works and teaches in hydrology. His father, Charles Allen, performed on station WJLS in Beckley, West Virginia, and it was a quest for a photo of his father's band that started his world-class collection of musical post cards.

GEORGE CARNEY is Regents Professor of Geography at Oklahoma State University. He is author of *The Sounds of People and Places: A Geography of American Folk and Popular Music* (1994), *Fast Food, Stock Cars, and Rock 'n' Roll: Space and Place in American Pop Culture* (1995), and *Baseball, Barns, and Bluegrass: A Geography of American Folklife* (1998).

DON CUSIC, a former Nashville journalist and songwriter, is a professor in the Curb Music Program at Belmont University and author of numerous books and articles on country and gospel music.

S. RENEE DECHERT is an assistant professor of English at Northwest College who has published articles and reviews on country and alt.country music and is co-creator of the syndicated radio program *The Country Music Moment*. She's also active in an effort to collect enough funds to buy the Drive-by Truckers their first road case.

JAMES I. ELLIOTT is an assistant professor of music business at Belmont University. In addition, he is a songwriter and music publisher, having co-written five number-one Christian songs. He is a recipient of the Dove Award, ASCAP Gospel Award, and eight gold- and platinum-album awards. He is a contributing writer on the *Century of Country: Definitive Country Music Encyclopedia* CD-ROM. He holds membership in ASCAP, NARAS, GMA, NSAI, and MEIEA.

GREG FAULK is an associate professor of finance at Belmont University. His research interests include valuation of financial assets. He has published articles in the *Review of Quantitative Accounting and Finance* and *The Journal of Accounting and Finance Research* in addition to having presented numerous papers at national and regional financial conferences. He holds membership in the American Finance Association and the Financial Management Association.

JOHN GARST is an emeritus professor of chemistry at the University of Georgia who has maintained a sixty-year interest in American vernacular music. Recently he has studied the historical background of several songs and ballads, including "Wayfaring Stranger," "Ella Speed," "Delia," and "John Henry."

JOHN GONAS is currently on leave from the Finance Department at Belmont University to pursue a doctorate in finance at the University of Kentucky. Prior to entering academe, Mr. Gonas was an investment banker and holds a Series 7 Certification.

DAVID HERRERA is an instructor of management/music business at Belmont University. He has experience in publishing, management, and concert promotion and currently directs the student-run record company, Acklen Records. Recently published in *The Journal of Arts Management, Law and Society,* he is pursuing a doctorate in Economics at Middle Tennessee State University.

GEORGE H. LEWIS is a professor of sociology at University of the Pacific. Long interested in music and culture, he has published extensively in the field, including an edited anthology on country music, *All That Glitters:*

Country Music in America. Lewis is audio review editor of *Popular Music and Society*, and when he is not listening to Southern rock opera, is still working on getting the "Carter scratch" down right on guitar.

DIANE PECKNOLD is a Ph.D. candidate in the Department of History at Indiana University.

DAVID B. PRUETT, a native of Concord, North Carolina, is currently pursuing a Ph.D. in ethnomusicology at Florida State University. He has presented his research on bluegrass and old-time music at a number of national venues, and has articles forthcoming in publications such as *The Encyclopedia of Appalachia*.

JIMMIE N. ROGERS is professor of communication at the University of Arkansas, Fayetteville. He is the author of *The Country Music Message: Revisited*.

ANDREW SMITH works as an educational statistician and has been collecting country music for over thirty years. He is currently researching the life of Tex Morton.

RICHARD D. SMITH's *Can't You Hear Me Callin': The Life of Bill Monroe, Father of Bluegrass* was Belmont University country music book of the year and won second place in the Ralph J. Gleason Memorial Prizes for best books on American music.

CHARLES K. WOLFE is author of some twenty books on folk and country music. His most recent works include *A Good-Natured Riot: The Birth of the Grand Ole Opry* and *Classic Country*.

Lecture Notes in Computer Science 1352
Edited by G. Goos, J. Hartmanis and J. van Leeuwen

Springer
*Berlin
Heidelberg
New York
Barcelona
Budapest
Hong Kong
London
Milan
Paris
Santa Clara
Singapore
Tokyo*